ANALYSIS FOR FINANCIAL MANAGEMENT

ANALYSIS FOR FINANCIAL MANAGEMENT

Robert C. Higgins

The University of Washington

1989   Second Edition

Homewood, Illinois 60430

Executive editor: *Gary L. Nelson*
Project editor: *Suzanne Ivester*
Production manager: *Irene H. Sotiroff*
Cover designer: *Maureen McCutcheon*
Compositor: *Weimer Typesetting Co., Inc.*
Typeface: *11/13 Century Schoolbook*
Printer: *R. R. Donnelley & Sons Company*

LIBRARY OF CONGRESS
Library of Congress Cataloging-in-Publication Data

Higgins, Robert C.
    Analysis for financial management / Robert C. Higgins.—2nd ed.
        p.   cm.
    Includes bibliographies and index.
    ISBN 0-256-06899-2 (pbk.)
    1. Corporations—Finance.   I. Title.

HG4026.H496 1989   88–12840
658.1'51—dc19   CIP
Printed in the United States of America

    5 6 7 8 9 0 DO 5 4 3 2 1 0

*In memory of Alex Robichek,
teacher, colleague, and friend.*

Preface

So you read prefaces too. I suppose, like myself, you find authors are frequently more forthcoming about the subject, scope, and intended uses of their book in the preface than anywhere else. Perhaps this is because prefaces are frequently written last, thus providing time for the author's perceptions of what he is truly about to ripen into something approaching coherence.

Like its predecessor, the second edition of *Analysis for Financial Management* is my conception of what today's manager needs to know about financial management. Its purpose is to present standard techniques and modern developments in a practical, intuitive manner. The book is intended for nonfinancial managers and business students interested in the practice of financial management, and it assumes no prior background beyond a rudimentary and perhaps rusty familiarity with financial statements. Emphasis throughout is on the managerial implications of financial analysis.

Analysis for Financial Management is an attempt to translate into another medium the enjoyment and stimulation I have experienced over the past two decades working with executives and college students. From this experience I have come to believe that modern developments in the field such as market efficiency, β-risk, and market signaling are important to practitioners; that financial techniques and concepts need not be abstract or obtuse; and that finance has much to say about the broader aspects of company management. I am also convinced that any activity in which so much money changes hands with such rapidity cannot fail to be of interest.

The story begins in Part I with a look at the management of existing resources, including the assessment of a company's financial health, its strengths, weaknesses, recent performance, and future prospects. This involves a review of financial statements and careful consideration of their use in evaluating financial performance. A recurring theme is that a business must be viewed as an integrated whole, and that effective financial management is possible only within the context of a company's broader operating characteristics and strategies.

The rest of the book deals in one way or another with the acquisition and management of new resources. Part II looks at financial forecasting and planning, with particular emphasis on managing growth and decline. Part III considers the financing of company operations, including a review of the principal security types, the markets in which they trade, and the proper choice of security type by the issuing firm. The latter topic requires a close look at financial leverage, and its impact on the firm and its shareholders.

Evaluation of investment opportunities is the topic of Part IV. Included here are the use of discounted cash flow techniques—such as the net present value and the internal rate of return—to estimate an investment's merit and a look at the difficult task of incorporating risk analysis into decision making. The book concludes with an examination of the corporate restructuring phenomenon presently engulfing American business.

In addition to the usual updates and expansions endemic to second editions, those familiar with the first edition of *Analysis for Financial Management* will note three major changes here: (1) what originally was Chapter 3, "Inflation and the Assessment of Company Performance," has been condensed and appears as an appendix to Chapter 1 (no one cares about inflation accounting when the inflation rate is below 5 percent); (2) Chapter 4, "Managing Growth," has been extensively revised to simplify the sustainable growth equation and to emphasize problems created by insufficient growth; and (3) a new chapter, "Business Valuation and Corporate Restructuring," has been added.

A word of caution: *Analysis for Financial Management* emphasizes the application and interpretation of analytic techniques in decision making. These techniques have proved useful for putting financial problems into perspective and for helping managers anticipate the consequences of their actions. But techniques do not substitute for thought. Even with the best technique it is still necessary to define and prioritize issues, to modify the analysis to fit specific circumstances, to strike the proper balance between quantitative analysis and more qualitative considerations, and to evaluate alternatives insightfully and creatively. Mastery of technique is only the necessary first step toward effective management.

I wish to express my gratitude to Loyd Heath, Bill Alberts, Nik Varaiya, Stephen Thode, and especially Megan Partch for commenting insightfully on earlier drafts. I also want to thank my family for tolerating an often distracted family member these several months, and my many students and colleagues at the University of Washington, the Pacific Coast Banking School, the University of Hawaii Advanced Management Program, Burlington Northern, Inc., SeaFirst Bank, Tekronix, Inc., and Bank of America, among others, for creating the hothouse in which the ideas expressed here took root.

Robert C. Higgins

Contents

Forecasting. Pro Forma Statements and
Financial Planning: *Sensitivity Analysis.*
Simulation. Cash Flow Forecasts. Cash
Budgets. The Techniques Compared. Planning
in a Large Company.

Appendixes

Part I

Assessing the Financial Health of a Firm

Chapter 1

Interpreting Financial Statements

*Financial statements are
like fine perfume; to be
sniffed but not swallowed.*

Abraham Brilloff

Accounting can usefully be thought of as the scorecard of business. It translates the activities of a company into a set of objective numbers that provide information about the firm's performance, problems, and prospects. Finance involves the interpretation of these accounting numbers for the assessment of performance and the planning of future actions.

The skills of financial analysis are important to a wide range of people, including investors, creditors, and regulators. Nowhere are they more important than within the company. Regardless of functional specialty or company size, managers who possess these skills are able to diagnose their firm's ills, prescribe useful remedies, and anticipate the financial consequences of their actions. Like a ball player who cannot keep score, an operating manager who does not fully understand accounting and finance works under an unnecessary handicap.

This chapter and the following one look at the use of accounting information for the assessment of financial health. We begin with an overview of the accounting principles governing financial statements and a discussion of one of the most abused and confused notions in all of finance—cash flow. In Chapter 2, we will look at measures of financial performance and ratio analysis.

THE CASH FLOW CYCLE

Finance can seem arcane and complex to the uninitiated. There are, however, a comparatively few basic principles that should guide your thinking. One is that *a company's finances and its operations are integrally connected.* A company's activities, method of manufacture, and competitive strategy all fundamentally shape its financial structure. The reverse is also true. Decisions that appear primarily financial in nature can significantly affect company operations. For example, the way a company finances its assets can affect the nature of the investments it is able to undertake.

The cash flow–production cycle appearing in Figure 1–1 illustrates the close interplay between company operations and finances. For simplicity, suppose the company shown is a new one that has raised money from owners and creditors, has purchased productive assets, and is now ready to begin operations. To do so, the company uses cash to purchase raw materials and hire laborers; they make the product and store it temporarily in inventory. What began as cash is now physical inventory. When the company sells an item, the physical inventory changes once again into cash. If the sale is made for cash, this occurs immediately; otherwise, cash is not realized until some time later when the account receivable is collected.

This simple movement of cash to inventory, to accounts receivable, and back to cash is the firm's *operating,* or *working capital cycle.* Another ongoing activity represented in Figure

FIGURE 1–1
The Cash Flow–Production Cycle

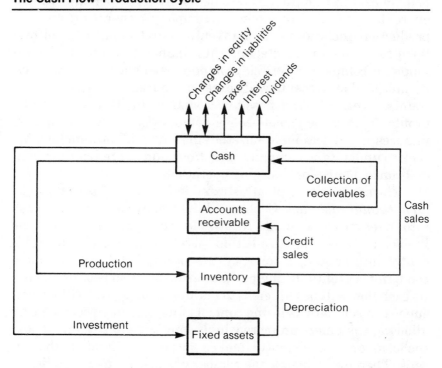

1–1 is investment. Over a period of time, the company's fixed assets are consumed, or worn out, in the manufacture of products. It is as if every item passing through the factory takes with it a small portion of the value of fixed assets. The accountant recognizes this process by continually reducing the accounting value of fixed assets and increasing the value of merchandise flowing into inventory by an amount known as depreciation. To maintain productive capacity, the company must invest part of its newly received cash in new fixed assets. The object of the exercise, of course, is to assure that the cash returning from the working capital cycle and the investment cycle exceeds the amount that started the journey.

We could further complicate Figure 1–1 by including accounts payable and by expanding on the use of debt and equity to generate cash, but the figure already demonstrates two basic principles. First, financial statements are an important window on reality. As already noted, a company's operating policies, production techniques, and inventory and credit-control systems fundamentally determine its financial profile. If, for example, a company requires prompter payment on credit sales, its financial statements will reveal a reduced investment in accounts receivable and possibly a change in its revenues and profits. This linkage between a company's operations and its finances is our rationale for studying financial statements. We seek to understand company operations and to predict the financial consequences of changing operations.

The second principle illustrated in Figure 1–1 is that *profits do not equal cash flow*. Cash—and the timely conversion of cash into inventories, accounts receivable, and back to cash—is the lifeblood of any company. If this cash flow is severed or significantly interrupted, insolvency can occur. Yet the fact that a company is profitable and perhaps growing is no assurance that its cash flow will be sufficient to maintain solvency. To illustrate, suppose a company is losing control of its accounts receivable by allowing customers an increasingly long time to pay, or suppose the company consistently makes more merchandise than it sells. Then even though the company is selling merchandise at a profit in the eyes of an accountant, its sales may not be producing enough cash inflows soon enough to replenish the cash outflows required for production and investment. When a company has insufficient cash to pay its maturing obligations, it is insolvent. As another example, suppose the company is managing its inventory and receivables carefully, but rapid sales growth is forcing an ever larger investment in these assets. Despite the fact that the company is profitable, it may have too little cash to meet its obligations. The company will literally be "growing broke." These brief examples illustrate why a manager must be concerned with cash flows at least as much as with profits.

We will return to these themes repeatedly in later chapters and will consider cash flow analysis in a few pages. But first it is necessary to review the basics of financial statements.

THE BALANCE SHEET

The most important source of information for evaluating the financial health of a company is its financial statements, consisting of a balance sheet, an income statement, and a cash flow statement. Let us look briefly at each in turn.

A balance sheet is a financial snapshot, taken at a given point in time, of all assets owned by the company and all claims against those assets. The basic relationship expressed is

Assets = Liabilities + Shareholders' equity.

It is as if a herd (flock? covey?) of auditors run through the company on the appointed day, making a list of everything the company owns, and assigning each item a value. Having tabulated the assets, the auditors next make a list of all outstanding company liabilities, where a liability is any form of an IOU. Having thus toted up what the company owns and what it owes, the auditors define the difference to be shareholders' equity. Shareholders' equity is the accountant's estimate of the value of the shareholders' investment in the firm. It is analogous to the situation of a home-owner, whose equity equals the value of the home less the mortgage outstanding against it. The term shareholders' equity is also known as *owners' equity, net worth,* or simply *equity.*

To illustrate the techniques and concepts presented throughout this book, I will refer whenever possible to Tektronix, Inc. (TEK)—a large manufacturer of sophisticated electronic test equipment—located just outside Portland, Oregon. Tables 1–1 and 1–2 present TEK's balance sheets and income statements for the fiscal years 1986 and 1987. The asset and liability categories appearing in Table 1–1 should be self-explanatory except possibly for current assets and current liabilities.

In most instances, the accountant defines any asset or liability that will be converted into cash within one year as current; all other assets or liabilities are long-term. Inventory is a current asset because it is reasonable to assume that it will be sold and will generate cash within the year. Accounts payable is a short-term liability because it must be paid within the year.

Table 1–1
TEKTRONIX, INC.
Balance Sheets
Fiscal Years 1986, 1987
($ millions)

	1986	1987	Change in Account
Assets			
Current assets:			
Cash and securities..............	$ 258	$ 243	(15)
Accounts receivable	240	252	12
Inventories.....................	165	146	(19)
Other current assets	64	56	(8)
Total current assets	727	697	
Land...........................	32	32	0
Plant and equipment	775	820	45
Accumulated depreciation	427	494	67
Net plant and equipment	348	326	
Other long-term assets	90	105	15
Total assets	$1,197	$1,160	
Liabilities and Shareholders' Equity			
Current liabilities:			
Short-term debt..................	$ 85	$ 3	(82)
Accounts payable................	113	109	(4)
Income taxes due................	24	42	18
Accrued compensation...........	97	96	(1)
Total current liabilities	319	250	
Long-term debt...................	11	51	40
Deferred tax liability.............	22	12	(10)
Other long-term liabilities	7	8	1
Total liabilities	359	321	
Shareholders' equity:			
Common shares..................	61	35	(26)
Retained earnings	777	804	27
Total shareholders' equity	838	839	
Total liabilities and shareholders' equity	$1,197	$1,160	

Table 1–2
TEKTRONIX, INC.
Income Statements
Fiscal Years 1986, 1987
($ millions)

	1986	1987
Net sales	$1,352	$1,396
Cost of sales	663	639
Gross profit	689	757
Operating expenses:		
Engineering expense	198	200
Selling expense	249	264
Administrative expense	138	139
Profit sharing	35	54
Operating income	69	100
Interest expense	16	10
Nonoperating income (expense)	(11)	12
Income before taxes	42	102
Provision for taxes	3	52
Earnings	$ 39	$ 50

Note that even though TEK is a manufacturing firm, over 60 percent of its assets are current. We will have more to say about this in the next chapter.

One common source of confusion is the large number of accounts appearing in the shareholders' equity portion of the

---

A Word to the Unwary

Nothing puts a damper on a good financial discussion (if such exists) faster than the suggestion that if a company is short of cash, it can always spend some of its shareholders' equity. Shareholders' equity appears on the liabilities side of the balance sheet, not the asset side. It represents owners' claims against existing assets. In other words, it is money that already has been spent.

balance sheet. TEK has two: common shares and reinvested earnings. Other frequently used accounts include paid-in capital and retained earnings. My advice is to forget these distinctions. They keep lawyers and accountants employed but seldom make any practical difference. Just add up everything that is not an IOU and call it shareholders' equity.

THE INCOME STATEMENT

A balance sheet is a snapshot at a point in time. An income statement, on the other hand, measures the flow of resources over time. The basic relationship is:

$$\frac{\text{Net}}{\text{sales}} - \frac{\text{Cost of}}{\text{sales}} - \frac{\text{Operating}}{\text{expenses}} + \frac{\text{Nonoperating}}{\frac{\text{Income}}{\text{(expense)}}} - \text{Taxes} = \text{Earnings}$$

Earnings measure the extent to which revenues generated during the accounting period exceeded expenses incurred in producing the revenues. For variety, earnings are also commonly referred to as *profits* or *income,* frequently with the word "net" stuck in front of them; and net sales are frequently known as *revenues,* or *net revenues.* I have never found a meaningful distinction between these terms.

Income statements are commonly divided into operating and nonoperating segments. As the names imply, the operating segment reports the results of the company's major, ongoing activities, while the nonoperating segment summarizes all secondary activities of the firm. In 1987 TEK reported operating income before tax of $100 million and nonoperating income of $12 million. Review of footnotes to TEK's annual report reveals that, among other things, the nonoperating income was composed of investment income and interest in earnings of a joint venture less charitable contributions.

Measuring Earnings

This is not the place for a detailed discussion of accounting. Because earnings, or the lack of same, are a critical indicator of financial health, however, several technical aspects of earnings measurement deserve mention.

Accrual Accounting. The measurement of accounting earnings involves two steps: the identification of revenues for the period and the matching of corresponding costs to revenues. Looking at the first step, it is important to note that revenue is not the same as cash received. According to the *accrual principle* (a cruel principle?) of accounting, revenue is recognized as soon as the effort required to generate the sale is substantially complete and there is a reasonable certainty that payment will be received. The accountant sees the timing of the actual cash receipts as only a technicality. For credit sales, the accrual principle means that revenue is recognized at the time of sale, not when the customer pays. This can result in a significant time lag between the generation of revenue and the receipt of cash. Looking at TEK, for instance, we see that revenue in 1987 was $1,396 million, but that accounts receivable increased $12 million over the year. We conclude that cash received from sales during 1987 was only $1,384 million ($1,396 million − $12 million); the other $12 million still awaits collection.

Depreciation. Fixed assets, and associated depreciation, present the accountant with a particularly thorny problem in matching. Suppose in 1985 a company purchases for $5 million a machine that has an expected productive life of 10 years. If the accountant assigns the full cost of this machine to expenses in 1985, operating income in that year will clearly plunge; and operating income in the following nine years will get a free ride in the sense that the new machine will contribute to revenue but will not add to expenses. Accounting for the cost of the new machine in this manner clearly distorts the company's reported profitability over time.

The preferred approach is to spread the cost of the machine over its expected useful life in the form of depreciation. Because the only cash outlay associated with the machine occurs in 1985, the annual depreciation listed as a cost on the company's income statement is not a cash outflow. It is a *noncash charge* used to match the 1985 expenditure with resulting revenue. Said differently, depreciation is the allocation of past expenditures to future time periods so as to match revenues and expenses. TEK buries its annual depreciation charge in cost of goods sold, but elsewhere in its financial statements we learn that depreciation was $84 million each year for 1986 and 1987.

To determine the amount of depreciation to be taken on a particular asset, three estimates are required: the asset's useful life, its salvage value, and the method of allocation to be employed. All of these estimates should be based on economic and engineering information, experience, and on any other objective data about the asset's likely performance. Broadly speaking, there are two methods of allocating an asset's cost over its useful life. Under the *straight-line* method, the accountant depreciates the asset by a uniform amount each year. If an asset costs $5 million, has an expected useful life of 10 years, and an estimated salvage value of $1 million, straight-line depreciation would be $400,000 per year [($5 million − $1 million)/10].

The second method of cost allocation is really a family of methods known as *accelerated depreciation*. Each technique charges more depreciation in the early years of the asset's life and correspondingly less in later years. Accelerated depreciation does not enable a company to take more depreciation in total; instead it alters the timing of the recognition. While the specifics of the various accelerated techniques need not detain us here, you should recognize that the life expectancy, the salvage value, and the allocation method used by a company can fundamentally affect reported earnings. In general, if a company is conservative and depreciates its assets rapidly, it will tend to understate current earnings, and vice versa.

Taxes. A second noteworthy feature of depreciation accounting involves taxes. Most companies, except the very small, keep at least two sets of financial records: one for managing the company and reporting to shareholders and another for determining its tax bill. The objective of the first set is, or should be, to portray accurately the financial performance of the company. The objective of the second is much simpler: to minimize taxes. Forget objectivity and minimize taxes. These differing objectives mean that the accounting principles used to construct the

---

Cash Cost of Merchandise Produced

TEK's cost of goods sold in 1987 was $639 million, but this is not the cash cost incurred to produce merchandise during the period. The difference is attributable to changes in accounts payable and inventories over the year and to depreciation. See if you can calculate TEK's cash cost of merchandise produced in 1987.

Answer: Accounts payable fell $4 million during 1987; thus, on balance TEK's payments to suppliers exceeded bills from suppliers by $4 million. This added to the cash cost. Inventory fell $19 million during the year, meaning that the cash costs incurred to produce some of the merchandise sold during 1987 were incurred in prior years. This reduced 1987's cash cost. Depreciation of $84 million is a noncash charge, but is included in the cost of goods sold. Cash costs are thus overstated by this amount on the income statement. In sum, the cash costs incurred by TEK to produce merchandise during 1987 were:

Cost of goods sold......................	$639 million
+ Change in accounts payable.........	+ 4
− Change in inventory................	−19
− Depreciation	−84
Cash paid to produce merchandise	$540 million

---

two sets of books differ substantially. Depreciation accounting is a case in point. Regardless of the method used for reporting to shareholders, company tax books will minimize current taxes by employing the most rapid method of depreciation over the shortest useful life allowed by the tax authorities.

This dual reporting creates some complications on a company's published financial statements. To illustrate, the provision for taxes of $52 million appearing on TEK's 1987 income statement corresponds to the taxes due according to the accounting techniques used in constructing TEK's published statements. Since TEK used different accounting techniques when reporting to the tax authorities—techniques intended to defer the recognition of tax liabilities until future years—$52 million is not the amount actually paid by TEK in 1987. To confirm this, note on TEK's balance sheet that deferred tax liability (a long-term liability), fell $10 million in 1987 and income taxes due (a short-term liability) rose $18 million. Here's what happened: Using legal tax-deferral techniques, TEK was able to delay payment of $8 million of tax liabilities from 1987 to future years. As shown below, cash disbursements for taxes were therefore only $44 million.

Provision for taxes...................... $52 million
  − Change in income taxes due .... − 18
  − Change in deferred tax liability .... −(−10)

Taxes paid............................. $44 million

Because these taxes are only postponed, not eliminated, they appear as an increase in liabilities on TEK's 1987 balance sheet. In the meantime, TEK has use of the money. In essence, tax-deferral techniques create the equivalent of an interest-free loan from the government.

CASH FLOW STATEMENT

Until recently, the third component of financial statements, in addition to an income statement and a balance sheet, was a creature known as "the statement of changes in financial position." Once described as a random collection of pluses and minuses, the statement of changes in financial position was so confusing that even accountants were not certain of its intended purpose.

Fortunately, the accounting profession has remedied this situation by abandoning the statement of changes in favor of a cash flow statement. But just to keep things interesting, two presentation formats have been deemed acceptable. The *direct method* is a straightforward statement of cash received and disbursed, while the *indirect method* arrives at the same end result by adjusting income statement data for noncash items. Our comments here will be confined to the direct method.

A cash flow statement has two principal virtues. Accounting neophytes, and those who have never really believed in accrual accounting, can understand it; and, more significantly, it directs attention to the important issue of the firm's solvency. By observing how a company spends its money and where the money comes from, one can gain important insights into the firm's operating strategies and the viability of these strategies over time.

Table 1–3 presents a 1987 cash flow statement for Tektronix.[1] Note that three categories of receipts and disbursements appear: cash flows from *operating activities,* from *investing activities,* and from *financing activities.* Most of the numbers are reasonably straightforward combinations of balance sheet, income statement, and occasional footnote data from TEK's annual report. Indeed, we calculated several of the more difficult entries in our discussion of accrual accounting above.

Reviewing these numbers, note that although TEK's reported earnings for 1987 were only $50 million, cash flow from operating activities was over $150 million. The company is clearly generating some very healthy operating cash flows. Further, the company spent some $70 million, almost half of TEK's operating cash flow, on new assets; and over $100 million on financing activities, chiefly repaying debt and repurchasing common stock. This is a very conservative financial profile, suggesting no solvency problems for TEK in the near future. In fact, TEK appears to have more cash than it knows what to do with.

One potentially confusing entry is "Effect of exchange rate changes on cash $19 million." It arose as follows. For tax reasons, Tektronix has sizable cash and marketable securities investments offshore, investments denominated in foreign currencies. Because the U.S. dollar declined substantially in value relative to most other currencies during 1987, the dollar value of these foreign denominated cash balances rose $19 million. The cash flow statement, therefore, tells us that the $15

---

[1]At the time of this writing, the chief accounting rulemaking body, the Financial Accounting Standards Board (FASB), has announced that cash flow statements will be required in 1988. Because Tektronix did not publish a cash flow statement in fiscal year 1987, Table 1–3 is my best guess of what TEK's cash flow statement would have looked like had they offered one.

Table 1–3
TEKTRONIX, INC.
Cash Flow Statement
Fiscal Year 1987
($ millions)

Cash flows from operating activities:		
Cash received from customers...............	$1,384	
Cash received from investments, etc...........	12	
Cash provided by operating activities...........		$1,396
Cash paid to produce merchandise...........	$ 540	
Cash paid to employees and suppliers........	650	
Interest paid...............................	10	
Taxes paid.................................	44	
Cash disbursed for operating activities..........		1,244
Net cash flow from operations.................		152
Cash flows from investing activities:		
Purchase of property & equipment	(67)	
Proceeds from sale of property & equipment...	12	
Purchase of other assets	(15)	
Net cash used by investing activities		(70)
Cash flows from financing activities:		
Stock sale.................................	27	
Stock repurchase	(81)	
Dividends	(21)	
Repayment of short-term debt	(82)	
Repayment of long-term debt	(1)	
New long-term borrowing....................	41	
Increase in other long-term liabilities..........	1	
Net cash used by financing activities		(116)
Net reduction in cash from operating, investing and financing activities....................		(34)
Effect of exchange rate changes on cash........		19
Net increase (decrease) in cash................		$(15)

million decline in cash evidenced on TEK's balance sheet is the result of a $34 million outflow due to operating, investing, and financing activities and a $19 million increase in the dollar value of cash held in other currencies.

Sources and Uses Statement

A sources and uses statement can be thought of as a poor man's cash flow statement. Although the information it reveals about a company's cash flows can be somewhat impressionistic, a sources and uses statement is easy to make and is often preferred by managers to a more formal cash flow statement. We will review this common tool here because knowledge of its construction is useful for thoroughly understanding the ties between a company's operations and its finances.

Constructing a sources and uses statement entails two very simple steps. First, place two company balance sheets for different dates side by side and note all changes occurring. The rightmost column of Table 1–1 contains the requisite changes for TEK during 1987. Second, segregate the changes into those that generated cash and those that consumed cash. The result is a sources and uses statement.

Here are the rules for deciding which balance sheet changes are sources of cash and which are uses.

A company generates cash in two ways: by reducing an asset or by increasing a liability. For example, the sale of used equipment, the liquidation of inventories, and the reduction of accounts receivable are all reductions in asset accounts and are all sources of cash to the company. On the liabilities side of the balance sheet, an increase in a bank loan or the sale of common stock are increases in liabilities, which again generate cash.

A company also uses cash in two ways: to increase an asset account or to reduce a liability account. To illustrate, adding to inventories or accounts receivable or building a new plant all increase assets and all use cash. Conversely, the repayment of a bank loan, the reduction of accounts payable, and an operating loss all reduce liabilities and all use cash.

Table 1–4
TEKTRONIX, INC.
Sources and Uses Statement
Fiscal year 1987 ($ millions)

Sources:

Reduction in cash and securities	$ 15
Reduction in inventories	19
Reduction in other current assets	8
Reduction in net plant and equipment	22
Increase in income taxes due	18
Increase in long-term debt	40
Increase in other long-term liabilities	1
Increase in retained earnings	27
Total sources	$150

Uses:

Increase in accounts receivable	$ 12
Increase in other assets	15
Reduction in short-term debt	82
Reduction in accounts payable	4
Reduction in accrued compensation	1
Reduction in deferred tax liability	10
Reduction in common shares	26
Total uses	$150

Naturally, total uses of cash over an accounting period must equal total sources; otherwise, the company would be spending money it didn't have.

Table 1–4 presents a sources and uses statement for TEK covering 1987. Note that the two largest sources of cash were a $40 million increase in long-term debt and a $27 million increase in retained earnings, while the two largest uses were an $82 million reduction of short-term debt and a $26 million reduction in common shares. The increase in retained earnings, of course, reflects TEK's retention of earnings, and the reduction in common shares is attributable to the company's stock repurchase. As with TEK's cash flow statement, we see a very

Cash Flow from Operations

A frequently used notion in finance is cash flow from operations, defined as

Cash flow from operations = Earnings ± Noncash items.

Cash flow from operations is intended to measure the cash generated by operations, as distinct from the earnings—a laudable objective. The formula says that as a first approximation, one should add noncash charges, principally depreciation, back to earnings to calculate the desired quantity. Thus, TEK's cash flow from operations in 1987 was $142 million, composed of $50 million in earnings, $84 million in depreciation, and $8 million in deferred taxes.

A problem with this reasoning is that it implies a very narrow definition of operations. In particular, earnings ± noncash items equals cash generated by operations only under the artificial assumption that all of the firm's working capital accounts remain constant over time. For example, earnings ± noncash items might be large and positive, but if operations cause inventories and accounts receivable to rise and accounts payable to fall, the actual result may be a reduction rather than an increase in cash. In TEK's case, the true effect of operations on cash in 1987, as revealed by the net cash flow from operating activities on the company's cash flow statement, was $152 million. In sum, the above measure of cash flow from operations has its uses, but its limitations must be kept in mind.

conservative financial profile. Earnings are positive, yet net plant and equipment is declining, as are liabilities and common shares. Notice too that although the cash flow statement and the sources and uses statement tell a similar tale, the cash flow statement provides considerably more detail.[2]

One potential source of confusion in Table 1–4 is that the reduction of cash and securities appears as a source of cash. How can a reduction in cash be a source of cash? It is the same

---

[2]Although it is possible to reconcile TEK's cash flow statement and its sources and uses statement, I would not recommend doing so unless you have plenty of time and a high tolerance for ambiguity.

as when you withdraw money from a checking account: you reduce your bank balance but generate cash to spend.

Quoth the Banker, "Watch Cash Flow"

Once upon a midnight dreary as I pondered weak and
    weary
Over many a quaint and curious volume of accounting lore,
Seeking gimmicks (without scruple) to squeeze through
    some new tax loophole,
Suddenly I heard a knock upon my door,
        Only this, and nothing more.

Then I felt a queasy tingling and I heard the cash a-
    jingling
As a fearsome banker entered whom I'd often seen before.
His face was money-green and in his eyes there could be
    seen
Dollar-signs that seemed to glitter as he reckoned up the
    score.
        "Cash flow," the banker said, and nothing more.

I had always thought it fine to show a jet black bottom line,
But the banker sounded a resounding, "No,
Your receivables are high, mounting upward toward
    the sky;
Write-offs loom. What matters is cash flow."
        He repeated, "Watch cash flow."

Then I tried to tell the story of our lovely inventory
Which, though large, is full of most delightful stuff.
But the banker saw its growth, and with a mighty oath
He waved his arms and shouted, "Stop! Enough!
        Pay the interest, and don't give me any guff!"

Next I looked for non-cash items which could add
    ad infinitum
To replace the ever-outward flow of cash,
But to keep my statement black I'd held depreciation back,
And my banker said that I'd done something rash.
        He quivered, and his teeth began to gnash.

When I asked him for a loan, he responded, with a groan,
That the interest rate would be just prime plus eight,
And to guarantee my purity he'd insist on some security—

All my assets plus the scalp upon my pate.
   Only this, a standard rate.

Though my bottom line is black, I am flat upon my back,
My cash flows out and customers pay slow.
The growth of my receivables is almost unbelievable;
The result is certain—unremitting woe!
And I hear the banker utter an ominous low mutter,
   "Watch cash flow."

Herbert S. Bailey, Jr.

FINANCIAL STATEMENTS AND THE VALUE PROBLEM

To this point we have reviewed the basics of financial statements and grappled with the distinctions between earnings and cash flow. As a further perspective and in anticipation of later materials, I want to conclude by examining a recurring problem in the use of accounting data for financial decision making.

Market Value versus Book Value

Part of what I will call the value problem involves the distinction between the market value and the book value of shareholders' equity. TEK's 1987 balance sheet states that the value of shareholders' equity is $839 million. This is known as the *book value* of TEK's equity. However, TEK is not worth $839 million to its shareholders or to anyone else, for that matter. There are two reasons why. One is that financial statements are *transactions based*. If a company purchased an asset in 1950 for $1 million, this transaction provides an objective measure of the asset's value, which becomes the value of the asset on the company's balance sheet. Unfortunately, it is a 1950 value that may or may not have much relevance today. Moreover, to further confound things, the accountant attempts to reflect the gradual deterioration of an asset over time by periodically subtracting depreciation from its balance sheet value. This practice makes sense as far as it goes, but depreciation is the only change in value recognized by the accountant. The $1 million asset purchased in 1950 may be technologically obsolete and therefore virtually worthless today; or owing to inflation, its current value may be much higher than its original purchase price. This is especially true of land, which can have a current value many times the original cost.

It is tempting to argue that accountants should forget the original cost of long-term assets and provide a more meaningful current value. The problem, however, is that objectively determinable current values of many assets do not exist. Faced with a trade-off between relevant, but subjective current values, and irrelevant, but objective historical costs, accountants have opted for irrelevant historical costs. This means it is the user's responsibility to make any adjustments to historical-cost asset values he deems appropriate.

To understand the second, more fundamental reason TEK is not worth $839 million, we need to recall that equity investors buy shares for the future income they hope to receive, not for the value of the firm's assets. Indeed, if all goes according to plan, most of the firm's existing assets will be consumed in generating future income. The problem with the accountant's measure of shareholders' equity is that it bears little relation to future income. The chief reason is that companies have many assets and liabilities that do not appear on their balance sheets, but that, nonetheless, affect future income. Examples of unrecorded assets include patents and trademarks limiting competition for the firm's products, customer loyalty fostered by a reputation for quality and service, entrenched market position created by effective advertising or superior technology, and, of course, better management. It is said that in many companies the most valuable assets go home to their spouses in the evening. Examples of unrecorded liabilities include pending lawsuits, inferior management, and obsolete production processes. The accountant's inability to measure assets and liabilities such as these means that book value is customarily a highly inaccurate measure of the value seen by shareholders.

For a publicly traded company, it is a simple matter to calculate the value of equity as seen by shareholders: Just multiply

TABLE 1–5
The Book Value of Equity Is a Poor Proxy
for the Market Value of Equity

Company	Date	Value of equity ($ millions) Book	Value of equity ($ millions) Market	Ratio, Market Value to Book Value
BankAmerica Corporation .	12/31/86	$ 3,330	$ 1,420	0.4
Bethlehem Steel	12/31/86	631	326	0.5
Biocraft Laboratories	3/31/86	29	255	8.9
Chemical Waste Mgt.	12/31/86	369	2,300	6.2
Columbia Savings & Loan .	12/31/86	492	174	0.4
IBM Corporation	12/31/86	34,400	72,700	2.1
Kellogg Company	12/31/86	898	7,950	8.9
Tektronix, Inc.	5/30/87	838	1,290	1.5

the number of common shares outstanding by the market price per share. On the last day of its fiscal year 1987, TEK's common shares closed on the New York Stock Exchange at $34.88 per share. With 37 million shares outstanding, this yields a value of $1,291 million, or more than 1.5 times the book value ($1,291 million/$839 million). This figure is known as the *market value* of equity.

Table 1–5 presents the market and book values of equity for eight representative companies. It demonstrates clearly that book value is a poor proxy for market value.

Economic Income versus Accounting Income

A second dimension of the value problem has its roots in the accountant's distinction between *realized* and *unrealized* income. To an economist, income is what you could spend during the period to end up as well off at the end as you were at the start. For example, suppose a woman's assets, net of liabilities, are worth $100,000 at the start of the year and rise to $120,000 by the end of the year. Suppose further that she received $30,000 in wages during the year, all of which she spent. The economist would say this individual's income for the year was $50,000 ($30,000 wages + $20,000 increase in net assets).

The accountant, on the other hand, would say this individual's income was only $30,000. The accountant would not recognize the $20,000 increase in the market value of assets as income because the gain was not *realized* by the sale of the assets. Because the market value of the assets could fluctuate in either direction before the assets are sold, the gain exists only on paper; and accountants generally do not recognize paper gains or losses (of course, money is *only* paper as well). Accountants consider *realization* the necessary objective evidence required to record the gain.

It is easy to criticize accountants' conservatism when measuring income. Certainly the amount the woman could spend, ignoring inflation, and be as well off as at the start of the year is the economist's $50,000, not the accountant's $30,000. Moreover, if the woman were to sell her assets for $120,000 and immediately repurchase them for the same price, the $20,000 gain would become realized in the accountant's eyes, and he would include it as part of income. That income could depend upon a sham transaction like this is enough to raise suspicions about the accountant's definition.

However, two points should be noted in the accountant's defense. First, if the woman described above holds her assets for several years before selling them, the gain or loss recognized by the accountant on the sale date will just equal the sum of the annual gains and losses recognized by the economist. So it's really not total income that is at issue here but just the timing of its recognition. A second point in the accountant's favor is that it is extremely difficult to measure the periodic change in the value of many assets unless they are actively traded. So even if an accountant wanted to include paper gains and losses in income, he would often have great difficulty doing so. In the corporate setting, this means the accountant must be content to measure realized rather than economic income.

Imputed Costs.   A similar but more subtle problem exists on the cost side of the income statement. It involves the cost of equity capital. TEK's auditors acknowledge that in 1987 the company had use of $839 million of shareholders' money, measured at book value. They would further acknowledge that TEK could not have operated without this money and that this money is not free. Just as creditors earn interest on loans, equity investors expect a return on their investment. Yet if you look again at TEK's income statement, Table 1–2, you will find no mention of the cost of this equity—interest expense appears but not comparable cost for equity.

While acknowledging that equity capital has a cost, the accountant does not record it on the income statement because the cost must be imputed—i.e., estimated. Because there is no piece of paper stating the amount of money TEK is obligated to pay owners, the accountant refuses to recognize any cost of equity capital. As before, the accountant would rather be reliably wrong than make a potentially inaccurate estimate. The result has been serious confusion in the minds of less knowledgeable observers and continuing "image" problems for corporations.

Below is the bottom portion of TEK's 1987 income statement as prepared by its accountants and as it might be prepared by an economist. Observe that while the accountant shows earnings of $50 million for the year, the economist records a $76 million loss. These numbers differ because the economist includes a $126 million cost of equity capital, while the accountant shows no cost. (We will consider ways to estimate a company's cost of equity capital in Chapter 8. Here I have assumed a 15 percent equity cost and applied it to the book value of TEK's equity [$126 million = 15% × $839 million].)

TEK's 1987 Income as Seen by an Accountant and by an Economist ($ millions)

	Accountant	Economist
Operating income	$100	$100
Interest expense	(10)	(10)
Cost of equity		(126)
Nonoperating income	12	12
Income before tax	102	(24)
Provision for taxes	52	52
Accounting earnings	$ 50	
Economic earnings		($ 76)

The distinction between accounting earnings and economic earnings might be only a curiosity if everyone understood that positive accounting earnings were not necessarily a sign of superior, or even commendable, performance. But when many labor unions and politicians view accounting profits as evidence that a company can afford higher wages or higher taxes or more onerous regulation, and when most managements view such profits as justification for distributing handsome performance bonuses, the distinction can be an important one. Keep in mind, therefore, that the right of equity investors to expect a competitive return on their investment is every bit as legitimate as a creditor's right to interest and an employee's right to wages. They all voluntarily contribute scarce resources, and they all are justified in expecting compensation. Remember too that a company is not shooting par unless its *economic* profits are zero or above. By this criterion TEK performed like a weekend duffer in 1987.

To summarize, the value problem means that financial statements will customarily provide distorted information about company earnings and market value. This limits their applicability for many important managerial decisions. However, financial statements are frequently the best information available, and if their limitations are borne in mind, they can be a useful starting point for analysis. In the next chapter, we consider the use of accounting data for evaluating financial performance.

APPENDIX

INFLATION AND THE ASSESSMENT OF COMPANY PERFORMANCE

'Tis the night before Christmas
and all through the nation
your bonus means nothing
because of Inflation

Mad Magazine

Assessing the financial performance of a company during inflation is like measuring the width of a table with a rubber band: the size of the yardstick keeps changing. Here we will consider briefly the ways in which inflation distorts historical-cost financial statements and the accounting techniques available to minimize these distortions.

INFLATION AND COMPANY PROFITS

Inflation distorts a company's income statement in three distinct ways. One involves historical-cost depreciation, another the valuation of inventory, and the third, accounting for interest expense under inflation. The first two sources of distortion are well known, while the third is less well known and frequently misunderstood.

Historical-Cost Depreciation

Because depreciation expense under historical-cost accounting must be based on the original cost of the asset, the annual amount charged against income during inflation understates the true decline in the value of assets. Or said differently, historical-cost depreciation is not sufficient to maintain the value of company assets during inflation. This understatement of annual depreciation causes an overstatement of reported earnings and an increase in corporate taxes due.

Inventory Valuation

An analogous problem arises with inventories. The two most widely used methods of inventory accounting in the United States are first-in, first-out (FIFO) and last-in, first-out (LIFO). In an inflationary environment, a company's reported earnings and its tax bill depend on which method it uses. To illustrate, suppose a company manufactures and sells boxes and that it keeps its inventory of finished boxes in a stack as shown in the figure below. Each time a new box is completed, it is added to the top of the pile. The dollar amounts to the left of the boxes are the cost incurred by the company in making each box. Since prices are rising, the cost of each successive box is higher, starting with the oldest box in inventory at $1 and rising to the most recently produced box at $1.50.

When the company sells a box for, say, $2.00, the accountant must match the cost of the box sold against the revenue. If the company uses FIFO, the assigned cost of goods sold will be $1; while if LIFO accounting is employed, the cost of goods sold will be $1.50. (Here, we ignore all practical problems associated with removing a box from the bottom of the stack.) As shown in the figure, the choice of the inventory valuation method significantly affects the company's tax liability and its reported earnings. In our numerical example, FIFO accounting produces earnings and taxes of $0.50 as opposed to $0.25 for LIFO accounting.

Which earnings figure is correct? Since the current cost of manufacturing one box is much closer to $1.50 than to $1.00, the LIFO earnings figure is the more accurate measure of true earnings under inflation. Yet for reasons we need not go into here, a great many cor-

Inventory Valuation, Taxes, and Earnings under Inflation

Cost of Production	Finished boxes		FIFO Accounting	LIFO Accounting
$1.50		Selling price	$2.00	$2.00
1.40		Cost of goods sold	1.00	1.50
1.30		Taxable income	1.00	.50
1.20		Tax @ 50%	.50	.25
1.10		Earnings after tax	$ .50	$ .25
1.00				

porations use FIFO accounting. For these companies, inflation again causes an overstatement of reported earnings and an increase in taxes.

Gains to Net Debtors

The third distortion to a company's income statement under inflation involves the way accountants measure interest expense on a loan. Suppose you borrow $100 from a bank for one year. In the absence of inflation, the banker might be content for you to repay $104 at year end, $100 in principal and $4 in interest. But in an environment of, say, 50 percent inflation, $104 will no longer be sufficient. The banker now will want his $100 principal back *plus* enough to maintain the purchasing power of the principal, or $50. In addition, he will want a return on the loan of $4 *plus* enough to maintain the purchasing power of the return, or $2. So in total you will be asked to repay $156 in one year. You and the banker both know that $150 of this amount is really the repayment of principal and only $6 represents interest on the loan. But the accountant, whether she knows the truth or not, does not report the transaction this way. Instead, she reasons that because you borrowed $100, this by definition is the principal, and the rest must be interest expense. This overstatement of interest expense causes an understatement of reported earnings and a reduction of taxes due. Of course, these effects apply only to companies that are "net debtors," that is, companies that have more IOUs outstanding than "you-owe-mes."

The Net Effect

The overstatement of reported earnings caused by historical-cost depreciation and FIFO inventory accounting are well known. Indeed, for some years U.S. national income accounts have included adjustments to aggregate corporate income required to remove these distortions. They are known as the inventory valuation adjustment (IVA) and the capital consumption adjustment (CCA).

However, the understatement of reported earnings caused by the mislabeling of interest expense is not known precisely. One study suggests that *on average* the understatement of company earnings due to the mislabeling of interest is about equal in magnitude, but opposite in sign to the *total* overstatement due to FIFO accounting and histori-

---

A Problem: Inflation Biases and Company Earnings

During a period of rapid inflation, Companies A and B both report earnings of $100 million. Company A uses LIFO accounting, has primarily current assets, and makes extensive use of debt financing. Company B uses FIFO accounting, has primarily fixed assets, and is very conservatively financed. Which company, in truth, is probably the more profitable?

Answer: Company A. FIFO accounting and historical-cost accounting cause reported earnings to exceed true earnings during inflation. Company A suffers comparatively little from these biases. Debt financing and the resulting misstatement of interest expense causes reported earnings to understate true earnings. Company A does suffer from this bias. Hence, true earnings are probably above $100 million. By the same reasoning, Company B's true earnings are probably below $100 million.

---

cal-cost depreciation.[1] This means that for the economy as a whole the three distortions to reported income approximately offset one another, leaving reported earnings about equal to true earnings. This, of course, does not suggest that such a conclusion applies to every company. For depending on the particular company's degree of capital intensity, accounting conventions, and capital structure, reported earnings can differ substantially from true earnings.

INFLATION AND COMPANY BALANCE SHEETS

The distortions to a company's balance sheet caused by inflation are the direct result of the three biases already discussed. Thus, historical-cost accounting tends to understate the balance sheet value of long-term assets. Similarly, a look back at the figure summarizing FIFO and LIFO inventory accounting will convince you that LIFO accounting understates the balance sheet value of company invento-

---

[1]F. Modigliani and R. Cohn, "Inflation, Rational Valuation and the Market," *Financial Analysts Journal* (March/April, 1979).

ries. Indeed, after the sale of one box in our example, finished goods inventory would be $6.50 under FIFO but only $6.00 under LIFO.

Finally, the accounting treatment of liabilities under inflation tends to overstate their balance sheet values. Consistent with the idea that borrowers repay debts with cheaper dollars during inflation, the true value of many liabilities declines during inflationary periods. However, this decline is ignored by the accountant, with the result that the apparent indebtedness of a company overstates reality.

Let me caution: I am not saying it is necessarily good to be a debtor during inflation. The true value of liabilities does decline, but if the inflation is anticipated, the interest rate rises to offset the decline. The accountant's error is that she includes the higher interest rate but ignores the fall in the value of the liabilities.

INFLATION ACCOUNTING

In the late 1970s and early 1980s as the U.S. inflation rate headed toward the moon, the accounting profession made a half-hearted attempt to remedy the problems cited here by requiring large corporations to report some of the effects of inflation on their historical-cost financial statements. However, the information was relegated to a footnote, was presented in a confusing format, and did not include gains to net debtors. Not surprisingly, it was seldom used, and as soon as the inflation rate dipped to a tolerable level, the reporting requirement was eliminated entirely.

The intent here is *not* to ridicule historical-cost financial statements but simply to remind you that historical-cost statements are especially misleading under inflation. At the same time, it must be admitted that inflation accounting is still new and controversial. One debate involves the extent to which it is proper to write up fixed assets under inflation, while another surrounds the question of whether gains to net debtors should appear on the income statement. Until these and related controversies are resolved, and as long as inflation remains low, many executives are prepared to acknowledge that inflation distorts historical-cost statements, while remaining skeptical about the objectivity and usefulness of available remedies.

CHAPTER SUMMARY

1. The purpose of this chapter has been to review the accounting principles governing financial statements and

to describe the relationship between earnings and cash flow.

2. A company's finances and its business operations are integrally related. We study a company's financial statements because they are a window on its operations.

3. Earnings are not cash flow. The financial executive watches both.

4. A balance sheet is a snapshot of a company's assets and liabilities at a point in time. An income statement records sales, related expenses, and earnings over a period. Both documents are transactions based and use the accrual principle. Because accounting statements are transactions based, long-term assets and depreciation are listed at historical cost, and paper gains and losses are ignored. Use of the accrual principle means that revenues and expenses do not always coincide with cash inflows and outflows.

5. A cash flow statement presents a company's cash receipts and disbursements over the accounting period.

6. Two steps are required to create a sources and uses statement: (a) calculate changes in balance sheet accounts over the accounting period, (b) segregate the sources from the uses.

7. There are two recurring problems in the use of accounting statements for financial analysis: (a) accounting book values seldom equal market values and (b) the accountant's refusal to recognize unrealized gains and losses and imputed costs makes accounting income differ from economic income.

ADDITIONAL READING

Callard, Charles G., and David C. Kleinman. "Inflation-Adjusted Accounting: Does It Really Matter?" *Financial Analysts Journal* (May–June, 1985): 51–59.

An empirical study of the relation between stock prices and accounting information. The authors conclude that inflation-adjusted accounting data correlate more closely with stock prices than do historical-cost data. They also point out the dangers to investors and managers of using less accurate historical-cost information.

Merrill Lynch, Pierce, Fenner & Smith, Inc. "How to Read a Financial Report." 5th ed. 1984. 30 pages.

First published in 1973, this brief pamphlet offers a clear, straightforward introduction to financial statements and their interpretation. See your nearest Merrill Lynch representative for a complimentary copy.

Kyd, Charles W. *Financial Modeling Using Lotus 1-2-3*. Berkeley, Calif.: Osborn McGraw-Hill, 1986. 422 pages.

Personal computers are playing an increasingly important role in financial analysis. Here is a thorough, lively introduction to the topic. Inasmuch as the author is a former student, you will find a certain family resemblance between Kyd's approach and that taken here.

Tracy, John A. *How to Read a Financial Report*. 2d ed. New York: John Wiley & Sons, 1983. 176 pages.

Subtitled "Wringing Cash Flow and Other Vital Signs out of the Numbers . . . for Managers, Entrepreneurs, Lenders, Lawyers, and Investors," this is a lively, practical introduction to the nuances of financial statements and their interpretation.

CHAPTER PROBLEMS

1. Why do you suppose financial statements are constructed on an accrual basis rather than a cash basis when cash accounting is so much easier to understand?

2. Below is selected information about XYZ Company's financial statements for 1988 and 1989. Use this information to do the following:
   a. Fill in the blanks in the company's 1989 data.
   b. Show that the increase in cash from operations in 1989 is the same whether one looks at the reporting books or the tax books.

	1988 Books of Account	
	Reporting Purposes	Tax Purposes
Accrued taxes	$ 150	$ 0
Gross fixed assets	1,000	1,000
Accumulated depreciation	300	700

	1989 Books of Account	
	Reporting Purposes	Tax Purposes
Net sales	$ 100	$ 100
Operating costs	50	50
Depreciation	10	30
Income before tax	40	20
Provision for tax @ 34%	Taxes due @ 34%	
Income after tax	$ ____	$ ____
Accrued taxes		
Gross fixed assets	1,000	1,000
Accumulated depreciation		
Net fixed assets	$ ____	$ ____

3. Using the information below, calculate ABC, Inc.'s Cash Flow From Operating Activities as it would appear on the company's cash flow statement.

	1988	1989
Net sales	$1,500	$2,000
Cost of goods sold	900	1,200
Gross income	600	800
Depreciation	100	100
General, selling expenses	200	200
Income before tax	$ 300	$ 500
Provision for taxes @ 34%	102	170
Income after tax	$ 198	$ 330
Accounts receivable	$ 123	$ 329
Inventory _	300	600
Accounts payable	200	70
Accrued taxes	100	60
Accrued wages	20	10

4. Table 3–1 in Chapter 3 presents financial statements over the period 1985–1988 for R&E Supplies, Inc.
   a. Construct a sources and uses statement for the company from 1985 through 1988 (one statement for all three years).
   b. What insights, if any, does the sources and uses statement give you about the financial position of R&E Supplies?

5. Explain briefly how each of the following transactions would affect a company's financial statements.
   a. Purchase of a new $10 million building, financed 20 percent with cash and 80 percent with a bank loan.
   b. Purchase of a new building for $10 million in cash.
   c. A $10,000 payment to trade creditors.
   d. Sale of $100,000 of merchandise for cash.
   e. Sale of $100,000 of merchandise for credit.

6. Assume you are the chief labor negotiator for a Fortune 500 company having total assets of $10 billion and equity of $5 billion. During intense labor negotiations, the General Secretary of your company's largest union pointedly observes that "the company earned a profit of over $400 million last year—due largely to the effort expended by union employees. So management can damn well afford a decent raise this year."

Chapter 2

Evaluating Financial Performance

*The difference between well-managed
companies and not-so-well managed
companies is the degree of attention
they pay to numbers, the temperature
chart of their business.*

Harold Geneen

The cockpit of a 747 airliner, if you have never seen one, looks like a three-dimensional video game. It is a sizable room crammed with meters, switches, lights, and dials requiring the full attention of three highly trained pilots. When compared to the cockpit of, say, a Piper Cub, it is tempting to conclude that the two planes are different species rather than distant cousins. Yet at a more fundamental level, the similarities probably exceed the differences. Despite the complexity and the technology, the 747 pilot controls his plane in the same way as the Piper Cub pilot: with a stick, a throttle, and flaps. And if either pilot

---

*I owe a special thanks to George Parker for help on this chapter.

wants to change the altitude of his plane, he does so by making simultaneous adjustments to the same few levers he has for controlling the plane.

Much the same is true of companies. Once you strip away the facade of apparent complexity, the levers by which managers affect the financial performance of their firms are comparatively few and are similar among firms. The executive's job is to control these levers to assure a safe and efficient flight. And like the pilot, he or she must remember that the levers are interrelated; one cannot change the business equivalent of the flaps without also adjusting the stick and the throttle.

THE LEVERS OF FINANCIAL PERFORMANCE

Our goal in this chapter will be to analyze financial statements for the purpose of evaluating performance and for understanding the levers of management control. We begin by studying the ties between a company's operating decisions—such as pricing policy, inventory control practices, and financing strategies—and its financial performance. These operating decisions are the levers by which management controls financial performance. Then we will broaden the discussion to consider the uses and limitations of ratio analysis as a tool for evaluating performance. To retain a practical perspective, we will again use the financial statements for Tektronix, Inc., presented in Tables 1–1 and 1–2 of the last chapter, to illustrate the techniques. The chapter will conclude with an evaluation of TEK's financial performance relative to its competition.

RETURN ON EQUITY

By far the most popular yardstick of financial performance among investors and senior managers is the return on equity (ROE), defined as

$$\text{Return on equity} = \frac{\text{Earnings}}{\text{Shareholders' equity}}.$$

Referring to Tables 1–1 and 1–2 in the last chapter, TEK's ROE for 1987 was

$$ROE = \frac{\$50}{\$839} = 6.0\%.$$

It is not an exaggeration to say that the careers of many senior executives rise and fall in harmony with their firm's ROE. ROE is accorded such importance because it is a measure of the *efficiency* with which the firm employs owners' capital. It is an estimate of the earnings per dollar of invested equity capital, or alternatively, the percentage return to owners on their investment in the firm. In short, it measures bang per buck.

Later in this chapter we will consider some significant problems with ROE as a measure of financial performance, but for now let us accept it provisionally as at least widely used and see what we can learn.

Three Determinants of ROE

To see how a company can increase its ROE, let us use some simple algebra to restate the ratio in terms of its three principal components.

$$ROE = \frac{\text{Earnings}}{\text{Shareholders' equity}}$$
$$= \frac{\text{Earnings}}{\text{Sales}} \times \frac{\text{Sales}}{\text{Assets}} \times \frac{\text{Assets}}{\text{Shareholders' equity}}.$$

In words,

$$\frac{\text{Return on}}{\text{equity}} = \frac{\text{Profit}}{\text{margin}} \times \frac{\text{Asset}}{\text{turnover}} \times \frac{\text{Financial}}{\text{leverage}}.$$

We find that TEK's ROE in 1987 was generated as follows:

$$\frac{\$50}{\$839} = \frac{50}{1,396} \times \frac{1,396}{1,160} \times \frac{1,160}{839}$$
$$6.0\% = 3.6\% \times 1.2 \times 1.4.$$

This expression says that management has three levers for controlling ROE. They are (1) the earnings squeezed out of each dollar of sales, or the *profit margin,* (2) the sales generated from each dollar of assets employed, or the *asset turnover,* and (3) the amount of debt used to finance the assets, or the *financial leverage.* With limited exception, whatever management does to increase these ratios increases ROE.

Note too the close correspondence between the levers of performance and company financial statements. The profit margin summarizes a company's income statement performance, while asset turnover and financial leverage do the same for the left-hand side and the right-hand side of the balance sheet, respectively. This is reassuring evidence that despite their simplicity, the three levers do capture the major elements of a company's financial performance.

Table 2–1 presents ROE decomposed into its three principal components for 11 widely diverse companies. It shows clearly that there are many paths to heaven: The ROE's of the companies are quite similar, but the combinations of profit margin, asset turnover, and financial leverage that produce this end result vary widely. Thus ROE ranges from a high of 16.7 percent for Exxon to a low of 6 percent for Tektronix, while the profit margin, to take one example, ranges from a low of 0.9 percent for Lucky Food Stores to a high of 13.8 percent for Pacific Gas & Electric. ROE differs by a factor of about 3 to 1, while the profit margin differs by a factor of over 15 to 1.

To understand why such diversity exists and how managerial decisions and a company's competitive environment combine to affect ROE, let us examine the levers of performance in more detail. In anticipation of our discussion of ratio analysis, which follows, it will also be useful to devote some attention to related, commonly used financial ratios.

The Profit Margin

The profit margin measures the portion of each dollar of sales that trickles down through the income statement to profits. The ratio is of particular importance to operating managers because it reflects the company's pricing strategy and its ability to control operating costs. As Table 2–1 indicates, profit margins differ greatly among industries and companies within an industry,

TABLE 2–1
ROE and the Levers of Performance for 11 Diverse Firms
(1986 except Tektronix, which is fiscal year 1987)

	Return on Equity (ROE) (percent)	=	Profit Margin (P) (percent)	×	Asset Turnover (A) (times)	×	Financial Leverage (T) (times)	Return on Assets (ROA) (percent)
Boeing Company...............	13.8%	=	4.1%	×	1.48	×	2.29	6.0%
Citicorp.....................	15.1	=	4.5	×	0.12	×	28.00	0.5
Exxon Corporation...........	16.7	=	7.7	×	1.01	×	2.17	7.7
IBM Corporation.............	13.9	=	9.3	×	0.89	×	1.68	8.3
K mart Corporation..........	14.4	=	2.1	×	2.27	×	3.05	4.7
Lucky Stores................	13.7	=	0.9	×	4.86	×	3.04	4.5
Norfolk Southern............	10.2	=	12.7	×	0.42	×	1.92	5.3
Pacific Gas and Electric.....	15.4	=	13.8	×	0.43	×	2.59	5.9
Southwest Airlines..........	9.8	=	6.5	×	0.71	×	2.11	4.6
Tektronix, Inc.	6.0	=	3.6	×	1.20	×	1.38	4.3
Xerox Corporation...........	10.4	=	5.2	×	0.88	×	2.26	4.6

depending on the nature of the product sold and the company's competitive strategy.

Note from the table that profit margin and asset turnover tend to vary inversely. This is no accident. In the manufacturing sector, companies like IBM, with unique products, or companies that add significant value to a product can demand high profit margins. Because maintaining unique products and adding significant value to a product usually require lots of assets, however, these same firms tend to have lower asset turns. Much the same is true at the retail level. Grocery stores like Lucky, which add little to product value and which minimize selling costs, have very low profit margins but high asset turns. At the other extreme, jewelry stores, which carry expensive inventories and spend heavily on display and selling, have low asset turns but much higher profit margins. It should be apparent, therefore, that a high-profit-margin company is not necessarily better than a low-margin company. It all depends on the combined effect of the profit margin and the asset turnover.

Return on Assets.   The product of these two ratios is known as the *return on assets* (ROA).

$$\text{ROA} = \frac{\text{Profit}}{\text{margin}} \times \frac{\text{Asset}}{\text{turnover}}$$

$$= \frac{\text{Earnings}}{\text{Sales}} \times \frac{\text{Sales}}{\text{Assets}}$$

$$= \frac{\text{Earnings}}{\text{Assets}}$$

TEK's ROA in 1987 was

$$\text{ROA} = \frac{50}{1,160} = 4.3\%.$$

This means that TEK earned an average of 4.3 cents on each dollar invested.

ROA is a basic measure of the efficiency with which a company allocates and manages its resources. It differs from ROE because ROA measures profit as a percentage of total assets while ROE measures profit as a percentage of shareholders' equity only.

Some companies, like PG&E and IBM, produce their ROAs by combining a high profit margin with a moderate asset turn, while others, like Lucky, adopt the reverse strategy. A high profit margin *and* a high asset turn is ideal, but can be expected to attract considerable competition, which will eventually drive the ROA down to a more normal level. Conversely, a low profit margin and a low asset turn will attract only bankruptcy lawyers.

Gross Margin.   When analyzing a company's profit margin, it is often interesting to distinguish between variable costs and fixed costs of manufacture. Variable costs are those that change as sales vary; fixed costs are those that remain constant. Companies with a high proportion of fixed costs are more vulnerable to sales declines than other firms because it is impossible to reduce fixed costs as sales fall. This means that falling sales will produce major profit declines.

The gross margin distinguishes, as far as possible, between fixed and variable costs. It is defined as

$$\text{Gross margin} = \frac{\text{Gross profit}}{\text{Sales}} = \frac{\$757}{\$1,396} = 54.2\%.$$

The accountant does not differentiate between fixed and variable costs when constructing an income statement. Most items in cost of goods sold are variable, however, while most of the other operating costs are fixed. Roughly speaking then, 54.2 percent of TEK's sales dollar is a *contribution to fixed costs and profits;* 54.2 cents of every sales dollar is available to pay for fixed costs and to add to profits.

Asset Turnover

The second principal determinant of ROE is the sales generated by each dollar of assets, or the asset turnover. TEK's asset turnover of 1.2 means that TEK generated $1.20 of sales for each dollar invested in assets. This ratio is a measure of capital intensity, with a low asset turnover signifying a capital-intensive business and a high turnover the reverse.

The nature of a company's products and its competitive strategy contribute significantly to the asset turnover it achieves. However, the process is not a mechanical one. Management diligence and creativity in controlling assets are also vital. When technology is similar among competitors, control of assets is often the margin between success and failure.

Control of current assets is especially critical. It may appear at first glance that distinguishing between current and fixed assets solely on the basis of whether the asset will revert to cash within one year is artificial. But there is more involved than this. Current assets, especially accounts receivable and inventory, have several unique properties that should be recognized. One is that if something goes wrong—if sales decline unexpectedly, if customers delay payment, or if a critical part fails to arrive—a company's investment in current assets can grow very rapidly. When you observe that even manufacturing companies routinely have one-half or more of their money invested in current assets, it is easy to appreciate that even modest alterations in the management of these assets can significantly affect company finances.

A second distinction is that unlike fixed assets, current assets can become a source of cash during downturns in the business cycle. As sales decline, a company's investment in accounts receivable and inventory should decline as well, thereby freeing cash for other uses. The fact that in a well-run company current assets move in accordion-like fashion with sales is appealing to creditors. For they know that during the upswing of a business cycle rising current assets will require loans, while during a downswing falling current assets will provide the cash to repay the loans. In bankers' jargon such a loan is said to be *self-liquidating* in the sense that the use to which the money is put creates the source of repayment.

Because control of current assets is so important in generating an acceptable ROE, it is useful to analyze each type of asset individually. This gives rise to what are known as *control ratios*. Although the form in which each ratio is commonly expressed varies, any control ratio is really just an asset turnover for a particular type of asset. In each instance, the firm's investment in an asset is compared to net sales or a closely related figure.

Why compare current assets to sales? The fact that a company's investment in, say, inventories has risen over time could be due to two forces: (1) perhaps sales have risen and simply dragged inventories along or (2) management may have slackened its control of inventories, allowing excess quantities to accumulate. Relating inventory to sales in a control ratio adjusts for changes in sales, enabling the analyst to concentrate on the more important effects of changing management control. Thus the control ratio distinguishes between sales-induced changes in investment and other, perhaps more sinister, causes. Below are presented a number of standard control ratios.

Inventory Turnover.   The inventory turnover ratio is defined as

$$\text{Inventory turnover} = \frac{\text{Cost of goods sold}}{\text{Ending inventory}} = \frac{\$639}{\$215} = 4.4 \text{ times.}$$

An inventory turn of 4.4 times means that an average item in TEK's inventory turns over 4.4 times per year; or said differently, the average item sits in inventory almost three months before being sold (12 months/4.4 times = 2.7 months).

Several alternative definitions of the inventory turnover ratio exist, including sales divided by ending inventory, and cost of goods sold divided by average inventory. Cost of goods sold is a more appropriate numerator than sales because sales include a profit markup that is absent from inventory. But beyond this, there is little to choose from among the various definitions.

The Collection Period.   The collection period provides information about a company's accounts receivable management. It is defined as

$$\frac{\text{Collection}}{\text{period}} = \frac{\text{Accounts receivable}}{\text{Credit sales per day}} = \frac{\$252}{\$1,396/365} = 65.9 \text{ days.}$$

Credit sales rather than net sales are used here because only credit sales generate accounts receivable. Because TEK is a manufacturer, virtually all of its sales are on credit, so we can use net sales in place of credit sales in this instance. Credit sales per day is defined as credit sales for the accounting period

---

A Problem

Sales of XYZ Company last year were $3.5 million, up 20 percent over the prior year. Meanwhile, accounts receivable have risen from $250,000 to $350,000. What portion of this increase in receivables would you say is due to sales growth and what portion to changing management of accounts receivable?

Answer: Sales are up 20 percent, so it is reasonable to expect that receivables will also increase 20 percent to $300,000 [$250,000 + (20% × $250,000)]. The remaining $50,000 increase, or 50 percent of the total, must be due to slackening control of the accounts. A look at the collection period tells a similar story. The collection period has risen from 31.3 days the prior year [$250,000/($3.5 million/1.2/365)] to 36.5 days last year [$350,000/($3.5 million/365)].

---

divided by the number of days in the accounting period. Because we are using TEK's annual statements, the divisor is 365 days.

It is possible to interpret TEK's 65.9-day collection period in either of two ways: We can say that TEK has an average of 65.9 days worth of credit sales tied up in accounts receivable, or we can say that the average time lag between sale and receipt of cash from the sale is 65.9 days.

If we liked, we could define a more conventional asset turnover ratio for accounts receivable as credit sales/accounts receivable. However, the collection-period format is more informative because it is possible to compare a company's collection period with its terms of sale. Thus if TEK sells on 60-day terms, a collection period of 65.9 days may not be bad, but if the terms of sale are 30 days, our interpretation would be quite different.

Day Sales in Cash.   This ratio is defined as

$$\frac{\text{Day sales}}{\text{in cash}} = \frac{\text{Cash and securities}}{\text{Net sales per day}} = \frac{\$243}{\$787/365} = 63.5 \text{ days}.$$

TEK has 63.5 days worth of sales in cash and securities. It is difficult to generalize about whether this amount is appropriate for TEK or not. Companies require modest amounts of cash to

---

A Word of Warning on Seasonal Companies

Interpreting many ratios of companies with *seasonal sales* can be quite difficult. For example, suppose a company's sales are seasonal, with a large peak at the end of the year. The sales peak will result in a high year-end accounts receivable balance. Yet in calculating credit sales per day, using annual financial statements, this peak will be averaged with periods of low sales. The result will be an apparently very high collection period. To avoid being misled, a better way to calculate the collection period for a seasonal company is to relate end-of-year accounts receivable to credit sales per day, based on the prior 60–90 days sales. This matches the accounts receivable to the credit sales that actually generated those receivables.

---

facilitate transactions and are often required to carry substantially larger amounts as compensating balances for bank loans. In addition, marketable securities can be an important source of liquidity to a firm, obviating the need to maintain backup borrowing facilities with banks. So the question of how much cash a company should carry is often closely related to broader financial policies. Nonetheless, over two months' sales in cash appears more than ample.

Payables Period. The payables period is a control ratio for a liability. It is just the collection period applied to accounts payable.

$$\frac{\text{Payables}}{\text{period}} = \frac{\text{Accounts payable}}{\text{Credit purchases per day}} = \frac{\$109}{\$639/365} = 62.3 \text{ days.}$$

The payables period is properly defined in terms of credit purchases because this is what generates accounts payable. Credit purchases are seldom available to the outside analyst, however, so it is frequently necessary to settle for the closest approximation—cost of goods sold. This is what I have done in the above figures for TEK. $639 million is TEK's cost of goods sold, not its credit purchases. Cost of goods sold can differ from credit purchases for two reasons. First, the company is producing, and hence purchasing material at a rate that differs from its sales rate; and second, the company adds labor and depreciation to material in the production process, thereby making cost of goods sold much larger than purchases. Because of these differences, it is not meaningful to compare a manufacturing company's payables period, based on cost of goods sold, to its purchase terms.

Fixed Asset Turnover. Fixed asset turnover reflects the capital intensity of a business. Changes in the ratio over time provide information about whether management is becoming more or less efficient in its utilization of fixed assets. It is defined as

$$\frac{\text{Fixed asset}}{\text{turnover}} = \frac{\text{Sales}}{\text{Net fixed assets}} = \frac{\$1,396}{\$358} = 3.9 \text{ times,}$$

where $358 million is the book value of TEK's land and net plant and equipment.

Financial Leverage

The third principal lever by which management affects ROE is financial leverage, defined as the substitution of debt for equity in company financing. Determining the appropriate degree of financial leverage for a particular company is a major responsibility of corporate financial officers (a topic to which we will later devote a full chapter). Here it is sufficient to recognize that while companies have considerable latitude in selecting a degree of leverage, there are economic and institutional constraints on their discretion. As Table 2–1 suggests, the nature of a company's business and its assets influence the financial leverage it can employ. In general, businesses that have highly predictable and stable operating cash flows can safely undertake more financial leverage than firms facing a high degree of market uncertainty. Public utilities—like PG&E in Table 2–1— are an example of such stable, highly levered firms. In addition, enterprises such as commercial banks, which have a diversified portfolio of liquid assets, can also safely use more financial

---

A Problem

The equation ROE = ROA × Financial leverage suggests that debt financing transforms—or levers—ROA into a higher ROE. Can you think of a situation in which more debt would lower ROE?

Answer: Suppose the firm's earnings are so low or the interest rate on the new debt so high that the decline in earnings due to the increased interest expense more than offsets the increase in leverage. Then increasing leverage would reduce ROE. We will explore the relation between ROE and financial leverage in considerable detail in Chapter 6.

---

leverage than the typical firm. By *liquid assets,* I refer to assets that can be readily sold without significant loss of value.

Another pattern evident in Table 2–1 is that ROA and financial leverage tend to be inversely related. Companies with low ROA generally employ more debt financing, and vice versa. This is consistent with the previous paragraph. Safe, stable, liquid investments tend to generate low returns but substantial borrowing capacity. Commercial banks are extreme examples of this pattern. Citicorp, as an example, combines what by manufacturing standards would be a horrible ROA of 0.5 percent with an astronomic leverage ratio of 28 to generate an attractive ROE of 15.1 percent. The key to this pairing is the safe, liquid nature of Citicorp's assets. The bank's loans to Mexico and other third-world debtors are, of course, another story—one that the bank would just as soon forget.

In following paragraphs we will discuss the more common ways to measure financial leverage and the related concept of liquidity. These ratios are useful to managers and creditors in appraising a company's debt capacity.

Balance Sheet Ratios. The most common way to measure financial leverage is to compare the book value of a company's liabilities to the book value of its assets or of its shareholders' equity. This gives rise to the debt-to-assets ratio and the debt-to-equity ratio, defined as

$$\text{Debt-to-assets ratio} = \frac{\text{Total liabilities}}{\text{Total assets}} = \frac{\$321}{\$1,160} = 27.7\%;$$

$$\text{Debt-to-equity ratio} = \frac{\text{Total liabilities}}{\text{Shareholders' equity}} = \frac{\$321}{\$839} = 38.3\%.$$

The first ratio says that 27.7 percent of TEK's assets, in book-value terms, come from creditors of one kind or another. The second ratio says the same thing in a slightly different way: Creditors supply TEK with 38.3 cents for every dollar supplied by shareholders.[1]

Coverage Ratios. There exist a number of variations on these balance sheet ratios. There is conceptually no reason to prefer one over the other, however, for they all focus on the balance sheet value of liabilities and, hence, all suffer from the same weakness. The financial burden imposed on a company by the use of debt financing ultimately depends not on the size of the liability relative to assets or to equity but on the ability of the company to meet the annual cash payments required by the debt. A simple example will illustrate the distinction. Suppose two companies have the same debt-to-assets ratio, but one is very profitable, while the other is losing money. The company that is losing money will probably have difficulty meeting the annual interest and principal payments required by its loans; yet the profitable company with the same debt-to-assets ratio may have no such difficulties. We conclude that balance sheet ratios are of primary interest only in liquidation, when the proceeds from the sale of assets are to be distributed to creditors and owners. In all other instances, we should be more interested in comparing the annual burden imposed by the debt to the cash flow available for debt service.

To measure the financial burden placed on a company by its use of leverage, it is useful to calculate what are known as

---

[1]The leverage ratio used earlier, assets/shareholders' equity, is just the debt-to-equity ratio plus one:

$$\frac{\text{Assets}}{\text{Equity}} = \frac{\text{Liabilities} + \text{Equity}}{\text{Equity}} = \frac{\text{Liabilities}}{\text{Equity}} + 1.$$

coverage ratios. The two most common coverage ratios, times interest earned and times burden covered, are defined as

$$\text{Times interest earned} = \frac{\text{Earnings before interest and taxes}}{\text{Interest expense}}$$

$$= \frac{\$112}{\$10} = 11.2 \text{ times;}$$

$$\text{Times burden covered} = \frac{\text{Earnings before interest and taxes}}{\text{Interest} + \left(\dfrac{\text{Principal repayment}}{1 - \text{Tax rate}}\right)}$$

$$= \frac{\$112}{\$10 + \left(\dfrac{\$0}{1 - 0.51}\right)} = 11.2 \text{ times.}$$

Both ratios compare income available to some annual measure of financial obligation. For both ratios the income available is *earnings before interest and taxes* (EBIT). This is the earnings generated by the company that can be used to make interest payments. EBIT is before-tax because interest payments are a before-tax expenditure, and we want to compare like quantities. TEK's times-interest-earned ratio of 11.2 means that the company earned its interest obligation 11.2 times over in 1987; EBIT was 11.2 times as large as interest.

The times-burden-covered ratio expands the definition of annual financial obligation to include repayments of debt principal as well as interest. If a company fails to make a principal repayment when due, the outcome is just as if it had failed to make an interest payment. In both cases, the company is in default, and creditors can force it into bankruptcy. When including principal repayment as part of the company's financial burden, we must remember to express the figure on a before-tax basis comparable to interest and EBIT. Unlike interest payments, principal repayments are not a tax-deductible expense. This means that if a company is in, say, the 50 percent tax bracket, it must earn $2 before taxes to have $1 after taxes to pay creditors. The other dollar goes to the tax collector. For other tax brackets, the before-tax burden of a principal repayment is found by dividing the repayment by one minus the company's tax rate. Adjusting the principal repayment in this manner to its before-tax equivalent is known in the trade as "grossing up" the principal, one of the better examples of financial jargon.

Looking at the supplementary information in TEK's annual report, we find that the company had no principal payments in 1987, so times burden covered equals times interest earned in this year.

An often-asked question is, Which of these coverage rates is more meaningful? The answer is that both are important. If a company could always roll over its maturing obligations by taking out new loans as it repaid old ones, the *net* burden of the debt would be just the interest expense. The problem with this logic is that the replacement of maturing debt with new debt is not an automatic feature of capital markets. In some instances, when capital markets are unsettled or the fortunes of a company decline, creditors may refuse to renew maturing obligations. In these cases, the burden of the debt is interest plus principal payments. This is what happened to Burmah Oil, a large British company, in 1974. Burmah took out a large, short-term Eurodollar loan to finance acquisition of Signal Oil Company in the United States, thinking they could roll over the maturing short-term debt into more permanent financing as it came due. Before Burmah was able to roll over the debt, however, Herstatt Bank in Germany failed, creditors became very conservative, and no one was willing to lend money to Burmah. A crisis was averted only when the British government bailed Burmah out by purchasing for cash a large block of British Petroleum stock owned by Burmah. In sum, it is fair to conclude that the times-burden-covered ratio is too conservative, assuming the company will pay its existing loans down to zero; but the times-interest-earned ratio is too liberal, assuming the company will roll over all its obligations as they mature.

Another frequent question is, How much coverage is enough? This question cannot be answered precisely, but several generalizations are possible. If a company has ready access to cash in the form of unused borrowing capacity, sizable cash balances, or readily salable assets, it can operate safely with lower coverage ratios than competitors without such sources of cash. The ready access to cash gives the company a means of payment it can use whenever operating earnings are insufficient to cover financial obligations. A second generalization is that coverage should increase with the *business risk* faced by the firm. TEK operates in a very dynamic environment characterized by rapid technological changes and high rates of product obsolescence. In view of this high business risk, TEK would be ill-advised to take on the added financial risk that accompanies low coverage ratios. Said another way, an electric utility that has very stable, predictable cash flows can operate safely with much lower coverage ratios than a company like TEK, which has trouble forecasting more than three or four years into the future.

Liquidity Ratios.   As noted earlier, one determinant of a company's debt capacity is the liquidity of its assets. An asset is liquid if it can be readily converted to cash, while a liability is liquid if it must be repaid in the near future. As the Burmah Oil debacle illustrates, it is risky to finance illiquid assets like fixed plant and equipment with liquid, short-term liabilities because the liabilities will come due before the assets generate enough cash to pay them. A company that mismatches the maturity of its assets and liabilities in this manner must roll over, or refinance, maturing liabilities to avoid insolvency.

Two common ratios intended to measure the liquidity of a company's assets relative to its liabilities are the *current ratio* and the *acid test,* defined as

$$\text{Current ratio} = \frac{\text{Current assets}}{\text{Current liabilities}}$$

$$= \frac{\$697}{\$250} = 2.8 \text{ times;}$$

$$\text{Acid test} = \frac{\text{Current assets} - \text{Inventory}}{\text{Current liabilities}}$$

$$= \frac{\$697 - \$146}{\$250} = 2.2 \text{ times.}$$

The current ratio compares the assets that will turn into cash within the year to the liabilities that must be paid within the year. A company with a low current ratio lacks liquidity in the sense that it cannot reduce its current asset investments to supply cash to meet maturing obligations. It must rely instead on operating income and outside financing.

You should recognize that this is a rather crude definition of liquidity for at least two reasons. First, rolling over some obligations, such as accounts payable, involves virtually no insolvency risk provided the company is at least marginally profitable; second, the size of a company's investment in current assets and its ability to reduce this investment to pay its bills are two different things. Unless sales decline, cuts in accounts receivable and inventory will usually diminish profits, sales, and production efficiency. Except in liquidation, companies do not customarily sell off large portions of their current assets to meet maturing obligations.

The acid-test ratio, which is sometimes called the quick ratio, is identical to the current ratio except that the numerator is reduced by the value of inventory. The reason for subtracting inventory is that it frequently is illiquid. Under distress conditions, a company or its creditors may not be able to realize much cash from the sale of inventory. In liquidation sales, the typical experience is that sellers receive 40 percent or less of the book value of inventory.

IS ROE A RELIABLE FINANCIAL YARDSTICK?

Until now we have assumed that management wants to increase its ROE, and we have analyzed three important levers of financial performance: profit margin, asset turnover, and financial leverage. We concluded that regardless of whether a company is General Motors or the corner drugstore, careful management of these levers can positively affect ROE. We also saw that determining and maintaining appropriate values of the levers is a challenging managerial task, involving an understanding of the nature of the company's business, the way it competes, and the interdependencies among the levers themselves.

It is time now to ask how reliable ROE is as a measure of financial performance. If Company A has a higher ROE than Company B, is its financial performance necessarily superior? If Company C increases its ROE, is this unequivocal evidence of improved financial performance?

As a measure of financial performance, ROE is prone to three problems: the timing problem, the risk problem, and the value problem. Seen in proper perspective, these potential difficulties mean that ROE is seldom an unambiguous measure of performance. ROE remains a useful and important indicator, but it must be interpreted in light of its limitations and no analyst should mechanically infer that a higher ROE is always better than a lower one.

The Timing Problem

Many business opportunities require the sacrifice of present earnings in anticipation of enhanced future earnings. This is true when a company introduces a new product involving heavy start-up costs. If we calculate the company's ROE just after introduction of the new product, it will appear depressed. But rather than suggesting poor performance, the low ROE is just the result of the company's new product introduction. Because ROE necessarily includes earnings for only one year, it frequently fails to capture the full influence of longer-term decisions.

The Risk Problem

Most business decisions involve the classic "eat well–sleep well" dilemma. If you want to eat well, you had best be prepared to take risks in search of higher returns. If you want to sleep well, you will likely have to forgo high returns in search of safety. Seldom will you find high returns and safety. (But when you do, please give me a call.)

The problem with ROE in this regard is that it says nothing about what risks a company has taken to generate its ROE. Consider a simple example. Take-a-Risk, Inc. earns an ROA of 6 percent from wildcat oil exploration in South Africa, which it combines with an assets-to-equity ratio of 5.0 to produce an ROE of 30 percent (6% × 5.0). Never-Dare, Ltd., meanwhile, has an ROA of 10 percent on its investment in government securities, which it finances with equal portions of debt and equity to produce an ROE of 20 percent (10% × 2.0). Which company is the better performer? My answer is Never-Dare. Take-a-Risk's ROE is high, but its high business risk and extreme financial leverage make it a very uncertain enterprise. I would prefer the more modest but eminently safer ROE of Never-Dare. Even if I preferred eating well to sleeping well, I would still choose Never-Dare and finance my purchase with a little personal borrowing to lever my return on the investment. In sum, because ROE looks only at return while ignoring risk, it can be an inaccurate yardstick of financial performance.

Return on Invested Capital.   To circumvent the distorting effects of financial risk on ROE, I recommend calculating return on invested capital (ROIC), also known as return on net assets (RONA).

$$\text{ROIC} = \frac{\text{EBIT}\,(1 - \text{Tax rate})}{\text{Debt} + \text{Equity}}.$$

TEK's 1987 ROIC was

$$\frac{\$112(1 - 52/102)}{\$3 + 51 + 839} = 6.1\%.$$

The numerator of this ratio is the earnings the firm would report if it were all-equity financed, while the denominator is the sum of all company capital on which a return must be earned. Thus, while accrued wages may be a source of capital to the firm, it is excluded because it carries no explicit cost. In essence, ROIC is the rate of return earned on the total capital invested in the firm without regard to whether that capital is called debt or equity.

To see the virtue of ROIC, consider the following example. Companies A and B are identical in all respects except that A is highly levered and B is all-equity financed. Because the two companies are identical except for capital structure, we would like a return measure that reflects this fundamental similarity.

The figures below show that ROE, and for that matter ROA, fails this test. Reflecting its extensive use of financial leverage, A's ROE is 18 percent, while B's zero-leverage position generates a lower, but better-quality, ROE of 7.2 percent. ROA goes to the other extreme, punishing Company A for its extensive use of debt and leaving B unaffected. Only ROIC is independent of the differing financing schemes employed by the two companies, showing a 7.2 percent return for both firms. ROIC thus reflects the fundamental earning power of the company before it is confounded by differences in financing strategies.

	A	B
Debt @ 10% interest.......	$ 900	$ 0
Equity..................	100	1,000
Total assets	$1,000	$1,000
EBIT....................	$ 120	$ 120
– Interest expense	90	0
Earnings before tax........	30	120
– Tax @ 40%	12	48
Earnings after tax	$ 18	$ 72
ROE	18.0%	7.2%
ROA	1.8%	7.2%
ROIC	7.2%	7.2%

The Value Problem

ROE measures the return on shareholders' investment, but the investment figure used is the *book value* of shareholders' equity, not the *market value*. This distinction is an important one. TEK's ROE in 1987 was 6.0 percent and, indeed, this is the annual return you could have earned had you been able to buy TEK's equity for its book value of $839 million. But that would have been impossible, for as noted in the previous chapter, the market value of TEK's equity was $1,291 million. At this price, your annual return would have been only 3.9 percent, not 6.0 percent ($50/$1,291 = 3.9%). The market value of equity is more significant to shareholders because it measures the current, realizable worth of the shares, while book value is only history. We conclude that because of possible divergence between the market value of equity and the book value, a high ROE may not be synonymous with a high return on investment to shareholders.

The Earnings Yield and the P/E Ratio. It might appear that we can circumvent the value problem by just replacing the book value of equity with its market value in the ROE. Such a ratio is known as the *earnings yield.*

$$\text{Earnings yield} = \frac{\text{Earnings}}{\text{Market value of shareholders' equity}}$$

$$= \frac{\text{Earnings per share}}{\text{Price per share}} = \frac{\$1.33}{\$34.88}$$

$$= 3.8\%.$$

Is it logical to say that earnings yield is a useful measure of performance and that managers should try to increase their earnings yield? No! The difficulty with earnings yield as a performance measure is that a company's stock price is very sensitive to investor expectations about the future. A share of stock entitles its owner to a portion of *future* earnings as well as present earnings. Naturally, the higher the investor's expectations of future earnings, the more he will be willing to pay for the stock. This means that a bright future, a high stock price, and a *low* earnings yield go together. Clearly, a high earnings yield is not a useful measure of performance. Said another way, the earnings yield suffers from a severe timing problem of its own that invalidates it as a performance measure.

Turning the earnings yield on its head produces the price-to-earnings ratio, or the P/E ratio.

$$\text{Price to earnings ratio} = \text{P/E ratio}$$

$$= \frac{\text{Price per share}}{\text{Earnings per share}} = \frac{\$34.88}{\$1.33}$$

$$= 26.2 \text{ times.}$$

The P/E ratio adds little to our discussion of performance measures, but because of its wide usage among investors, it deserves comment. The P/E ratio measures the amount of money investors are willing to pay for one dollar of current earnings. It is a means of standardizing stock prices to facilitate comparison among companies with different earnings. In May 1987, investors were paying $26.20 for each dollar of TEK's current earnings. Speaking broadly, a company's P/E ratio depends on two things: its future earnings prospects and the risk associated with those earnings. As noted in the previous paragraph, stock price, and hence the P/E ratio, rises as a company's prospects for future growth improve. Risk has the opposite effect. A high degree of uncertainty about a company's future earnings prospects will result in a low P/E ratio. In general, the P/E ratio tells you little about a company's current financial performance, but it is a useful indicator of what investors feel about the company's future prospects.

ROE or Market Price?

For years academicians and practitioners have been at odds over the proper measure of financial performance. Academicians criticize ROE for the reasons cited above and argue that the correct measure of financial performance is the firm's stock price. Moreover, they contend that management's goal should be to maximize stock price. Their logic is persuasive: Stock price represents the value of the owners' investment in the firm. Assuming the objective of managers is to further the interest of owners, managers should take actions that increase value to owners. Indeed, the notion of "value creation" has become a central theme in the writings of many academicians and consultants.

Practitioners acknowledge the logic of this reasoning but maintain that it is not practical. One problem is the difficulty of specifying precisely how operating decisions affect stock price. If we cannot say what effect a change in, say, financial leverage will have on a company's stock price, the goal of increasing price becomes ambiguous. A second problem is that managers typically know more about their company than outside investors. Why then should managers consider the assessments of less-informed investors when making business decisions? Yet

Can ROE Substitute for Share Price?

The accompanying graphs (Figures 2–1 and 2–2) suggest that the gulf between academicians and practitioners over the proper measure of financial performance may not be as wide as many believe. The graphs plot the market value of equity divided by book value of equity against ROE for two representative industries. ROE is measured as a weighted average of the past five years' ROEs. The smooth line in each figure is a regression line indicating the general relation between the two variables. The strong positive relationship visible in both graphs suggests that high-ROE firms tend to have high stock prices relative to book value, and vice versa. Hence, working to increase ROE in these industries is largely consistent with working to increase stock price.

The proximity of the company dots to the fitted regression lines is also interesting. It shows the importance of factors other than ROE in determining a company's market-to-book ratio. As we should expect, these other factors play a significant role in determining the market value of a specific firm's shares.

For interest, I have indicated the position of several companies on the graphs. Note in Figure 2–1 that Tektronix is right on the regression line with a weighted-average ROE of about 8.6 percent and market-to-book ratio of 1.1. The stock prices used here are those following the October 19, 1987, crash, which explains why this ratio is well below that calculated in Chapter 1. Note too that EG&G, Inc., has a lofty 22 percent ROE and is accorded the highest market-to-book ratio of almost 3.5. In Figure 2–2, Zondervan Corporation is clearly an indication that "hope springs eternal." Although their ROE has not exceeded three percent in the last four years, investors are still willing to pay well above book value for their shares.

To summarize, these graphs offer tantalizing evidence that despite its weaknesses, ROE may be a useful proxy for share price in measuring financial performance.

another practical problem with stock price as a performance measure is that it depends on a whole array of factors outside the company's control. One can never be certain whether an increase in stock price reflects improving company performance or an improving external economic environment. For these rea-

FIGURE 2–1

The Ratio of Market Value to Book Value of Equity versus Return on Equity in the Precision Instruments Industry

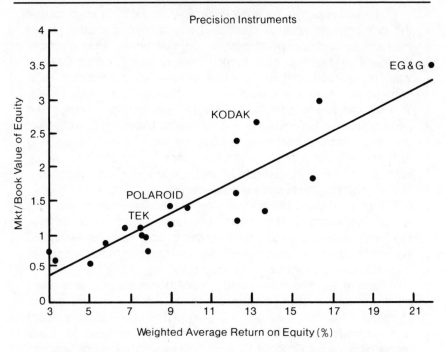

Source: © *Value Line Investment Survey* (December 25, 1987); used by permission of Value Line, Inc. ROE figures for 1987 are Value Line estimates.

sons, practitioners continue to use ROE as an admittedly imperfect measure of financial performance. Academicians and financial consultants, meanwhile, work to make value creation a more practical financial objective.

RATIO ANALYSIS

In the course of our discussion of the levers of financial performance, we defined a number of financial ratios. It is time now to broaden the discussion to consider the systematic use of such ratios to analyze financial performance. This involves nothing more than calculating a number of diverse ratios and comparing

FIGURE 2–2
The Ratio of Market Value to Book Value of Equity versus Return on Equity in the Publishing Industry

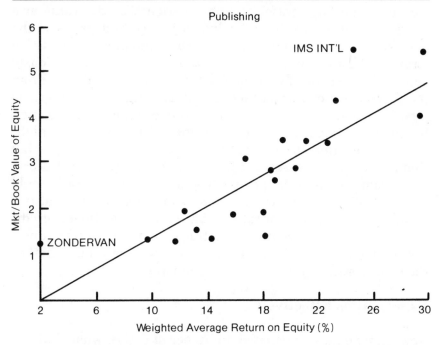

Source: © *Value Line Investment Survey* (December 11, 1987); used by permission of Value Line, Inc. ROE figures for 1987 are Value Line estimates.

them to certain standards, in search of insights into the company's operations and its financial health.

Ratio analysis is widely used by managers, creditors, regulators, and investors. Used with care and imagination, the technique can reveal much about a company and its operations. But there are a few things to bear in mind about ratios. First, a ratio is just one number divided by another, so it is unreasonable to expect that the mechanical calculation of one ratio, or even several ratios, will automatically yield important insights into anything as complex as a modern corporation. It is useful to think of ratios as clues in a detective story. One or even several ratios might be misleading, but when combined with other knowledge of a company's management and economic circumstances, ratio analysis can tell an interesting story.

A second point to bear in mind is that there is no single correct value for a ratio. The observation that the value of a particular ratio is too high, too low, or just right depends on the perspective of the analyst and on the company's competitive strategy. As an example, consider the current ratio, previously defined as the ratio of current assets to current liabilities. From the perspective of a short-term creditor, a high current ratio is a positive sign because it suggests ample liquidity and a high likelihood of repayment. Yet an owner of the company might look on the same current ratio as a negative sign, suggesting that the company's assets are too conservatively deployed. Moreover, from an operating perspective, a high current ratio could be a sign of conservative management or it could be the natural result of a competitive strategy that emphasizes liberal credit terms and sizable inventories. In this case, the important question is not whether the current ratio is too high, but whether the chosen strategy is best for the company.

Using Ratios Effectively

Now that we have calculated a number of ratios, what shall we do with them? If there are no universally correct values for ratios, how do you interpret them? How do you decide whether a company is healthy or sick? There are three approaches: compare the ratios to rules of thumb, compare them to industry averages, or look for changes in the ratios over time. Comparing a company's ratios to rules of thumb has the virtue of simplicity, but has little to recommend it conceptually. The appropriate values of ratios for a company depend too much on the analyst's perspective and on the company's specific circumstances for rules of thumb to be very useful. The most positive thing to be said in their support is that over the years, companies conforming to these rules of thumb tend to go bankrupt somewhat less frequently than those that do not.

Comparing a company's ratios to industry ratios provides a useful feel for how the company measures up to its competitors. But it is still true that company-specific differences can result in entirely justifiable deviations from industry norms. There is also no guarantee that the industry as a whole knows what it is doing. The knowledge that one railroad was much like its competitors was cold comfort in the depression of the 1930s, when virtually all railroads got into financial difficulties.

The most useful way to evaluate ratios involves trend analysis. Calculate ratios for a company over several years and take note of how they change over time. Trend analysis eliminates company and industry differences, enabling the analyst to draw firmer conclusions about the company's financial health and its variation over time. Moreover, the levers of performance suggest one logical approach to trend analysis. First, observe the trend in ROE over the recent past; second, determine what changes in the three levers of performance account for the observed pattern; and third, depending on the source of the observed change in ROE, study individual income statement or balance sheet accounts in search of a more specific explanation. For example, if ROE has fallen because of a decline in asset turnover, study the control of individual asset accounts in search of the culprit, or culprits.

Ratio Analysis of Tektronix

As a practical demonstration of ratio analysis, let us see what the technique can tell us about Tektronix, Inc. Table 2–2 presents what are known as common-size financial statements for TEK over the period 1983–87 as well as industry averages for 1986. The comparison industry consists of the four firms from the Electronics-Instrumentation industry represented in the Standard and Poor's 500 stock averages.[2] A common-size balance sheet simply presents each asset and liability as a percentage of total assets. A common-size income statement is

---

[2]The companies represented are Gould Inc., Hewlett-Packard, Perkin-Elmer, and Tektronix. The fact that TEK is itself a member of the industry averages attenuates the differences observed between TEK and the industry. Figures for a broader cross section of firms are available, but they appear to be dominated by much smaller companies. Despite the small number of firms represented, the sample chosen appears to provide the most relevant comparison with TEK.

TABLE 2–2
TEKTRONIX, INC.
Common-Size Financial Statements, 1983–1987 and Industry Averages for 1986

	1983	1984	1985	1986	1987	Industry Average
ASSETS						
Current assets:						
Cash and securities..........	9.1%	14.2%	19.0%	21.6%	20.9%	NA
Accounts receivable	19.3	23.0	22.9	20.1	21.7	20.9%
Inventories................	26.9	21.3	17.9	13.8	12.6	17.4
Other current assets	3.6	2.9	2.8	5.3	4.8	5.4
Total current assets	58.9	61.5	62.5	60.7	60.1	61.2
Net plant and equipment	36.4	33.5	32.6	31.7	30.9	31.8
Other long-term assets.......	4.7	5.1	4.9	7.5	9.1	7.0
Total assets	100.0%	100.0%	100.0%	100.0%	100.0%	100.0%
LIABILITIES AND SHAREHOLDERS' EQUITY						
Current liabilities:						
Short-term debt	3.1	2.4	1.6	7.1	0.3	5.2
Accounts payable	7.2	7.7	8.1	9.4	9.4	5.2
Income taxes due	1.4	0.9	1.4	2.0	3.6	2.5
Accrued expenses...........	6.4	7.0	7.5	8.1	8.3	12.6
Total current liabilities ...	18.1	17.9	18.6	26.6	21.6	25.5
Long-term debt	14.0	13.9	7.5	0.9	4.4	5.8
Deferred tax liability	4.0	1.7	2.0	1.8	1.0	2.6
Other long-term liabilities	2.9	2.4	2.0	0.6	0.7	2.7
Total liabilities	39.1	35.9	30.1	30.0	27.7	37.0
Shareholders' equity.........	60.9	64.1	69.9	70.0	72.3	63.0
Total liabilities and shareholders' equity ...	100.0%	100.0%	100.0%	100.0%	100.0%	100.0%

TABLE 2–2 (concluded)
TEKTRONIX, INC.
Common-Size Financial Statements, 1983–1987 and Industry Averages for 1986

	1983	1984	1985	1986	1987	Industry Average
Net sales	100.0%	100.0%	100.0%	100.0%	100.0%	100.0%
Cost of sales	52.4	51.2	49.1	49.0	45.8	
Gross profit	47.6	48.8	50.9	51.0	54.2	
Operating expenses:						
Engineering expense	10.7	11.4	13.3	14.6	14.3	14.5
Selling expense	15.6	14.9	15.8	18.4	18.9	0.2
Administrative expense	9.5	9.2	8.8	10.2	10.0	
Profit sharing	2.4	3.4	4.1	2.6	3.9	
Operating income	9.4	9.9	8.9	5.1	7.2	14.5
Interest expense	2.2	2.0	1.3	1.2	0.7	0.2
Nonoperating income (expense)	−2.1	0.1	0.8	−0.8	0.9	
Income before taxes	5.1	8.0	8.4	3.1	7.3	10.2
Provision for taxes	1.2	−0.5	2.1	0.2	3.7	3.5
Earnings	3.9%	8.5%	6.3%	2.9%	3.6%	6.7%

NA = Not available.

Source: *Standard & Poor's Analysts Handbook: Official Series, 1987 Annual Edition*, p. 53. Sample consists of the four firms in the S&P 500 stock index from the Electronics-Instrumentation industry. The companies represented are Gould Inc., Hewlett-Packard, Perkin-Elmer, and Tektronix.

analogous, except that all items are scaled in proportion to net sales instead of total assets. The motivation for scaling financial statements in this fashion is to concentrate on underlying trends by abstracting from changes in the dollar figures caused by growth or decline. In addition, common-size statements are useful in removing simple scale effects when comparing companies of differing size.

Looking first at TEK's balance sheet, note that although TEK is a manufacturing company, over 60 percent of its assets are short-term—primarily cash and accounts receivable. Note too that inventories have fallen dramatically over the period from 26.9 percent of assets in 1983 to only 12.6 percent in 1987—a figure that compares very favorably with the industry average of 17.4 percent. This improvement is due to a major company initiative that included, among other things, the institution of just-in-time (JIT) inventory management. Developed originally in Japan, JIT attempts to eliminate raw material and work-in-process inventories by scheduling materials to arrive just as needed in the production process. Experience indicates that reduced inventory investment is only a secondary benefit of JIT. The real payoff is in the production process itself, for JIT uncovers basic production inefficiencies and bottlenecks that might otherwise be obscured by the buffering effect of work-in-process inventories.

Another noteworthy trend is the sharp increase in cash and securities to over one-fifth of total assets. This may be a source of comfort to TEK's short-term creditors, but to managers and owners it is a worrisome sign that the company is not generating sufficient investment opportunities. Indeed, the lack of attractive investments is clearly reflected in TEK's growth rate. Between 1977 and 1982, TEK's sales grew at an annual compound rate of 21.3%, while this same number over the last five years has been only 3.1%, less even than the inflation rate. More will be presented on this topic in Chapter 4.

Looking at the liabilities side of the balance sheet, we see TEK's financial leverage falling steadily over the period until by 1987 equity constitutes almost three-quarters of total assets—approximately 10 percentage points above the industry average. This is yet another sign of the company's inability to find worthwhile investments.

The most noteworthy thing about TEK's common-size income statement is its volatile and mediocre profit margin. At 3.6 percent in 1987, it stands at little more than one-half the industry average, and a far cry from the halcyon days of 1979, when the ratio was almost 10 percent. Two offsetting trends appear to be at work: Improving manufacturing efficiency has steadily increased the gross margin, but these gains have been more than offset by increasing selling and engineering expenses. Compared to 1979, the improving gross margin has only returned the company to prior levels, while selling and engineering expenses far exceed those of earlier years.

Has TEK lost control of engineering and selling expenses, or is the pattern we see a conscious strategy of sacrificing short-run profits in pursuit of some longer-run goal? I believe it is the latter. Management appears to be spending increasing sums on research and marketing in hopes of rekindling growth. Indeed, TEK could have boosted its 1987 profit margin from 3.6 percent to 6.8 percent by simply throttling engineering expense back to its 1979 value relative to sales. This would clearly have improved near-term performance but at the expense of longer-run growth. TEK has wisely taken the longer-run perspective.

Continuing our ratio analysis of TEK, Table 2–3 presents 18 previously discussed ratios for the company over the years 1983–87 and, where possible, industry-average ratios for 1986. Table 2–4, at the end of the chapter, presents similar ratios for other representative industries, including median, upper quartile, and lower quartile values for the represented ratios.[3]

Looking first at TEK's ROE, we note again that it is only about half that of its competitors. To see why, look at the levers of performance. Financial leverage and asset turnover differ only modestly from industry averages, while the profit margin is well below par—clear confirmation that TEK's financial problems are to be found on its income statement. Looking at the

---

[3]For any ratio, if we were to array all of the values for the companies in the industry from the highest to the lowest, the figure falling the middle of the series is the *median;* the ratio halfway between the highest value and the median is the *upper quartile;* while the ratio halfway between the lowest value and the median is the *lower quartile.* Data are taken from *Industry Norms and Key Business Ratios: Library Edition 1986–1987* (New York: Dun & Bradstreet Credit Services, 1986).

TABLE 2–3
TEKTRONIX, INC.
Ratio Analysis of Tektronix, Inc. 1983–1987 and Industry Averages for 1986

	1983	1984	1985	1986	1987	Industry Average*
Profitability ratios:						
Return on equity (%)	7.1	14.4	10.6	4.7	6.0	11.1
Return on assets (%)	4.3	9.2	7.4	3.3	4.3	7.0
Return on invested capital (%)	7.9	14.3	10.9	5.8	6.1	9.6
Profit margin (%)	3.9	8.5	6.3	2.9	3.6	6.7
Gross margin (%)	47.6	48.8	50.9	51.0	54.2	—
Price to earnings (×)	30.3	9.8	13.2	31.4	26.2	30.5†
Leverage and liquidity ratios:						
Assets to equity (×)	1.6	1.6	1.4	1.4	1.4	1.6
Debt to assets (%)	39.1	35.9	30.1	30.0	27.7	37.0
Debt to equity (%)	64.1	56.1	43.1	42.8	38.3	58.7
Times interest earned (×)	3.3	5.1	7.4	3.6	11.2	59.3
Times burden covered (×)	2.9	4.6	6.5	3.6	11.2	—
Current ratio (×)	3.3	3.4	3.4	2.3	2.8	2.4
Acid test (×)	1.8	2.2	2.4	1.8	2.2	1.7
Turnover-control ratios:						
Asset turnover (×)	1.1	1.1	1.2	1.1	1.2	1.0
Inventory turnover (×)	2.1	2.6	3.2	4.0	4.4	5.1
Collection period (days)	64.7	76.9	71.1	64.8	65.9	73.3
Days sales in cash (days)	30.6	47.6	59.1	69.7	63.5	—
Payables period (days)	46.2	50.3	51.2	62.2	62.3	—
Fixed asset turnover (×)	3.0	3.3	3.6	3.6	3.9	3.3

† June 30, 1987.

*Source: *Standard & Poor's Analysts Handbook: Official Series, 1987 Annual Edition*, p. 53. Sample consists of the four firms in the S&P 500 stock index from the Electronics-Instrumentation industry. The companies represented are Gould Inc., Hewlett-Packard, Perkin-Elmer, and Tektronix.

TABLE 2–4
Selected Ratios for Representative Industries (Upper quartile, median, and lower quartile values)

Lines of business and number of firms reporting	Current ratio	Total liabilities to net worth	Collection period (days)	Net sales to inventory (times)	Total assets to net sales	Profit margin	Return on assets	Return on equity
Agriculture, construction, and mining:								
Dairy farms (178)	4.8%	25.5%	16.1	30.0	78.9%	16.9%	9.7%	20.7%
	1.7	65.2	25.0	7.6	135.1	7.3	5.6	6.9
	0.8	125.8	32.5	3.7	243.5	2.2	1.0	1.6
Drilling, oil and gas wells (359)	3.9	19.2	30.7	73.7	49.4	9.9	9.6	22.1
	1.5	63.2	52.1	27.9	86.1	2.6	1.2	3.0
	0.8	169.5	85.4	15.6	193.4	(8.0)	(8.0)	(12.0)
General contractors, single family homes (2,342)	3.5	33.7	8.8	107.4	17.7	11.6	23.0	59.7
	1.7	91.6	23.7	28.6	33.0	4.9	9.6	23.5
	1.1	223.5	48.9	7.6	65.6	1.5	2.4	7.4
Manufacturing:								
Semiconductors and related devices (322)	4.9	22.1	35.5	11.7	39.6	10.7	12.7	24.5
	2.7	60.9	49.6	6.7	56.9	4.8	4.8	9.8
	1.5	145.5	69.4	3.9	113.0	(0.3)	(4.1)	(10.2)
Wood household furniture, except upholstered (413)	4.1	31.2	18.5	16.9	25.5	8.9	18.1	37.7
	2.2	75.9	31.0	9.0	40.2	4.5	9.8	17.2
	1.3	181.4	48.9	5.9	57.7	2.2	3.8	7.2
Men's, youths' and boys' suits, coats, and overcoats (117)	3.5	46.1	26.6	9.0	30.1	4.1	8.6	16.4
	2.2	94.4	40.5	6.0	44.5	1.3	2.3	8.8
	1.5	185.2	59.9	3.7	60.0	0.4	0.7	2.3
Motor vehicle parts and accessories (483)	3.8	30.8	27.0	12.3	34.7	8.8	14.2	30.8
	2.2	86.6	40.6	6.9	47.7	4.4	7.6	17.5
	1.4	196.0	54.0	4.6	67.4	1.9	3.1	7.4

TABLE 2–4 (concluded)

Lines of business and number of firms reporting	Current ratio	Total liabilities to net worth	Collection period (days)	Net sales to inventory (times)	Total assets to net sales	Profit margin	Return on assets	Return on equity
Retailing:								
Department stores (1,032)	6.2%	19.7%	8.9	6.2	39.2%	4.2%	6.9%	13.2%
	3.2	64.4	30.1	4.6	50.6	1.8	3.6	6.7
	2.1	151.9	57.9	2.9	69.1	0.2	0.5	1.1
Grocery stores (2,295)	4.3	31.2	1.0	24.7	12.7	3.6	12.7	32.8
	2.2	84.0	2.6	16.8	19.4	1.6	6.6	14.8
	1.3	207.0	6.5	10.7	32.4	0.4	1.5	5.3
Jewelry stores (1,762)	7.3	18.1	11.7	3.6	51.7	13.5	15.4	29.9
	3.4	54.5	26.6	2.4	71.1	5.4	6.3	12.2
	2.0	144.2	59.7	1.6	102.0	1.4	1.6	3.4
Services:								
Automotive, rental, and leasing (612)	2.9	78.7	10.5	129.7	76.9	14.9	10.9	44.4
	1.2	221.5	22.2	18.9	132.3	6.8	5.2	19.0
	0.6	443.1	45.6	3.2	208.8	2.3	1.3	10.2
Colleges, universities, and professional schools (412)	6.1	9.4	8.8	9.7	144.2	9.1	5.4	7.3
	2.2	21.9	18.5	67.7	205.6	1.7	0.9	1.4
	1.1	65.9	36.0	38.6	269.7	(0.4)	(0.2)	(0.4)
Wholesaling:								
Sporting and recreational goods and supplies (738)	4.4	29.2	18.3	8.6	29.1	6.6	11.2	343.6
	2.1	89.5	33.5	5.0	41.0	2.8	5.8	243.9
	1.4	217.1	53.2	3.3	58.4	0.8	1.3	171.2
Electrical appliances, television, and radios (735)	3.0	48.2	17.9	14.4	22.0	5.7	9.6	454.5
	1.7	120.7	31.7	7.6	31.7	1.9	4.8	315.5
	1.3	262.5	46.7	4.8	47.1	0.6	1.3	212.3

Source: *Industry Norms and Key Business Ratios: Library Edition 1986–87*, Dun and Bradstreet Credit Services, 1986.

Problem

What increase in ROE could TEK attain if it increased financial leverage up to the industry average of 1.6 while leaving the other levers of performance unchanged?

Answer: ROE = .036 × 1.6 × 1.2 = 6.9%. This compares to 6.0% presently.

---

turnover ratios, we see again the marked improvement in inventory control as the turnover ratio rises from 2.1 to 4.4 times over the period. On balance, however, asset turnover improves only modestly, principally because days sales in cash has more than doubled. It is as if cash has sopped up every dollar provided by improved inventory management.

In sum, ratio analysis of TEK suggests a growth company that has at least temporarily lost its way. ROE and the profit margin are low because management is pumping increasing dollars into research and marketing in the attempt to stimulate renewed growth. In the meantime, idle cash and unused borrowing capacity are piling up, despite a large share repurchase. To TEK's benefit, sharply improved inventory control and significant improvements in manufacturing cost have helped to buy time while the company searches for growth.

APPENDIX

EVALUATING DIVISIONAL PERFORMANCE

Senior managers typically spend much more time assessing the financial performance of divisions or profit centers in their own company than they do evaluating other firms. To appreciate the magnitude of such "internal financial analysis," it is useful to note that ITT once had 250 separate profit centers, each reporting its financial performance to top management on at least a quarterly basis. It is therefore of interest to ask whether the techniques already presented for analyzing entire companies are also appropriate for assessing the financial health of individual divisions within a company. You will be relieved to learn that the techniques are indeed appropriate—but with several important provisos.

Management has at least three objectives in mind when evaluating division performance: to learn which divisions need help and what type of help is required, to learn which divisions are doing exceptionally well so that investment in these activities can be increased, and to learn which division managers are doing well so their superior achievement can be rewarded.

The evaluation of division performance is obviously closely related to the topics already discussed in this chapter. Both a company and a division invest resources in pursuit of profits, and the challenge is to measure their success in this activity. There are, however, some differences. One is that divisions seldom have debt or equity of their own. Instead, all financing is done at the corporate level, so it is impossible to define a ROE for a division. A second difference is that in divisional performance appraisal, the managerial incentives created by the evaluation are usually a prominent concern.

Return on Investment.   It should come as no surprise to learn that the most common technique for assessing the financial performance of divisions is a variation of Return on Assets known as return on investment, or ROI:

$$\frac{\text{Return on}}{\text{investment}} = \text{ROI} = \frac{\text{Division earnings}}{\text{Division assets}}.$$

Considering again the levers of performance, ROI, in effect, acknowledges an important division of labor between operating units and company headquarters. As illustrated below, ROI makes operating units responsible for generating decent profit margins and asset turnovers, while headquarters worries about the appropriate degree of financial leverage. Together, the operating divisions and headquarters attempt to produce attractive ROEs. The logical yardstick for measuring operating performance, then, is ROA (Profit margin × Asset turnover), or its close cousin, ROI.

	Divisional responsibility		Headquarters' responsibility
ROE =	Profit margin	× Asset turnover ×	Financial leverage

Many differing definitions of earnings and assets exist among companies using ROI for division performance appraisal. TEK, for example, calculates what they call "return on operations," or ROO, defined as unit operating income before tax divided by assets over which the operating manager has direct control. Jardine Fleming, a Hong Kong–based company, uses a similar quantity they call "return on operating funds," or ROOF, and reminds managers of its importance with the homily "A house without a ROOF provides no shelter."

Companies use variants of ROA rather than ROA itself for several largely technical reasons. First, operating executives frequently do not control all of the assets assigned to their unit. Cash, for example, is usually centrally managed, and hence, removed from the asset base on which the manager is evaluated. Second, as already noted during our discussion of ROIC, ROA and financial leverage are not truly independent of one another. Indeed, ROA declines as leverage rises. Use of ROA in performance appraisal, therefore, would suggest that operating managers had performed poorly whenever leverage increased. ROI and its relatives get around this problem by using income before interest expense in the numerator.

ROI as a Measure of Division Performance.   Just as with ROE, ROI suffers from timing, risk, and value problems when used as a performance measure. The timing problem is especially critical because it encourages managers to take a short-run focus. If you anticipate being a division manager for only five years, the natural incentive is to do whatever you can to boost near-term ROI and to ignore everything beyond this horizon. American industry has received considerable criticism of late for just such a myopia, and perhaps an over-reliance on ROI is one of the root causes of this problem.

Residual Profits.   A second incentive problem with ROI involves new investment. Suppose division managers are rewarded according to their divisions' ROI and that division A has an ROI of 25 percent, while division B's ROI is only 5 percent. Now assume that each division is presented with an opportunity to invest in a project yielding a 20 percent return.

Although 20 percent is a rather attractive return, the manager of division A will likely reject the investment because it will reduce his ROI, while the manager of B will jump at the chance to make the investment because it will increase his ROI. In fact, he'll undertake any investment promising more than five percent. The net effect of this distortion is that successful divisions will tend to underinvest and unsuccessful ones will overinvest.

There is no simple way to circumvent the timing, risk, and value problems inherent in the use of accounting ratios, but it is possible to eliminate the distortion described above by using what is known as residual profits rather than ROI as the performance measure. It is defined as

$$\frac{\text{Residual}}{\text{profits}} = \frac{\text{Division}}{\text{earnings}} - \left(K \times \frac{\text{Division}}{\text{assets}} \right)$$

where K is a percentage number representing the minimum acceptable rate of return on investment in the profit center, as defined by senior management. In later chapters we will refer to K as the cost of capital and will explain how it can be estimated.

To illustrate the use of residual profits, consider again divisions A and B, faced with an investment promising a 20 percent return. If both divisions have assets of $100 and if K equals 15 percent, then residual profits are

Division A	Division B
$\dfrac{\text{Residual}}{\text{profits}}$ = $25 − (15% × 100) = $10	$\dfrac{\text{Residual}}{\text{profits}}$ = $5 − (15% × 100) = −$10

Then, supposing the new 20 percent investment costs $50, its contribution to residual profits will be +$2.50 regardless of which division makes the investment ($2.50 = 20% × $50 − 15% × $50). Now, both division managers will want to make any investment promising a return greater than 15 percent regardless of their existing ROI or residual profits.

A closing comment regarding the evaluation of profit center performance: U.S. managers appear to be relearning an important lesson. It is short-sighted to manage anything strictly by the numbers. Executives need to take a broader, more qualitative view of the evaluation process, even when such a perspective reduces objectivity and dilutes incentives. Corporations are too complicated to allow the substitution of mechanical rules for creative thought. Numerical measures of performance are valuable tools, but their use must be kept in perspective.

SOURCES FOR BUSINESS RATIOS

Check your library for:

Annual Statement Studies. Philadelphia: Robert Morris Associates, published annually.

Common-size financial statements and widely used ratios for companies in many business lines, with companies classified into four sizes by net worth. Also contains comparative historical data. One limitation is that only companies with assets of $100 million or less are included. Excellent bibliography entitled "Sources of Composite Financial Data."

Industry Norms and Key Business Ratios. New York: Dun & Bradstreet Credit Services, published annually.

Percentage balance sheets and 14 ratios for over 800 lines of business. Median and upper- and lower-quartile values.

Analysts Handbook. New York: Standard & Poor's, published annually with quarterly updates.

Income statement, balance sheet, and share price data by industry for all companies included in the S&P 500 stock averages.

CHAPTER SUMMARY

1. Although a major corporation and the corner drugstore may seem vastly different, the levers by which managers in both firms affect performance are similar and few in number. The purpose of this chapter has been to study the ties between these levers and the firm's financial performance.

2. Return on equity is the most popular single yardstick of financial performance, although it does suffer from timing, risk, and value problems.

3. The primary components of return on equity are the profit margin, the asset turnover ratio, and financial leverage. The profit margin summarizes income statement performance; the asset turnover ratio focuses on the left-hand side of the balance sheet and indicates how efficiently management has used the firm's assets; financial leverage looks at the right-hand side of the balance sheet and how the company has financed its assets.

4. Turnover-control ratios are very important for operating managers. They indicate the efficiency with which the company uses a specific type of asset, such as accounts receivable or inventories.

5. More financial leverage is not always better than less. Financial leverage can be measured by using balance sheet ratios or coverage ratios. The latter are usually superior for long-term debt.
6. Ratio analysis is the systematic examination of a number of company ratios in search of insights into the firm's operations and its financial vitality. Used creatively, ratios are useful tools; but they can be misleading if applied mechanically.

ADDITIONAL READING

Bernstein, Leopold A. *Financial Statement Analysis: Theory, Application, and Interpretation.* 3d ed. Homewood, Ill.: Richard D. Irwin, 1983. 784 pages.

A detailed examination of financial statements and their uses from an accounting perspective. Not what I would call exciting reading, but particularly levelheaded and thorough.

Kyd, Charles W. "Forecasting Bankruptcy with Z Scores." *Lotus* (September 1985): 43–47.

In 1968 Professor Edward I. Altman developed a technique using financial ratios and a statistical technique called discriminant analysis to predict corporate bankruptcy. His results indicated that ratios could be used to predict bankruptcy up to two years in advance. In this article, Kyd shows how the Altman model can be run on a personal computer using Lotus 1-2-3. See the *Journal of Finance,* September 1968, for Altman's original paper.

CHAPTER PROBLEMS

1. Table 2–1 indicates that Exxon's ROE in 1986 was 16.7 percent and Southwest Airlines' was only 9.8 percent.
   a. Does this suggest that Exxon is a better managed company than Southwest Airlines? Why or why not?
   b. From an equity investor's perspective, do these differing ROEs suggest that Exxon's common stock is a better buy than Southwest Airlines'? Why or why not?

2. Table 3–1 presents financial statements over the period 1985–1988 for R&E Supplies, Inc.
   a. Calculate the return on equity, profit margin, asset turnover and financial leverage ratios for each year.
   b. Calculate return on assets and return on invested capital for each year.
   c. What insights, if any, do these figures provide about R&E Supplies? As a manger or a shareholder, would you be concerned?

3. In 1988 Acorn Services had assets of $100 million and liabilities of $70 million. Interest expense was $5 million, earnings before interest and taxes were $15 million, the tax rate was 34 percent, sinking fund payments were $3 million, and annual dividend payments were 20 cents per share on 10 million common shares outstanding.
   a. Calculate:
      (1) Acorn's liabilities-to-assets ratio,
      (2) liabilities-to-equity ratio,
      (3) times interest earned,
      (4) times burden covered.
   b. What percentage decline in earnings before interest and taxes could Acorn have sustained before failing to cover
      (1) interest expense,
      (2) sinking fund requirements,
      (3) common dividend payments?

4. Given the following information, complete the balance sheet shown below.

Collection period	50 days
Days sales in cash	15 days
Current ratio	2.4 times
Inventory turnover	6 times
Liabilities to assets	80 percent
Payables period	28 days

(All sales are on credit. All calculations assume a 365-day year. Payables period based on cost of goods sold.)

Assets	
Current:	
Cash	$500,000
Accounts receivable	
Inventory	1,000,000
Total current assets	
Net fixed assets	
Total assets	$5,000,000
Liabilities and shareholders' equity	
Current liabilities:	
Accounts payable	$
Short-term debt	
Total current liabilities	
Long-term debt	
Shareholders' equity	
Total liabilities and equity	$

Part II

Planning Future Financial Performance

Part II

Planning Future Financial Performance

Chapter 3
Financial Forecasting

Planning is the substitution of error for chaos.

Anonymous

To this point we have looked at the *past,* evaluating existing financial statements and assessing past performance. It is time now to look to the *future.* We begin in this chapter with an examination of the principal techniques of financial forecasting and a brief overview of planning and budgeting as practiced by modern large corporations. The following chapter will look at planning problems unique to the management of company growth. Throughout this chapter our emphasis will be on the *techniques* of forecasting and planning; so as a counterweight, it will be important for you to bear in mind that proper technique is only a part of effective planning. At least as critical is the development of creative market strategies and operating policies that underlie the financial plans.

PRO FORMA STATEMENTS

Finance is central to a company's planning activities for at least two reasons. First, much of the language of forecasting and planning is financial. Plans are stated in terms of financial statements, and many of the measures used to evaluate the plan are financial. Second, and more importantly, the financial executive is responsible for a critical resource: money. Because virtually every corporate action has financial implications, a critical part of any plan is the determination of whether it is attainable, given the company's limited resources.

Companies typically prepare a wide array of plans and budgets. Some, such as production plans and staff budgets, focus on a particular aspect of the firm, while others, such as pro forma statements, are much broader in scope. Our strategy here will be to begin with the broader techniques and to talk briefly about more specialized procedures later when addressing planning in large corporations.

The preparation of pro forma financial statements is the most widely used technique for financial forecasting. A pro forma statement is nothing more than a prediction of what a company's financial statements will look like at the end of the forecast period. These predictions may be the culmination of intensive, detailed operating plans and budgets or nothing more than rough, back-of-the-envelope projections. Either way, the pro forma format displays the information in a logical, internally consistent manner. A major use of pro forma forecasts, as will become apparent below, is to estimate the company's future need for external financing.

Percent-of-Sales Forecasting

One simple, yet effective way to project company financial performance is to tie many of the income statement and balance sheet figures to future sales. The rationale for the percent-of-sales approach is the tendency, noted earlier, for all variable costs and most current assets and current liabilities to vary directly with sales. Obviously, this will not be true for all of the entries in a company's financial statements, and certainly some independent forecasts of individual items will be required.

Nonetheless, the percent-of-sales method does provide simple, logical estimates of many important variables.

The first step in a percent-of-sales forecast should be an examination of historical data to determine which financial statement items have varied in proportion to sales in the past. This will enable the forecaster to decide which items can safely be estimated as a percent of sales and which must be forecast by using other information. The second step is to forecast sales. Because so many other items will be linked mechanically to the sales forecast, it is critically important to estimate sales as accurately as possible. Also, once the pro forma statements are completed, it is a good idea to test the sensitivity of the results to reasonable variations in the sales forecast. The final step in the percent-of-sales forecast is to estimate individual financial statement items by extrapolating the historical patterns to the newly estimated sales. For instance, if inventories have historically been about 20 percent of sales, and if next year's sales are forecasted to be $10 million, we would expect inventories to be $2 million. It's that simple.

To illustrate the use of the percent-of-sales method, consider the problem faced by Suburban National Bank. R&E Supplies, Inc., a modest-sized wholesaler of plumbing and electrical supplies, has been a customer of the bank for a number of years. The company has maintained average deposits of approximately $30,000 and has had a $50,000 short-term, renewable loan for five years. The company has prospered, and the loan has been renewed annually with only cursory analysis.

In late 1988, the president of R&E Supplies visited the bank and requested an increase in the short-term loan for 1989 to $500,000. The president explained that despite the company's growth, accounts payable had increased steadily and cash balances had declined. A number of suppliers had recently threatened to put the company on COD for future purchases unless payments were received more promptly. When asked why he was requesting $500,000, the president replied that this amount seemed about right and that it would enable him to pay off his most insistent creditors and to rebuild his cash balances.

Knowing that the bank's credit committee would never approve a loan request of this magnitude without careful financial projections, the lending officer suggested that he and the president prepare pro forma financial statements for 1989. He explained that these statements would provide a more accurate indication of R&E's credit needs.

The first step in preparing the pro forma projection was to examine the company's financial statements for the years 1985 to 1988, shown in Table 3–1, in search of stable patterns. The results of this ratio analysis appear in Table 3–2. The president's concern about declining liquidity and increasing trade payables is well founded; cash and securities as a percent of sales have fallen from 6 to 2 percent, while accounts payable have risen from 9 to 16 percent. In terms of the payables period, defined as accounts payable divided by cost of goods sold per day, the increase has been from 39 days to 66 days. Another worrisome trend is the increase in cost of goods sold and general, selling, and administrative expenses in proportion to sales. Earnings clearly are not keeping pace with sales.

The last column in Table 3–2 contains the projections agreed to by R&E's president and the lending officer. In line with recent experience, sales are predicted to increase 25 percent over 1988. General, selling, and administrative expenses will continue to rise as a result of an unfavorable labor settlement. The president feels that cash and securities should rise to at least 5 percent of sales, or 18 days sales. Since much of this money will sit in his bank, the lending officer concurs. The president also feels that accounts payable should decline to no more than 14 percent, giving the company a payables period of 59 days.[1] The tax rate and the dividends-to-earnings ratio are expected to stay constant.

The resulting pro forma financial statements appear in Table 3–3. Looking first at the income statement, the implication of the above assumptions is that earnings after tax will decline to $234,000, down 20 percent from the prior year. The only entry on this statement requiring further comment is net interest expense. Net interest expense will clearly depend on the size of the loan required by the company. However, because we do not

---

[1]$\text{Payables period} = \dfrac{\text{Accounts payable}}{\text{Cost of goods sold per day}} = \dfrac{14\% \text{ Sales}}{86\% \text{ Sales/365}}$

TABLE 3–1
R&E SUPPLIES, INC.
Financial Statements, 1985–1988
($000)

Income Statements
December 31,

	1985	1986	1987	1988*
Net sales...................	$11,190	$13,764	$16,104	$20,613
Cost of goods sold...........	9,400	11,699	13,688	17,727
Gross profit.................	1,790	2,065	2,416	2,886
Expenses:				
General, selling, and administrative expenses....	1,019	1,239	1,610	2,267
Net interest expense.........	100	103	110	90
Income before tax	671	723	696	529
Tax........................	302	325	313	238
Earnings after tax.............	$ 369	$ 398	$ 383	$ 291

Balance Sheets
Assets

Current assets:				
Cash and securities.........	$671	$551	$644	$412
Accounts receivable.........	1,343	1,789	2,094	2,886
Inventories.................	1,119	1,376	1,932	2,267
Prepaid expenses...........	14	12	15	18
Total current assets........	3,147	3,728	4,685	5,583
Net fixed assets	128	124	295	287
Total assets..................	$3,275	$3,852	$4,980	$5,870

Liabilities and owners' equity

Current liabilities:				
Bank loan	$50	$50	$50	$50
Accounts payable...........	1,007	1,443	2,426	3,212
Current portion long-term debt	60	50	50	100
Accrued wages.............	5	7	10	18
Total current liabilities......	1,122	1,550	2,536	3,380
Long-term debt...............	960	910	860	760
Common stock...............	150	150	150	150
Retained earnings	1,043	1,242	1,434	1,580
Total liabilities and owners' equity	$3,275	$3,852	$4,980	$5,870

*Estimate.

TABLE 3–2
Selected Financial Statement Items as a Percentage
of Sales for R&E Supplies, Inc., 1985–1989

	1985	1986	1987	1988*	1989†
Annual increase in sales.	—	23%	17%	28%	25%
Percent of sales:					
Cost of goods sold	84	85	85	86	86
General, selling, and					
administrative expenses . .	9	9	10	11	12
Cash and securities	6	4	4	2	5
Accounts receivable	12	13	13	14	14
Inventories.	10	10	15	16	14
Accounts payable.	9	10	15	16	14
Tax/Income before tax‡.	0.45	0.45	0.45	0.45	0.45
Dividends/Earnings after tax . .	0.50	0.50	0.50	0.50	0.50

*Estimate.
†Forecast.
‡Including state and local taxes.

know this yet, net interest expense has initially been assumed to equal last year's value with the understanding that this assumption may have to be modified later.

Estimating the Plug. To most operating executives, a company's income statement is more interesting than its balance sheet because the income statement measures profitability. The reverse is true for the financial executive. When the object of the exercise is to estimate future financing requirements, the income statement is interesting only in so far as it affects the balance sheet. To the financial executive, the balance sheet is key.

The first entry on R&E's pro forma balance sheet (Table 3–3) requiring comment is prepaid expenses. Like accrued wages, prepaid expenses is a small item that increases erratically with sales. Since the amounts are small and a high degree of precision in the forecast is not required, rough estimates will suffice. When asked about new fixed assets, the president indicated that a capital budget in the amount of $43,000 had already been approved for 1989. Further, depreciation for the year would

TABLE 3–3
R&E SUPPLIES, INC.
Pro Forma Financial Statements, 1989
($000)

Income Statement

	December 31, 1989	Comments
Net sales	$25,766	25% increase
Cost of goods sold	22,159	86% of sales
Gross profit	3,607	
Expenses:		
General, selling, and administrative expenses	3,092	12% of sales
Net interest expense	90	Initially constant
Income before tax	425	
Tax	191	At 45%
Earnings after tax	$234	

Balance Sheet
Assets

Current assets:		
Cash and securities.	$1,288	5% of sales
Accounts receivable	3,607	14% of sales
Inventories	2,577	10% of sales
Prepaid expenses	20	Rough estimate
Total current assets	7,492	
Net fixed assets.	280	See text discussion
Total assets	$7,772	

Liabilities and owners' equity

Current liabilities:		
Bank loan.	PLUG	
Accounts payable	3,607	14% of sales
Current portion long-term debt.	100	See text discussion
Accrued wages	22	Rough estimate
Total current liabilities	3,729 + PLUG	
Long-term debt	660	
Common stock.	150	
Retained earnings.	1,697	See text discussion
Total liabilities and owners' equity . . .	$6,236 + PLUG	

be $50,000, so net fixed assets would decline $7,000 to $280,000 ($280,000 = $287,000 + $43,000 − $50,000).

Note that the bank loan is labeled PLUG. This is the unknown in our problem. We will calculate the bank loan that must be plugged into the balance sheet to make total assets equal liabilities and owners' equity. Continuing down the balance sheet, current portion of long-term debt is just the principal repayment due in 1990. It is a contractual commitment specified in the loan agreement. As this required payment becomes a current liability, the accountant shifts it from long-term debt to current portion of long-term debt.

The last entry in need of explanation is retained earnings. Since the company does not plan to sell new equity in 1989, common stock remains constant. Retained earnings are determined as follows:

$$\text{Retained}_{\text{earnings}} \text{ '89} = \text{Retained}_{\text{earnings}} \text{ '88} + \text{Earnings}_{\text{after tax}} \text{ '89} - \text{Dividends '89}$$

$$\$1,697,000 = \$1,580,000 + \$234,000 - \$117,000$$

Sometimes companies will complicate this equation by charging nonrecurring gains or losses directly to retained earnings. But this is not a problem here.

The final step in constructing R&E's pro formas is to determine the size of the plug. We know from the principles of double-entry bookkeeping that

$$\text{Total assets} = \text{Liabilities} + \text{Owners' equity.}$$

Using the forecasted amounts, this means that

$$\$7,772,000 = \$6,236,000 + \text{PLUG};$$
$$\text{PLUG} = \$1,536,000.$$

According to our forecast, R&E Supplies needs not $500,000 but *over $1.5 million* to achieve the president's objectives.

The lending officer for Suburban National Bank is apt to be of two minds about this result. On one hand, R&E has a projected 1989 accounts receivable balance in excess of $3.5 million, which would probably provide excellent security for a $1.5 million loan. On the other hand, R&E's cavalier attitude toward financial planning and the president's obvious lack of knowledge about where his company is headed would be definite negatives.

PRO FORMA STATEMENTS AND FINANCIAL PLANNING

To this point R&E's pro forma statements have just displayed the financial implications of the company's operating plans. This is the forecasting half of the exercise. Now R&E management is ready to begin financial planning. This involves review of the forecasts and consideration of whether the operating plans should be modified. The first step is to decide whether the initial pro formas are satisfactory. This involves assessment of the financial health of the company as revealed in the pro formas, with special attention devoted to whether the estimated plug is too large. If the answer is yes, either because R&E does not want to borrow $1.5 million or because the bank is unwilling to grant such a large loan, management must modify its plans to conform to the financial realities. This is where operating plans and financial plans merge to create a coherent strategy.

To illustrate, suppose R&E management wants to reduce the size of the plug. It might then decide to test the following revisions in its operating plans for their effects on the company's external financing needs: (1) moderate the buildup in liquidity so that cash and securities are only 4 percent of sales instead of 5, (2) tighten up collection of accounts receivable so that receivables are 12 percent of sales rather than 14 percent, and (3) settle for a more modest improvement in trade payables so that payables equal 15 percent of sales rather than 14 percent. In combination, these reductions in assets and increases in liabilities would reduce R&E's plug by just under $1 million [(3% reduction in assets + 1% increase in liabilities) $\times$ net sales = $1 million].

Although each of these actions reduces R&E's need for external financing, each clearly has some offsetting disadvantages; so we cannot say for certain that the revised operating plan is necessarily better than the original one. It should be evident, however, that the pro forma format is useful for evaluating the financial dimensions of alternative operating strategies.

Sensitivity Analysis

Sensitivity analysis is the formal name for "what if" questions: What if R&E's sales grow by 15 percent instead of 25 percent? What if cost of goods sold is 84 percent of sales instead of 86 percent? It involves systematically changing one of the assumptions on which the pro forma statements are based and observing how the forecast responds. The exercise is useful for at least two reasons. First, it provides information about the range of possible outcomes. For example, suppose that sensitivity analysis reveals that, depending on the future sales volume attained, a company's need for external financing could vary between $1 and $2 million. This tells management that it had better provide enough flexibility in its financing plans to add another $1 million in new debt as the future unfolds. A second use of sensitivity analysis involves management by exception. Sensitivity analysis enables managers to determine which assumptions most strongly affect the forecast and which are secondary. This enables management to concentrate their data gathering and forecasting efforts on the most critical assumptions. Subsequently, during the implementation of the plan, it enables management to focus their efforts on those factors most critical to the success of the plan.

Personal computers and financial spreadsheets, such as Lotus 1-2-3, have greatly increased the popularity of sensitivity analysis in many business decisions. Once the basic pro forma forecast has been created, additional trials based on different values of the input variables can be spun out in seconds. Indeed, with modern technology, the scarce resource is no longer information, but the ability to interpret it.

Simulation

Simulation is an elaborate, computer-assisted, extension of sensitivity analysis. To perform a simulation we begin by assigning a probability distribution to each uncertain parameter in the forecast. The distribution describes the possible values that the parameter could conceivably take on, and it states the probability of each value's occurring. The next step is to ask a computer randomly to pick a value for each uncertain parameter consistent with the assigned probability distribution and to generate a set of pro forma statements based on the selected values. This creates one *trial*. Performing the last step many times produces a large number of trials. The output from a simulation is a table summarizing the results of many trials. For example, the output from a simulation study of R&E's loan needs for 1989 involving 1,000 trials might be the following.

Projected Loan Need	Number of Trials Occurring	Percent of Trials Occurring
$ 751,000–$1,000,000	150	15%
1,000,001– 1,250,000	200	20
1,250,001– 1,500,000	300	30
1,500,001– 1,750,000	200	20
1,750,001– 2,000,000	100	10
More than $2,000,000	50	5
Total	1,000	100%

The principal advantage of simulation over sensitivity analysis is that all of the uncertain input values are allowed to vary at once. Another advantage is that interdependencies among the uncertain parameters can be included. For example, if selling price and quantity sold are two uncertain parameters, simulation enables us to specify that the two parameters vary inversely; that is, a high selling price will be associated with a low quantity sold, and vice versa.

The principal disadvantage of simulation, in my experience, is that the results are often hard to interpret. One reason is that few executives are used to thinking about future events in terms of a range of possible outcomes or probabilities of outcomes. In terms of the above chart, should the company be prepared to raise in excess of $2 million, or is the 5 percent chance that this need will occur too remote to warrant concern? What is a reasonable maximum loan need the company should be prepared to meet?

A second reason simulation is less useful than sensitivity analysis in practice recalls President Eisenhower's dictum: "It's not the plans, but the planning." With simulation much of the "planning" occurs inside the computer, and management sees only the results. Consequently management does not develop the depth of insight into the plans that occurs when simpler techniques are used.

Interest Expense.   One thing that bothers novices about pro forma forecasting is the circularity involving interest expense and indebtedness. As noted above, interest expense cannot be estimated accurately until the plug has been determined. Yet because the plug depends in part on the amount of interest expense, it would appear one cannot be accurately estimated without the other.

There are two ways around this dilemma. One is to define a set of simultaneous equations to solve for interest expense and the plug together. If you are using a computer spreadsheet, this is equivalent to asking the computer to work through the statements several times, with each pass coming closer to the simultaneous solution. The other, more pragmatic approach is to forget the whole problem with the expectation that the first pass solution will be close enough. Given the likely errors in predicting sales and other variables, the additional error caused by a failure to determine interest expense accurately is usually not all that important.

To illustrate, R&E Supplies' first-pass pro formas assume a net interest expense of $90,000, whereas the balance sheet indicates total interest-bearing debt of over $2.2 million. At an assumed interest rate of 10 percent, this volume of debt implies an interest expense of $220,000, not $90,000. If we subtract, say, $20,000 for interest earned on newly purchased securities, net interest expense should be about $200,000, or $110,000 higher than our first-pass estimate. But think what happens as we trace the effect of a $110,000 addition to interest expense through the income statement. As shown below, the increase in net interest expense reduces the addition to retained earnings by only \$31,000 and increases the plug by a like amount. But when the plug is already over \$1.5 million, what's another \$31,000 among friends? Granted, increased interest expense has a noticeable percentage impact on earnings, but by the time the increase filters through taxes and dividend payments, the impact on the plug is quite modest.

	Original	Revised	Difference
Gross profit	\$3,607	\$3,607	—
General, selling, and administrative expenses	3,092	3,092	—
Net interest expense	90	200	+110
Income before tax	425	315	−110
Tax	191	142	−49
Earnings after tax	234	173	−61
Dividend at 50%	117	87	−30
Addition to retained earnings	\$ 117	\$ 86	−\$31

Seasonality. A more serious potential problem with pro forma statements and, indeed, all of the forecasting techniques mentioned in this chapter, is that the results are applicable only on the forecast date. The pro formas in Table 3–3 present an estimate of R&E Supplies' loan requirements on December 31, 1989. They say nothing about the company's need for financing on any other date before or after December 31. If a company has seasonal financing requirements, knowledge of year-end loan needs may be of little use in financial planning, since the year-end may bear no relation whatever to the date of the company's peak financing need. To protect against this, you should make monthly or quarterly forecasts rather than annual ones. Alternatively, if the date of peak borrowing need is known, you can simply make this date the forecast horizon.

CASH FLOW FORECASTS

A cash flow forecast is just a listing of all anticipated sources of cash to the company and uses of cash by the company over the forecast period. The difference between forecasted sources and

TABLE 3–4
R&E SUPPLIES, INC.
Cash Flow Forecast, 1989
($000)

Sources of cash:
Cash from operations:
    Earnings after tax $234
    Depreciation   50
Spontaneous sources of cash:
    Increase in accounts payable   395
    Increase in accrued wages   4
Total sources of cash $683

Uses of cash:
Investments:
    In fixed assets   43
    In current assets 1,909
Financial payments:
    Dividends   117
    Long-term debt repayment   100
    Short-term debt repayment   50
    Total uses of cash $2,219

Determination of PLUG:
Total sources + PLUG = Total uses
    $683,000 + PLUG = $2,219,000
              PLUG = $1,536,000

forecasted uses is the plug, which must be financed externally. Table 3–4 shows a 1989 cash flow forecast for R&E Supplies. The assumptions underlying the forecast are the same as those used to construct R&E's pro forma statements. Note that the sources and uses are grouped in categories. One category, spontaneous sources of cash, deserves mention. In most businesses, some sources of cash arise in the normal course of trade. The company pays no directly measurable fee for these sources, nor must they negotiate for them. Instead they arise spontaneously; examples include accounts payable, accrued wages, and accrued taxes.

Cash flow forecasts are quite straightforward and easily understood. Their principal weakness compared to pro forma statements is that they are less informative. R&E's pro forma statements not only indicate the size of the loan required, they also provide information that is useful for evaluating the company's creditworthiness. Thus, the loan officer can assess the company's future financial position by analyzing the pro forma statements. Because the cash flow forecast presents only *changes* in the quantities represented, a similar analysis using cash flow forecasts would be much more difficult.

CASH BUDGETS

A cash budget is a list of all anticipated receipts of cash and disbursements of cash over the forecast period. It can be thought of as a detailed cash flow forecast in which all traces of accrual accounting have been eliminated.

Table 3–5 presents a monthly cash budget of Trans-International Manufacturing (TIM) for the third quarter of 1988. To purge the accounting data of all accrual effects, it is necessary to remember that a period of time elapses between a credit sale or a credit purchase and the receipt or disbursement of the associated cash. In TIM's case, a 60-day collection period on accounts receivable means there is an average lag of 60 days between a credit sale and the receipt of cash. Consequently, cash collections in any month equal credit sales two months prior. The analogous lag for credit purchases is one month. Note that depreciation does not appear on a cash budget because it is not a disbursement of cash.

The bottom portion of TIM's cash budget illustrates the determination of cash needs. Observe that the ending cash for one month becomes the beginning balance for the next month. Comparing the ending cash balance to the desired minimum balance, as determined by management, yields an estimate of TIM's monthly cash surplus or deficit. The deficit corresponds to the plug in a pro forma forecast; it is the amount of money that must be raised on the forecast date to cover disbursements and to leave ending cash at the desired minimum. A forecasted cash surplus means that the company will have excess cash on that date and that ending cash will exceed the desired minimum by the forecasted amount.

TABLE 3–5

Cash Budget for TransInternational Manufacturing, 3rd Quarter, 1988 ($000)

	Actual		Forecast		
	May	June	July	August	September
Raw Data					
Credit sales........	$10,000	$14,000	$16,000	$19,000	$15,000
Credit purchases....	$ 5,000	$ 6,000	$ 5,000	$12,000	$ 6,000
Cash Budget					
Cash receipts:					
Sales for cash			$ 1,000	$ 1,000	$ 1,000
Collections from credit sales............			10,000	14,000	16,000
(assumes 60-day lag, sale to collection)					
Sale of used machinery...............				19,000	
Total cash receipts			11,000	34,000	17,000
Cash disbursements:					
Purchases for cash			1,000	1,000	2,000
Payment for credit purchases...........			6,000	5,000	12,000
(assumes 30-day lag, purchase to payment)					
Wages and salaries...................			4,000	4,000	4,000
Interest payments					12,000
Principal payments					26,000
Dividends...........................					8,000
Tax payments.......................			3,000		
Total cash disbursements...........			14,000	10,000	64,000
Net cash receipts (disbursements)			($3,000)	$24,000	($47,000)
Determination of cash needs:					
Beginning cash			$15,000	$2,000	$16,000
Net receipts (disbursements)			(3,000)	24,000	(47,000)
Ending cash........................			12,000	26,000	(31,000)
Minimum cash desired (assumed)			10,000	10,000	10,000
Cash surplus (deficit)			$2,000	$16,000	($41,000)

Because a cash budget focuses so narrowly on the cash account, it is seldom used by operating executives as a general forecasting tool. Its principal application is by treasury specialists for managing the company's cash balances. TIM's cash budget suggests that surplus cash will be available for investment in July and August but that the investments chosen had better be liquid, because all of the excess cash, plus $41 million from other sources, will be required in September.

THE TECHNIQUES COMPARED

Although the formats differ, it should come as a relief to learn that all of the forecasting techniques considered in this chapter produce the same results. That is, as long as the assumptions are the same and no arithmetic or accounting mistakes occur, all of the techniques will produce the same plug. Moreover, if your accounting skills are up to the task, it is possible to reconcile one format with another.

A second reassuring fact is that regardless of which forecasting technique is used, the resulting estimate of new financing needs is not biased by inflation. Consequently, there is no need to resort to elaborate inflation adjustments when making financial forecasts in an inflationary environment. This is not to say that the need for new financing is independent of the inflation rate. Indeed, as will become apparent in the next chapter, the financing needs of most companies rise with the inflation. Rather, we are saying that direct application of the previously described forecasting techniques will correctly indicate the need for external financing even in the presence of inflation.

Mechanically, then, the three forecasting techniques are equivalent, and the choice of which to use can depend on the purpose of the forecast. For most planning purposes and for credit analysis, I recommend pro forma statements because they present the information in a form suitable for additional financial analysis. For short-term forecasting and the management of cash, the cash budget is appropriate. A cash flow forecast is somewhere between the other two. It presents a broader picture of company operations than a cash budget and is easier to construct and more accessible to accounting novices than pro formas.

Problem

XYZ Corporation is forecasting its financing needs for next year. The original forecast shows a plug of $10 million. On reviewing the forecast, the production manager recommends increasing depreciation next year—for reporting purposes only, not for tax purposes—by $1 million. He reasons that this will reduce net fixed assets $1 million, and a reduction of an asset is a source of cash, which will reduce the plug by a like amount. Explain why the production manager is incorrect.

> **Answer:** Increasing depreciation will reduce net fixed assets. However, it will also reduce provision for taxes and earnings after tax by the same amount. Since both reduce liability accounts and reduction of a liability is a use of cash, the whole exercise is a wash with respect to the size of the plug. This is consistent with cash budgeting, which ignores depreciation entirely. Here is a numerical example:

	Original Depreciation	Increased Depreciation	Change in Liability Account
Operating income	$10,000	$10,000	
Depreciation	4,000	5,000	
Earnings before tax	6,000	5,000	
Provision for tax @ 40%	2,400	2,000	−400
Earnings after tax	3,600	3,000	
Dividends	1,000	1,000	
Additions to retained earnings	$2,600	$2,000	−$600
Total change in liabilities			−$1,000

PLANNING IN A LARGE COMPANY

In a well-run company, financial forecasts are only the tip of the planning iceberg. Executives throughout the organization devote substantial time and effort toward developing strategic and operating plans that eventually become the basis for the company's financial plans. This formalized planning process is especially important in large, multi-division corporations because it is frequently a key means of coordination and communication within the organization.

Effective planning in a large company usually involves three formal stages that recur on an annual cycle. In broad perspective, these stages can be viewed as a progressive narrowing of the strategic choices under consideration. In the first stage, headquarters executives and division managers hammer out a corporate strategy. This involves a broad-ranging analysis of the market threats and opportunities facing the company, an assessment of the company's own strengths and weaknesses, and a determination of the performance goals to be sought by each of the company's business units. At this initial stage, the process is creative and largely qualitative. The role of financial forecasts is limited to outlining in general terms the resource constraints faced by the company and to testing the financial feasibility of alternative strategies.

In the second stage, division managers and department personnel translate the qualitative, market-oriented goals established in stage 1 into a set of internal division activities that is deemed necessary to achieve the agreed-upon goals. For example, if a stage 1 goal is to increase product X's market share by a least 2 percent in the next 18 months, the stage 2 plans define what division management must do to achieve this objective. At this point, top management will likely have indicated, in general terms, the resources to be allocated to each division, although no specific spending plans will have been authorized. So division management will find it necessary to prepare at least rough financial forecasts to make certain their plans are generally consistent with senior management's resource commitments.

In the third stage of the planning process, department personnel develop a set of quantitative plans and budgets based on the activities defined in stage 2. This essentially involves putting a price tag on the agreed-upon division activities. The price tag appears in two forms: operating budgets and capital budgets. Although each company has its own definition of which expenditures are to appear on which budget, capital budgets customarily include expenditures on costly, long-lived assets, whereas operating budgets include recurring expenditures, such as materials, salaries, and so on.

The integration of these detailed divisional budgets at headquarters produces the corporation's financial forecast. If management has been realistic about available resources throughout the planning process, the forecast will contain few surprises. If not, headquarters executives may discover that in aggregate the spending plans of the divisions exceed available resources and that some revisions in division budgets will be necessary.

In Chapters 7 and 8 we will consider the financial analysis of investment opportunities in some detail. For now it is sufficient to acknowledge that corporate investment decisions are not made in a vacuum but rather are an integral part of the planning process described. This means, among other things, that even though a capital expenditure opportunity may appear financially attractive, it is likely to be rejected by senior management unless it furthers the attainment of agreed-upon corporate objectives. The proper perspective with regard to investment analysis, therefore, is that a company's strategic plans should create an umbrella under which operating and capital budgeting take place.

CHAPTER SUMMARY

1. The purpose of this chapter has been to present the principal techniques of financial forecasting and planning.
2. Pro forma statements are the best all-around means of financial forecasting. They are a projection of the company's income statement and balance sheet at the end of the forecast period.
3. Percent-of-sales forecasting is a simple but useful technique in which most income statement and many balance sheet entries are assumed to change in proportion to sales.

4. Most operating managers are concerned chiefly with the income statement. When the goal is forecasting the need for outside financing, the income statement is of interest only insofar as income affects the balance sheet.
5. Financial forecasting involves the extrapolation of past trends and agreed-upon changes into the future. Financial planning occurs when management evaluates the forecasts and considers possible modifications.
6. A cash budget is a less general way to forecast than pro forma statements. It consists of a list of anticipated cash receipts and disbursements and their net effects on the firm's cash balances. Done correctly and using the same assumptions, cash budgets and pro forma statements generate the same estimated need for outside financing.
7. Planning in most large companies involves three continuing cycles: (a) a strategic planning cycle in which senior management is most active, (b) an operational cycle in which divisional managers translate qualitative strategic goals into concrete plans, and (c) a budgeting cycle that essentially puts a price tag on the operational plans. Financial forecasting and planning are increasingly important in each succeeding stage of the process.

ADDITIONAL READING

Helfert, Erich A. *Techniques of Financial Analysis*. 6th ed. Homewood, Ill.: Richard D. Irwin, 1987. 458 pages.
A well-written introduction to financial analysis for managers. Chapters 3 and 4, Projection of Financial Requirements and Dynamics of the Business System, are especially good. Available in paperback.

Harrington, Diana R., and Brent D. Wilson. *Corporate Financial Analysis*. 2d ed. Plano, Texas: Business Publications, Inc., 1986. 239 pages.
See Chapter 3, Forecasting Future Needs. Available in paperback.

CHAPTER PROBLEMS

1. The financial manager of Ace Enterprises, a wholesale distributor of novelty toys, was interested in estimating the company's financing needs for the last three months of 1989. The following data are available:

Sales (one-half for cash, one-half on 60-day terms):	
August actual	$ 70,000
September actual	200,000
October forecast	100,000
November forecast	40,000
December forecast	40,000
Purchases (all on 30-day credit terms):	
September actual	200,000
October forecast	90,000
November forecast	20,000
December forecast	20,000
Wages payable each month	30,000
Interest and principal payments due in December	50,000
Dividends payable in December	50,000
Taxes payable in November	30,000
Cash balance October 1	200,000
Minimum desired cash balance	50,000

Construct a cash budget to estimate Ace's financing needs for the last three months of 1989.

2. Below are 1988 financial statements for Champion Drugs. For 1989 assume that:

Sales will increase 25 percent.

Investment in fixed assets will be $25 million.

Cost of goods sold, accounts receivable, inventories and accounts payable will rise in proportion to sales.

Dividends will equal 80 percent of profit after tax.

General selling expenses, depreciation, tax rate, long-term debt, and common stock will not change.

a. If Champion wants to maintain a minimum cash balance of at least $5 million, how large a bank loan will be required at year-end 1989? You may ignore any increases in interest expense.

Champion Drugs
Income Statement and Balance Sheet
December 31, 1988
($ millions)

Net sales	$100
Cost of goods sold	60
Gross profit	40
General selling expenses	10
Depreciation	10
Interest expense	5
Profit before tax	15
Tax at 34%	5
Profit after tax	10
Dividends paid	8
Additions to retained earnings	$ 2

Assets

Current assets:	
Cash	$ 10
Accounts receivable	17
Inventories	23
Total current assets	50
Gross fixed assets	130
Accumulated depreciation	60
Net fixed assets	70
Total assets	$120

**Liabilities and
shareholders' equity**

Current liabilities:	
Accounts payable	$ 8
Bank loan	22
Total current liabilities	30
Long-term debt	50
Common stock	20
Retained earnings	20
Total liabilities and shareholders' equity	$120

    b. How large a bank loan will Champion need if its collection
        period rises to 90 days? (Assume all sales are on credit.)
    c. How large a bank loan will Champion need if its collection
        period rises to 90 days **and** the company eliminates its
        dividend?

Chapter 4

Managing Growth

*Alas, the road to success is
always under repair.*

Anonymous

Growth and the management of growth present special problems in financial planning, in part because many executives see growth as something to be maximized. Their reasoning is simply that as growth increases, the firm's market share and profits should rise as well. From a financial perspective, however, growth is not always a blessing. Rapid growth can put considerable strain on a company's resources, and unless management is aware of this effect and takes active steps to control it, rapid growth can lead to bankruptcy. Companies can literally grow broke. It is a sad truth that almost as many companies go bankrupt because they grow too fast as do those who grow too slowly. It is doubly sad to realize that those companies that grew too fast met the market test by providing a product people wanted and failed only because they lacked the financial acumen to manage their growth properly.

At the other end of the spectrum, companies that grow too slowly have a different, but no less pressing, set of financial concerns. As will become apparent, if these companies fail to appreciate the financial implications of slow growth, they become potential candidates for takeover by more perceptive raiders. In either case, the financial management of growth is a topic worthy of inspection.

We begin our look at the financial dimensions of growth by defining a company's *sustainable growth rate*. This is the maximum rate at which company sales can increase without depleting financial resources. Then we will look at the options open to management when a company's target growth rate exceeds its sustainable growth rate and, conversely, when growth falls below sustainable levels. An important conclusion will be that growth is not necessarily something to be maximized. In many companies, it may be necessary to limit growth to conserve financial strength. This is a hard lesson for operating managers used to thinking that more is better; it is a critical one, however, because nonfinancial managers bear major responsibility for managing growth.

SUSTAINABLE GROWTH

It is possible to think of successful companies as passing through a predictable life cycle. The cycle begins with a start-up phase, in which the company loses money while developing products and establishing a foothold in the market. This is followed by a rapid growth phase, in which the company is profitable but is growing so rapidly it needs regular infusions of outside financing. The third phase is maturity, characterized by a decline in growth and a switch from absorbing outside financing to generating more cash than the firm can profitably reinvest. The last phase is decline, during which the company is perhaps marginally profitable, generates more cash than it can reinvest internally, and suffers declining sales. Mature and declining companies frequently devote considerable time and money to seeking investment opportunities in new products or firms that are still in their growth phase.

Our discussion will begin by looking at the growth phase, when financing needs are most pressing. Later we will consider the growth problems of mature and declining firms. Central to our discussion is the notion of sustainable growth. Intuitively, sustainable growth is just a formalization of the old adage, "It takes money to make money." Increased sales require more assets of all types, which must be paid for. Retained profits and the accompanying new borrowing generate some cash, but only in limited amounts. Unless the company is prepared to sell common stock, this limit puts a ceiling on the growth a company can achieve without straining its resources. This is the firm's sustainable growth rate.

The Sustainable Growth Equation

Let's begin by writing a simple equation to express the dependence of growth on financial resources. For this purpose, assume the following:

1. The company wants to grow as rapidly as market conditions permit.
2. Management is unwilling or unable to sell new equity.
3. The company has a target capital structure and a target dividend policy that it wants to maintain.

I will say more about these assumptions in a few pages. For now it is sufficient to realize that although they are certainly not appropriate for all firms, the assumptions are descriptive of a great many.

The variables to be used are:

P = Profit margin on sales (profits after tax/net sales);
A = Asset turnover ratio (net sales/total assets);
T = Target financial leverage ratio (total assets/equity);
R = Target earnings retention ratio (retained profits/profits);
S = Annual sales;
ΔS = Increase in sales during the year.

The variables T and R describe the company's target capital structure and dividend policy, respectively.

FIGURE 4–1
New Sales Require New Assets, which Must Be Financed

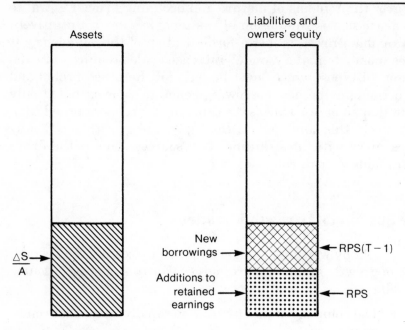

Uses of cash = Sources of cash

$$\frac{\Delta S}{A} = RPS + RPS(T-1)$$

$$\frac{\Delta S}{A} = RPST$$

$$g^\star = \frac{\Delta S}{S} = PRAT$$

To develop the sustainable growth equation, refer to Figure 4–1, which shows a company's balance sheet as two rectangles, one for assets, the other for liabilities and owners' equity. The two long, unshaded rectangles represent the company's balance sheet at the beginning of the year. Now if the company wants to increase sales by $\$\Delta S$ during the year, it must also increase assets. Assuming the asset turnover ratio, A, is constant over time, the required increase in assets is just $\Delta S/A$. If, for example, each $1 of assets can support $2 of sales, a $10 million increase in sales will require $5 million of new assets. This is shown in the figure as the cross-hatched area in the assets column.

Because the company is not selling new equity by assumption, the cash to finance this increase in assets must come from retained profits and new borrowings. The retained profits are just

Retained profits = Retention ratio × Profits
= Retention ratio × Profit margin
× Total sales
= *RPS*.

Further, because each dollar added to equity can support T dollars of new assets without deviating from the target capital structure, the total increase in assets the firm can afford is

Possible increase in total assets = *RPST*.

As a reality check, suppose the firm's profit margin is 5 percent, net sales are $100 million, and the earnings retention ratio is 60 percent. Then retained profits for the year will be $3 million. If the target assets-to-equity ratio is 2.5, this increase in equity can support $7.5 million in new assets.

The final step is to recognize that the use of cash represented by the increase in assets must equal the two sources of cash, retained profits and new borrowings.

Uses of cash = Sources of cash;
Increased assets = Retained profits + New borrowings;
$\Delta S/A$ = *RPST*.

Using a little algebra to rewrite this expression:

$$\Delta S/S = g^* = PRAT.$$

This is the sustainable growth equation.[1] Let's see what it tells us. $\Delta S/S$ is the growth rate in company sales, which we will refer to as g^*. It is the firm's sustainable growth rate. The equation says that, given the assumptions noted above, a company's growth rate in sales must equal the product of four ratios P, R,

---

[1] I shall refrain from admonishing you to avoid "prat"falls.

A, and *T*. Further, *g** is *the only growth rate in sales that is consistent with stable values of the four ratios.* If a company increases sales at any rate other than *g**, one or more of the ratios *must* change. For example, suppose a company grows at a rate in excess of its sustainable growth rate. Then it must either improve operations by increasing the profit margin or the asset turnover ratio, or it must alter its financial policies by increasing its retention ratio or its financial leverage.

TOO MUCH GROWTH

This is the crux of the sustainable growth problem for rapidly expanding firms: Because increasing operating efficiency is not always possible and altering financial policies is not always wise, we see that it is entirely possible for a company to grow too fast for its own good. This is particularly true among smaller companies, which may do too little financial planning. Such companies see sales growth as something to be maximized and think too little of the financial consequences. They do not realize that rapid growth has them on a treadmill; the faster they grow, even if they are profitable, the more cash they need. They can meet this need for a time by increasing leverage, but eventually the company will reach its debt capacity, lenders will refuse additional credit requests, and the company will find itself without the cash to pay its bills. All of this can be prevented if managers understand that growth above the company's sustainable rate creates financial problems that must be anticipated and solved. We will return to strategies for managing growth after looking at some numerical examples.

Tektronix's Sustainable Growth Rate

To illustrate the sustainable growth equation, let us return to Tektronix, Inc., the company discussed in Chapters 1 and 2. As luck would have it, TEK provides examples of the problems created both by too much growth and too little growth. In the late 1970s, TEK's chief problem was too much growth, while in more recent years a change of fortunes has made the absence of

---

Sustainable Growth and ROE

Three of the four ratios appearing in the sustainable growth equation are nothing more than the levers of performance discussed in earlier chapters. And because the levers of performance equal ROE, we can also write the sustainable growth equation as

$$g^* = R \times \text{ROE}$$

This version of the equation suggests another interpretation of sustainable growth. In essence, we are talking about a company in which everything is expanding at the same rate, and we are asking what determines the rate at which the system expands. Growing sales necessitate a proportional increase in assets, which in turn require an equal increase in liabilities and owners' equity. And because the rate at which liabilities expand depends on the growth rate of equity, we see that the growth rate of equity is the limiting factor. And how rapidly does equity increase? In the absence of new equity financing, it grows at a rate equal to retained profits divided by equity, or $R \times \text{ROE}$.

---

growth a critical concern. Looking first at the effects of too much growth, Table 4–1 presents TEK's actual and sustainable annual growth rates in sales for the period 1976 to 1979. For each year, the sustainable growth rate was calculated by plug-

TABLE 4–1
Tektronix, Inc., Sustainable Growth Calculations for the Period
1976–1979 (percent)

	1976	*1977*	*1978*	*1979*
Required ratios:				
Profit margin (*P*)	8.2	9.7	9.5	9.8
Retention ratio (*R*)	93.0	91.0	81.2	88.8
Asset turnover (*A*)	106.3	109.5	122.0	122.9
Financial leverage (*T*)	148.7	151.5	150.2	159.6
TEK's sustainable growth rate (*g**)	12.1	14.6	14.1	17.1
TEK's actual growth rate (*g*)	8.9	24.1	31.6	31.4

ging the four required ratios for that year into the sustainable growth equation. Two patterns are evident in the table. One is that TEK increased its sustainable growth rate by more than 40 percent over the period. It did this on the operating side by increasing P and A and on the financial side by increasing T. These changes outweighed the modest decline in R. The second pattern is that despite increasing g^*, actual growth in sales was well above the sustainable growth rate in the last three years.

What do these numbers suggest? As of 1979, TEK could have increased sales at a 17.1 percent annual rate forever without changing the four critical ratios. If TEK's actual growth rate were to exceed this rate, one or more of the ratios would have had to change. Of particular concern to management at the time was the noticeable increase in leverage. TEK had always been a conservatively financed company and wanted to stay that way. However, if rapid growth were to continue, management could envision increasing pressure to raise financial leverage or restrict growth. TEK management did not relish having to decide exactly how much growth they could afford. As we will see, TEK solved this problem, but not in a manner they would have chosen.

R&E Supplies' Sustainable Growth Rate

R&E Supplies, the wholesale distributor considered in the last chapter, finds itself in an even more dangerous situation. Table 4–2 shows that the gap between R&E's actual growth rate and its sustainable growth rate is steadily widening, primarily because of a falling profit margin. The result has been an increasing reliance on debt financing. Note that the assets-to-equity ratio has increased from 2.75 times in 1985 to a pro forma 1989 figure of 4.21. As noted in the last chapter, the pro forma bank loan required for 1989 may be possible to obtain, but the trend is a very unhealthy one. In the near future, R&E will reach its debt capacity and will be unable to raise added debt without a significant increase in equity. At this point, R&E will be without the money necessary to pay for added growth. If R&E and its

TABLE 4–2
R&E Supplies, Inc., Sustainable Growth Calculations (percent)

	1985	1986	1987	1988	Pro Forma 1989
Required ratios:					
Profit margin (P)	3.3	2.9	2.4	1.4	0.9
Retention ratio (R)	50.0	50.0	50.0	50.0	50.0
Asset turnover (A)	341.0	357.0	323.6	350.9	331.1
Financial leverage (T)	275.0	277.0	314.0	339.0	421.0
R&E's sustainable growth rate (g*)	15.5	14.3	12.2	8.3	6.3
R&E's actual growth rate (g)	—	23.0	17.0	28.0	25.0

What if?

	Profit Margin 1.9%	Retention Ratio 80%	Asset Turnover 400.0%	All of These Occur
R&E's sustainable growth rate in 1989	13.2%	10.0%	7.6%	25.6%

creditors realize what is happening in the near future, remedial action is possible; if not, the probable outcome will be bankruptcy.

"What If" Questions

Once management realizes that it has problems with sustainable growth, the sustainable growth equation can be useful in searching for solutions. This is done through a series of "what if" questions, as shown in the bottom portion of Table 4–2. We see, for example, that if R&E Supplies can increase its profit margin by one percentage point, its sustainable growth rate in 1989 will rise from 6.3 percent to 13.2 percent. Similarly, an increase in the retention ratio to 80 percent, holding everything else constant, increases sustainable growth to 10 percent, while raising the asset turnover to four times increases sustainable growth only marginally, to 7.6 percent. If R&E did all of these things at the same time, sustainable growth would rise to 25.6

percent, thereby solving the problem. As noted in the last chapter, "What If" questions such as these are an example of sensitivity analysis.

WHAT TO DO WHEN ACTUAL GROWTH EXCEEDS SUSTAINABLE GROWTH

We have now developed the sustainable growth equation and illustrated its use for rapidly growing businesses. The next question is, What should management do when actual growth exceeds sustainable growth? The first step is to determine how long the situation will continue. If the company's growth rate is likely to decline in the near future as the firm reaches maturity, the problem is only a transitory one that probably can be solved by further borrowing. Then in the future, when the actual growth rate falls below the sustainable rate, the company will switch from an absorber of cash to a generator of cash, and the loans can be repaid. For longer-term sustainable growth problems, some combination of the strategies described below will be necessary.

Sell New Equity

If a company is willing and able to raise new equity capital by selling shares, its sustainable growth problems vanish. The increased equity, plus whatever added borrowing is possible as a result of the increased equity, are sources of cash with which to finance further growth.

The problem with this strategy is that it is not available to many companies and unattractive to many others. In most countries throughout the world, equity markets are poorly developed or nonexistent. To sell equity in these countries, companies must go through the laborious and expensive task of seeking out investors directly to buy the new shares. This is a difficult undertaking because, without active stock market trading of the shares, new investors will become minority owners of illiquid securities. Consequently, those investors interested in buying the new shares will be limited largely to friends and acquaintances of existing owners.

TABLE 4–3
Sources of Capital to U. S. Nonfinancial Corporations, 1965–1986

Internal:		
Retained profits	17.24%	
Depreciation	43.83	
Subtotal		61.08
External:		
Increased liabilities	38.75	
New equity issues	0.17	
Subtotal		38.92
Total	100.00%	

Sources: Federal Reserve System, *Flow of Funds Accounts 1949–78,* and *Flow of Funds Accounts,* various issues.

Even in countries with well-developed stock markets, such as the United States, many companies find it very difficult to raise new equity. This is particularly true of smaller concerns, which, unless they have a glamorous product, find it difficult to secure the services of an investment banker to help them sell the shares. Without such help, the firms might just as well be in a country without developed markets. For a lack of trading in the stock will again restrict potential buyers largely to friends and acquaintances.

Finally, even many companies that are able to raise new equity prefer not to. This is evidenced in Table 4–3 showing the sources of capital to U.S. nonfinancial corporations over the period 1965–86. Observe that internal sources, depreciation and increases in retained earnings, were by far the most important sources of corporate capital over this period, accounting for about 60 percent of the total. At the other extreme, new equity has averaged *less than one percent* of total sources over the period.

Figure 4–2 shows the value of new equity issues, net of share repurchases, on a year-by-year basis. The highest figure reached was about $28 billion in 1983, while in more recent years, new equity has been a very large negative source, or a use, of capital. Indeed, in 1986, stock repurchases by corpora-

FIGURE 4–2
Corporate Net New Equity Issues, 1965–1986

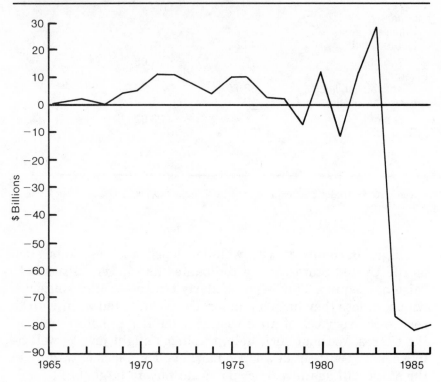

Sources: Federal Reserve System, *Flow of Funds Accounts 1949–78,* and *Flow of Funds Accounts,* various issues.

tions exceeded new issues by *$81 billion.* Ironically, U.S. companies' reliance on new equity appears to have varied *inversely* with stock prices. In direct opposition to the old buy low–sell high strategy, companies sold very few shares during the late 1960s, when stock prices were high, relied more heavily on new equity in the early 1970s as prices fell, and then in the mid-1980s massively repurchased shares during one of the strongest bull markets in history. This does not speak well of executives' ability to time new equity issues.

Like the fellow who drowned crossing the stream because he had heard it was only five feet deep on average, it is important to note that the equity figures presented are the *net* result

FIGURE 4–3
Gross New Equity Issues, 1970–1985

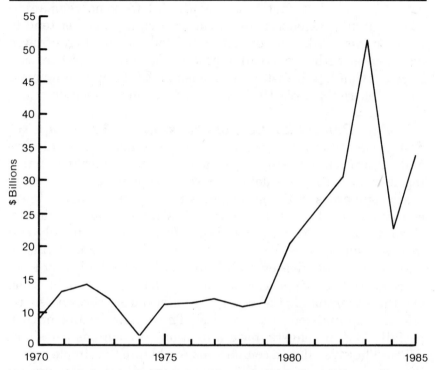

Note: New equity includes limited partnerships, preferred stock, and other equity.

Source: Federal Reserve System, *Annual Statistical Digest,* various issues.

of new issues and repurchases. Figure 4–3 shows the gross proceeds from new common stock sales, including limited partnerships, from 1970 to 1985. The 16-year average is $18.4 billion, and the peak is just over $50 billion in 1983. To put these numbers in perspective, gross proceeds from new stock issues equaled 6.4 percent of total sources of capital to corporations over the period. If one were to exclude public utilities (because the regulatory process appears to encourage new equity issues) and real estate and financial enterprises (because their numbers are dominated by limited partnerships), the figure would fall to 3.4%.

The appropriate conclusion appears to be that in aggregate the stock market is not an important source of capital to corporate America, but that it is meaningful to some companies. Those making extensive use of the new equity market tend to be companies with what brokers call "story paper," high-growth enterprises with a particular product or concept brokers can hype to stimulate investor enthusiasm. R&E Supplies and most likely Tektronix, circa 1979, would not be among such firms.

Why Don't U.S. Corporations Issue More Equity? There are a number of reasons. We will consider several here and will return to the topic in Chapter 6 when reviewing financing decisions in more detail. First, it appears that in recent years companies in the aggregate simply have not needed new equity. Retained profits and new borrowing have been sufficient. Second, equity is expensive to issue. Issue costs commonly run in the neighborhood of 5 to 10 percent of the amount raised, with the percentage even higher on small issues. This is at least twice as high as the issue costs for a comparable-size debt issue. On the other hand, the equity is outstanding forever, so its effective annualized cost is modest. Third, many managers, especially U.S. managers, have a fixation on earnings per share (EPS). They translate a complicated world into the simple notion that whatever increases EPS must be good, and whatever reduces EPS must be bad. In this view, a new equity issue is bad because, at least initially, the number of shares outstanding rises but earnings do not. EPS is said to have been *diluted.* Later, as the company makes productive use of the money it raised, earnings should increase, but in the meantime EPS has suffered. Moreover, as we will see in a later chapter, EPS is almost always higher when debt financing is used in favor of equity.

A fourth reason companies do not raise more equity is what might be called the "market doesn't appreciate us" syndrome. When a company's stock is selling for $10 a share, management has a tendency to think that the price will be a little higher in the future as soon as the current strategy begins to bear fruit. When the price rises to $15, management begins to believe this is just the beginning and that the price will be even higher in the near future. An inherent enthusiasm on the part of managers for their company's prospects produces a feeling that the firm's shares are undervalued at whatever price they currently command, and it creates a bias toward forever postponing new equity issues. This syndrome is borne out by a 1984 Louis Harris poll of top executives from more than 600 firms. Fewer than one-third thought the stock market correctly valued their stock, and only two percent felt their stock was overvalued, while fully 60 percent felt it was undervalued.[2]

A fifth reason managers appear to shy away from new equity issues is the feeling that the stock market is basically an unreliable funding source. In addition to uncertainty about the price a company can get for new shares, managers also face the possibility that during some future periods the stock market will not be receptive to new equity issues on any reasonable terms. In finance jargon, the "window" is said to be shut at these times. Naturally, executives are reluctant to develop a growth strategy that is dependent on such an unreliable source of capital. Rather, the philosophy is to formulate growth plans that can be financed from retained profits and accompanying borrowing, and to relegate new equity financing to a minor backup role. More on this topic in later chapters.

Increase Leverage

If selling new equity is not a solution to a company's sustainable growth problems, two other financial remedies are possible. One is to cut the dividend payout ratio, and the other is to increase leverage. A cut in the payout ratio raises sustainable growth by increasing the proportion of earnings retained in the business, while increasing leverage raises the amount of debt the company can add for each dollar of retained profits.

We will have considerably more to say about leverage in the next two chapters. It should be apparent already, however, that there are limits to the use of debt financing. As previously

---

[2]As reported in Alfred Rappaport, "Stock Market Signals to Managers," *Harvard Business Review* (November–December 1987) p. 57.

noted, all companies have a creditor-imposed debt capacity that restricts the amount of leverage the firm can employ. Moreover, as leverage increases, the risks borne by owners and creditors rise, as do the costs of securing additional capital.

Reduce the Payout Ratio

Just as there is an upper limit to leverage, there is a lower limit of zero to a company's dividend payout ratio. In general, owners' interest in dividend payments varies inversely with their perceptions of the company's investment opportunities. If owners believe that the retained profits can be put to productive use earning attractive rates of return, they will be willing to forgo current dividends in favor of higher future ones. If the investment opportunities do not promise attractive returns, a reduction in current dividends or in the payout ratio will cause a decline in stock price. An added concern for closely held companies is the impact of changing dividends on the owners' income and tax liabilities.

Profitable Pruning

Beyond modifications in financial policy, there are several operating adjustments a company can make to manage rapid growth. One is called "profitable pruning." During much of the 1960s and early 1970s, some financial experts emphasized the merits of product diversification. The idea was that companies could reduce risk by combining the income streams of businesses in different product markets. As long as these income streams were not affected in exactly the same way by economic events, the thought was that the variability inherent in each stream would "average out" when combined with others. We now recognize two problems with this conglomerate diversification strategy. One is that although it may reduce the risks seen by management, it does nothing for the shareholders. For if shareholders want diversification, they can get it on their own by just purchasing shares of different independent companies. The second problem with conglomerate diversification is that because companies have limited resources, they cannot be important competitors in a large number of product markets at the same time. Instead, they are apt to be followers in many markets, holding small shares and remaining unable to compete effectively with the dominant firms.

Profitable pruning is the opposite of conglomerate merger. It recognizes that when a company spreads its resources across too many products, it may not be able to compete effectively in any. Better to sell off marginal operations and plow the money back into remaining businesses.

Profitable pruning reduces sustainable growth problems in two ways: It generates cash directly through the sale of marginal businesses, and it reduces actual sales growth by eliminating some of the sources of the growth. This strategy was successfully used by Cooper Industries, a large Texas company, in the mid-1970s. Cooper sold several of its divisions during this time, not because they were unprofitable, but rather because Cooper did not believe it had the resources to become a dominant factor in the markets involved.

Profitable pruning is also possible for a single-product company. Here, the idea is to prune out slow-paying customers or slow-turning inventory. This lessens sustainable growth problems in three ways. It frees up cash, which can be used to support new growth; it increases asset turnover; and it reduces sales. The strategy will reduce sales because tightening credit terms and reducing inventory selection will drive away some customers.

Sourcing

Sourcing involves the decision of whether to perform an activity in-house or to purchase it from an outside vendor. A company can increase its sustainable growth rate by sourcing more and doing less in-house. When a company sources, it releases assets that would otherwise be tied up in performing the activity, and it increases its asset turnover. Both diminish growth problems. An extreme example of this strategy is a franchisor who sources out virtually all of the company's capital intensive activities to franchisees and who, as a result, has very little investment.

The key to effective sourcing is determining where the company's unique abilities lie. If these abilities can be identified and if peripheral activities are not critical to the maintenance of this competitive edge, they can be sourced.

Pricing

An obvious inverse relationship exists between price and revenue. When sales growth is too high relative to a company's financing capabilities, it may be necessary to raise prices to reduce the growth. If higher prices increase the profit margin, the price increase will also raise the sustainable growth rate.

Looking again at R&E Supplies' growth problem, it is possible that R&E has been, in effect, buying sales by underpricing competition. This is consistent with the rapid sales growth and the declining profit margin. A price increase might establish a proper balance between sales growth and profitability.

Is Merger the Answer?

When all else fails, it may be necessary to look for a partner. Two types of companies are capable of supplying the needed cash. One is a mature company, known in the trade as a "cash cow," looking for profitable investments for its excess cash flow. The other is a conservatively financed company that would bring liquidity and borrowing capacity to the marriage. Acquiring another company or being acquired by another company is a drastic solution to growth problems. But it is better to merge when a company is still financially strong than to wait until excessive growth forces the issue.

TOO LITTLE GROWTH

From the preceding discussion, it may appear that only rapidly expanding companies have growth problems, but this is not the case. Slow-growth firms—those for which the sustainable growth rate exceeds actual growth—have problems, too, but they are of a different kind. Rather than struggling continually

TABLE 4–4
Tektronix, Inc., Sustainable Growth Calculations for the Period 1983–1987 (percent)

	1983	1984	1985	1986	1987
Required ratios:					
Profit margin (P)	3.9	8.5	6.3	2.9	3.6
Retention ratio (R)	59.6	83.2	79.1	51.3	62.0
Asset turnover (A)	109.0	109.1	117.4	112.9	120.3
Financial leverage (T)	164.1	156.1	143.1	142.8	138.3
TEK's sustainable growth rate (g*)	4.2	12.0	8.4	2.4	3.7
TEK's actual growth rate (g)	−0.4	11.9	7.9	−6.0	3.3

for fresh cash to stoke the fires of growth, slow-growth companies face the dilemma of what to do with profits in excess of company needs. This might appear to be a trivial or even enviable problem, but to an increasing number of enterprises it is a very real and occasionally frightening one.

To look at the problem more closely, Table 4–4 presents sustainable growth calculations for Tektronix over the period 1983–87. Contrary to the late 1970s, TEK's growth in this more recent period was too slow. Although its sustainable growth rate has fallen noticeably, principally because of a deteriorating profit margin, actual growth is even lower. The predictable result is a buildup of idle resources. Despite steadily increasing dividends and a $128 million share repurchase in 1986 and 1987, cash and securities are up almost $150 million over the period, and financial leverage is down. TEK's problem in 1987 was to rekindle growth, or failing that, to find other productive uses for its idle resources.

WHAT TO DO WHEN SUSTAINABLE GROWTH EXCEEDS ACTUAL GROWTH

The first step in addressing problems of inadequate growth is to decide whether the situation is temporary or longer-term. If temporary, management can simply continue accumulating resources in anticipation of future growth.

When the difficulty is longer-term, the issue becomes whether the lack of growth is industry-wide—the natural result of a maturing market—or unique to the company. In the latter case, the reasons for inadequate growth, and possible sources of new growth, are to be found within the firm. This is Tektronix's diagnosis. After concluding that their company's problems were not industry-wide, management initiated several organizational changes and noticeably increased engineering and development expenses in hopes of stimulating future growth. The nerve-wracking concern, of course, is that these changes must bear fruit in the foreseeable future, or management will be forced to seek other, often more painful, solutions.

When a company is unable to generate sufficient growth from within, it has three options: ignore the problem, return the money to shareholders, or buy growth. Let us consider each briefly in turn.

Ignore the Problem

This response comes in two forms. Management can continue investing in its core businesses despite the lack of attractive returns, or it can simply sit on an ever-larger pile of idle resources. The difficulty with either response is that like dogs to a fire hydrant, underutilized resources attract raiders. Poorly utilized resources depress a company's stock price and make it feasible and attractive for a raider to strike. If she has done her sums correctly, the raider can redeploy the firm's resources more productively, and earn a substantial profit in the process. And among the first resources to be redeployed in such a raid is incumbent management, who find themselves suddenly reading help-wanted ads. Chapter 9 will go into corporate takeovers in more detail.

Return the Money to Shareholders

The most direct solution to the problem of idle resources is just to return the money to owners by increasing dividends or repurchasing shares. Indeed, TEK has done both in recent years, and as Figure 4–3 attests, share repurchase has become increasingly common. Returning the money to investors appears not to be the strategy of choice among many managements, however, for several reasons. One is that the U.S. tax code encourages earnings retention by fully taxing dividends at the corporate and again at the personal level, so that even mediocre investments by corporations can be more attractive to shareholders than increased dividends.

More importantly, many executives appear to have a bias in favor of growth, even when the growth has little or no effect on earnings. At the personal level, many managers resist paying large dividends because the practice hints of failure. Shareholders entrust managers with the task of profitably investing their capital, and for management to return the money suggests an inability to perform a basic managerial function. A cruder way to say the same thing is that dividends reduce the size of management's empire, an act counter to basic human nature.

Gordon Donaldson and others also document a bias toward growth at the organizational level.[3] In a carefully researched review and synthesis of the decision-making behavior of senior executives in a dozen large companies, Donaldson noted that executives commonly opt for growth, even uneconomic growth, out of concern for the long-run viability of their organization. As seen by senior managers, growth contributes importantly to company morale by fostering stimulating career opportunities for employees throughout the organization. And when growth slackens, the enterprise risks losing many of its best people.

Buy Growth

This leads naturally to the third strategy. Motivated by pride in their ability as managers, concern for retaining key employees, and fear of raiders, managers commonly respond to excess cash flow by diversification. Management systematically searches for worthwhile growth opportunities in other, more vibrant industries. And because time is a factor, this usually involves acquir-

---

[3]Gordon Donaldson, *Managing Corporate Wealth* (New York: Praeger Publishers, 1984).

ing existing companies rather than starting from scratch. Implementing an acquisition program is a complex and challenging task involving such issues as discovering superior growth opportunities, determining which opportunities are most consistent with existing managerial skills, estimating an appropriate acquisition price and financing package, and integrating the new acquisition into existing operations.

This is not the place for a lengthy discussion of these topics. Two points, however, are worth noting. First, important aspects of the growth-management problems of mature or declining companies are mirror images of those of rapidly growing firms. It is natural, therefore, that both types of companies will frequently solve their problems by merging with one another, so that the excess cash generated by one organization can finance the rapid growth of the other. Second, after a flurry of optimism in the 1960s and early 1970s, accumulating evidence increasingly suggests that from the shareholders' perspective, buying growth is distinctly inferior to returning the money to owners. More often than not, the superior growth prospects of potential acquisitions are fully reflected in the target's stock price; so that after paying a substantial premium for control, the acquirer is left with a mediocre investment, or worse. The conflict between managers and owners in this regard will be considered in more detail in Chapter 9.

SUSTAINABLE GROWTH AND INFLATION

Growth comes from two sources: increasing volume and increasing prices. Unfortunately, the amount of money a company must invest to support a dollar of inflationary growth is about the same as the investment required to support a dollar of real growth. Imagine a company that has no real growth—it makes and sells the same number of items every year—but is experiencing 10 percent inflationary growth. Then even though it has the same number of units in inventory, each unit will cost more in nominal terms to build, so the total investment in inventory will be higher. The same is true with accounts receivable. The same volume of customers will purchase the same number of units, but because each unit has a higher nominal selling price, the total investment in accounts receivable will be higher.

A company's investment in fixed assets behaves similarly under inflation but with a delay. When the inflation rate increases, there is no immediate need for more fixed assets. The existing fixed assets can produce the same number of units. As the existing assets wear out and are replaced at higher prices, however, the company's investment in fixed assets rises.

This inflationary increase in assets must be financed just as if it were real growth. It is fair to say then that inflation worsens a rapidly expanding company's growth-management problems. The degree to which this occurs depends primarily on the degree to which management and creditors understand the effect of inflation on company financial statements.

Inflation does at least two things to company financial statements. First it increases the amount of external financing required, and second, in the absence of new equity financing it increases the company's debt-to-equity ratio when *measured on its historical-cost financial statements*. This combination can spell trouble. If management or creditors require that the company's historical-cost debt-to-equity ratio stay constant over time, inflation will lower the company's real sustainable growth rate. If the sustainable growth rate is 15 percent without inflation, the real sustainable growth rate will fall to about 5 percent when the inflation rate is 10 percent. Intuitively, under inflation, cash that would otherwise support real growth must be used to finance inflationary growth.

If managers and creditors understand the effects of inflation, this inverse relation between inflation and the sustainable growth rate need not exist. It is true that the amount of external financing required does rise with the inflation rate, but because the real value of company liabilities is declining as companies are able to repay their loans with depreciated dollars, the *net* increase in external financing may be little affected.

In sum, with historical-cost financial statements, inflationary growth appears to substitute for real growth on almost a one-for-one basis—each one percentage point increase in inflation appears to reduce the real sustainable growth rate by the same amount. More accurate, inflation-adjusted financial statements show, however, that inflation turns out to have relatively little effect on sustainable growth. Let us hope that executives can convince their bankers of this fact.

SUSTAINABLE GROWTH AND PRO FORMA STATEMENTS

It is important to keep the material presented here in perspective. I find that comparison of a company's actual and sustainable growth rates reveals a great deal about the principal financial concerns confronting senior management. For nonfinancial types the sustainable growth equation is also useful for highlighting the tie between a company's growth rate and its financial resources. The sustainable growth equation, however, is essentially just a simplification of pro forma statements. It is therefore possible to learn as much or more about a company's growth-management problems from pro forma statements as from sustainable growth analysis. The appeal of the sustainable growth equation is its simplicity and its focus on the company's steady-state growth potential.

CHAPTER SUMMARY

1. The purpose of this chapter has been to study the financial management of growth and decline.
2. Unless a company is willing and able to raise new equity, more growth is not always a blessing. Without careful financial planning, companies can literally grow broke.
3. A company's sustainable growth rate is the maximum rate it can grow without depleting financial resources. More precisely, it equals the product of four ratios: the profit margin, the retention ratio, the asset turnover ratio, and financial leverage. Alternatively, it equals the retention ratio times return on equity. If a company's sales expand at any rate other than the sustainable rate, one or some combination of the four ratios must change.
4. If a company's actual growth rate *temporarily* exceeds

its sustainable rate, the required capital can likely be provided by increased borrowing.

5. When actual growth exceeds sustainable growth for longer periods, management must formulate a financial strategy from among the following options: sell new equity, permanently increase financial leverage, reduce dividends, liquidate marginal operations, source more activities, increase prices, or find a merger partner with deep pockets.

6. For a variety of reasons, some of which are yet to be discussed, most businesses are reluctant to sell new equity. Indeed, since 1985 corporations have repurchased far more shares in terms of market value than they have issued.

7. When actual growth is less than the sustainable growth rate, management's principal financial problem is finding productive uses for the excess cash flows. This problem has become more acute as corporate raiders have increasingly targeted such slow-growth, excess-cash-flow, companies for takeover. The options are to increase dividends, reduce liabilities, increase liquid assets, repurchase common shares, or acquire other firms for their growth opportunities.

8. If managers and creditors base decisions on historical-cost financial statements, inflation reduces a company's sustainable growth rate. If they adjust for the effects of inflation, inflation has comparatively little effect on sustainable growth.

ADDITIONAL READING

Donaldson, Gordon. *Managing Corporate Wealth.* New York: Praeger Publishers, 1984. 199 pages.

This book is the result of an ambitious study undertaken by Donaldson and several colleagues at Harvard in which they reviewed the major resource allocation decisions of 12 large corporations over the course of a decade. The collaborators' synthesis of the behavior they observed provides a detailed portrait of how late-20th-century corporations really function, including the important role played by sustainable growth.

Higgins, Robert C. "Sustainable Growth under Inflation," *Financial Management* (Autumn 1981): 36–40.

A look at the dependence of a company's sustainable growth rate on the inflation rate. The paper concludes that inflation will reduce sustainable growth only if an 'inflation illusion' exists.

CHAPTER PROBLEMS

1. The following information is available about Shannon Enterprise's operations in the most recent year:

Sales	$100
Profit margin	15%
Asset turnover	1
Debt-to-equity ratio	1
Retention ratio	1/3 of profits.

a. What were Shannon's
   (1) Assets?
   (2) Equity?
   (3) Debt?
b. What was Shannon's
   (1) Assets-to-equity ratio?
   (2) Sustainable growth rate?
c. Suppose next year Shannon's sales increase 10 percent. Show that this growth rate is sustainable.
d. Suppose next year Shannon's sales increase 20 percent. Show that this growth rate is not sustainable.

2. Below are financial data for Becton Dickinson and Company, manufacturer and seller of a broad range of products for use by health-care professionals, medical research institutions, and the general public.

	($ millions. 1987 is 3rd qtr. annualized)				
	1987	1986	1985	1984	1983
Income	$ 140	$ 122	$ 88	$ 63	$ 36
Net sales	1,501	1,312	1,144	1,127	1,120
Total assets	1,796	1,691	1,241	1,129	1,107
Dividends	30	27	24	24	24
Equity	828	804	681	607	598
Liabilities	968	887	560	522	509

  a. Calculate Becton Dickinson's sustainable growth rate in each year.
  b. Comparing the company's sustainable growth rate to its actual growth rate in sales, what growth problems, if any, does the company appear to have faced over this period?
  c. How does the company appear to have coped with these problems?
  d. If in 1986 Becton Dickinson had cut its dividend to $20 million, what impact would this change have had on the company's sustainable growth rate in that year?

3. Cypress Electronics is a small, rapidly growing telecommunications company. Plans for 1990 called for a substantial increase in sales from a current level of $50 million and a corresponding $8 million increase in assets. The profit margin was forecasted to be 10 percent. Management was determined to keep the total debt-to-equity ratio at 25 percent. Cypress did not pay dividends.
  a. Must Cypress raise new equity to finance the necessary increase in assets? If so, how much?
  b. If Cypress presently has 10 million common shares outstanding, what would earnings per share be in the absence of new equity?
  c. If Cypress' earnings per share last year were $.40 and if it sells new shares at a price-to-earnings ratio of 18 based on these earnings, what impact will the new equity issue have on earnings per share calculated in (b)? (You may

assume that the 10 percent profit margin is after subtracting all relevant interest expense.)

d. As a shareholder, how would you react to this change in pro forma earnings per share? What do you think would happen to Cypress' stock price when it announced the new equity issue?

Part III

Financing Operations

Chapter 5

Financial Instruments and Markets

Don't tell mom I'm an investment banker.
She still thinks I play piano in a brothel.

Bruce McKern

A major part of the financial executive's job is raising external capital to finance current operations and future growth. In this capacity, the financial manager acts much like a marketing manager. He or she has a product—claims on the company's future income—that must be packaged and sold to yield the highest price to the company. The financial manager's customers are creditors and investors who put money into the business in anticipation of future income. In return these customers receive a *financial security,* such as a stock certificate or a bond, that describes the nature of their claim on the firm's future income.

In packaging his product, the financial executive must select or design a financial security that meets the needs of the company and is attractive to potential creditors and investors. To do this effectively requires knowledge of financial instruments, of the markets in which they trade, and of the merits of each instrument to the issuing company. In this chapter we consider the first two topics—financial instruments and markets—and the next chapter looks at the proper choice of a financing instrument from the company's perspective.

FINANCIAL INSTRUMENTS

Fortunately, lawyers and regulators have not yet removed all creativity from raising money. When selecting a financial instrument for sale in securities markets, a company is *not* significantly constrained by law or regulation. The company is largely free to select or design any instrument, provided only that it appeals to investors and meets the needs of the company. Securities markets in the United States are regulated by the Securities and Exchange Commission (SEC) and, to a lesser extent, by state authorities. SEC regulation creates a lot of red tape and delay, but the SEC does not pass judgment on the investment merits of a security. It requires only that investors have access to all information relevant to valuing the security and that they have adequate opportunity to evaluate it before purchase. This freedom has given rise to such unusual securities as Foote Minerals' $2.20 cumulative, if earned, convertible preferred stock; Sunshine Mining's silver-indexed bonds; and Arley Merchandising Corporation's common stock with attached "puts." The Arley stock entitles the holder to sell the stock back to the company in two years after the date of issue for cash or an equivalent amount of debt.

But do not let the variety of securities obscure the underlying logic. When designing a financial instrument, the financial executive works with three broad variables: the investor's claim on future income, his right to participate in company decisions, and his claim on company assets in liquidation. Below we will describe the more popular security types in terms of these three variables. In reading the descriptions, bear in mind that the characteristics of a specific financial instrument are determined by the terms of the contract between issuer and buyer, not by law or regulation. So the descriptions below should be thought of as indicative of general security types rather than exact definitions of specific securities.

Bonds

A bond, like any other form of indebtedness, is a *fixed-income* security. The holder receives a specified annual interest income and a specified amount at maturity, no more and no less—unless the company goes bankrupt. The difference between a bond and other forms of indebtedness, such as trade credit, bank loans, and private placements, is that bonds are sold to the public in small increments, usually $1,000 per bond. After issue the bonds can be traded by investors on organized security exchanges.

Three variables characterize a bond: its *par value, coupon rate,* and *maturity date.* For example, a typical bond might have a $1,000 par value, a 14 percent coupon rate, and a maturity date of December 31, 1999. The par value is the amount of money the holder will receive on the bond's maturity date. By custom, the par value of bonds issued in the United States is usually $1,000. The coupon rate is the percentage of par value the holder will receive annually as interest income. The above bond will pay $140 per year in interest (14% × $1,000), usually in two semiannual payments of $70 each. On the maturity date, the company will pay the bondholder $1,000 per bond and will cease further interest payments.

On the issue date, companies usually try to set the coupon rate on the new bond equal to the prevailing interest rate on other bonds of similar maturity and quality. This assures that the bond's initial market price will about equal its par value. After issue, the market price of a bond can differ substantially from its par value as market interest rates change. As we will see in a later chapter, when interest rates rise, bond prices fall, and vice versa.

Most forms of long-term indebtedness require periodic repayment of principal. This principal repayment is known as a *sinking fund.* Technically, a sinking fund is a sum of money set aside by the company to meet a future obligation, and this is the way bonds used to work, but no more. Today, a bond sinking fund is a direct payment to creditors that reduces principal. Depending on the indenture agreement, there are several ways a firm can meet its sinking fund obligation. It can repurchase a certain number of bonds in securities markets, or it can retire a certain number of bonds by paying the holders par value. When a company has a choice, it will naturally repurchase bonds if the market price of the bonds is below par value. This occurs whenever interest rates have risen since the bond's issue date.

Call Provisions. Virtually all corporate bonds contain a clause giving the issuing company an option to retire the bonds prior to maturity. For example, although a bond might mature on December 31, 2001, the company may have the option to call the bonds for retirement prior to maturity. Frequently, the call price for early retirement will be at a modest premium above par. Many bonds also have a *delayed call,* meaning the company may not call the bond until it has been outstanding for a specified period, usually 5 or 10 years. An important difference between corporate and U.S. government bonds is that government bonds do not have call options.

Companies want call options on bonds for two reasons. One is that if interest rates fall, the company can pay off its existing bonds and issue new ones at a lower interest cost. The other is that the call option gives a company flexibility. If changing market conditions or changing company strategy requires it, the call option enables management to rearrange its capital structure.

At first glance, it may appear that a call option works entirely to the company's advantage. If interest rates fall, the company can call the bonds and refinance at a lower rate; but if rates rise, investors have no similar option. They must either accept the low interest income or sell their bonds at a loss. It look like "heads I win, tails you lose," but investors are not so stupid. As a general rule, the more attractive the call provisions are to the company, the higher the coupon rate on the bond.

Covenants. Under normal circumstances, no creditors, including bondholders, have a direct voice in company decisions.

Bondholders and other long-term creditors exercise control through *protective covenants* specified in the indenture agreement. Typical covenants include a lower limit on the company's current ratio, an upper limit on its debt-to-equity ratio, and perhaps a requirement that the company may not acquire or sell major assets without prior creditor approval. Creditors have no say in company operations as long as the firm is current in its interest and sinking fund payments and no covenants have been violated. If the company falls behind in its payment or violates a covenant, it is in *default,* and creditors gain considerable power. If they choose, creditors can force the company into bankruptcy, leaving the courts to decide whether the company should be reorganized for the benefit of creditors or simply be liquidated. In liquidation, the courts will sell company assets and use the proceeds to pay off creditors.

Rights in Bankruptcy. The distribution of liquidation proceeds in bankruptcy is determined by the *rights of absolute priority.* At the head of the line are, naturally, the government for past-due taxes and the bankruptcy lawyers who wrote the law. Among investors, the first to be repaid are *senior* creditors, then *general* creditors, and finally *subordinated* creditors. Preferred stockholders and common shareholders bring up the rear. Because each class of claimant is paid off in full before the next class receives anything, equity shareholders frequently get nothing in bankruptcy.

Secured Creditors. A secured credit is a form of senior credit in which the loan is collateralized by a specific company asset or group of assets. In liquidation, proceeds from the sale of this asset go only to the secured creditor. If the cash generated from the sale exceeds the debt to the secured creditor, the excess cash goes into the pot for distribution to general creditors. If the cash is too little, the lender becomes a general creditor for the remaining liability.

Bonds as an Investment. For many years, investors thought bonds to be very low risk. Interest income is specified and chances of bankruptcy are remote. However, bonds are a

TABLE 5–1
Rate of Return on Selected Securities, 1926–1987

Security	Return*
Common stocks	12.0%
Long-term corporate bonds	5.2
Long-term government bonds	4.6
Short-term government bills	3.5
Consumer price index	3.2

* Arithmetic mean of annual returns, ignoring taxes and assuming reinvestment of all interest and dividend income.

Source: Roger G. Ibbotson and Rex Sinquefield, *Stocks, Bonds, Bills, and Inflation (SBBI)* (Chicago: Ibbotson Associates, 1982—updated in *SBBI 1987 Yearbook*), p. 25.

monetary asset. Consequently, changes in the rate of inflation have a major effect on real and nominal bond returns. This has led to a growing perception that bonds can be quite risky in an inflationary world.

Table 5–1 presents the rate of return earned by investors in selected securities over the period 1926–87. Looking at long-term corporate bonds, you can see that had an investor purchased a representative portfolio of corporate bonds in 1926 and held them through 1987 (while reinvesting all interest income and principal payments in similar bonds), his annual return would have been 5.2 percent over the entire 62 years. By comparison, the annual return on an investment in long-term U.S. government bonds would have been 4.6 percent over the same period. We can attribute the 0.6 percent difference to a "risk premium." This is the added return an investor in corporate bonds earns over government bonds to compensate for the risk that corporations might default on their liabilities or deprive investors of attractive returns by calling their bonds prior to maturity.

These returns are *nominal,* meaning they are not adjusted for inflation. The bottom entry in Table 5–1 contains the annual percentage change in the consumer price index over the period. Subtracting the annual inflation rate from 1926 through 1987 of 3.2 percent from these nominal returns yields real, or inflation-adjusted, returns of 2.0 percent for corporates and 1.4 percent for governments. Long-term bonds have done little more than keep pace with inflation over this period.

Bond Ratings. Several investment companies in the United States analyze the investment qualities of many publicly traded bonds and publish their findings in the form of bond ratings. A bond rating is a letter grade, like AA, assigned to an issue, which reflects the analyst's appraisal of the bond's default risk. These ratings are determined by using many of the techniques discussed in earlier chapters, including analysis of the company's balance sheet debt ratios and its coverage ratios relative to competitors. Table 5–2 presents the debt rating definitions of Standard & Poor's, a major rating firm. Table 6–4 in the next chapter presents the differences in key performance ratios by rating category.

Junk Bonds. The rating a company receives on a new bond issue is important because it affects the interest rate the firm must offer. In addition, many institutional investors, such as pension funds, are prohibited from investing in bonds that are rated less than "investment" grade, usually defined as BBB – and above. As a result, there have been periods in the past when companies having less than a BBB – rating have had extreme difficulty raising debt capital in public markets. Bonds rated below BBB – are known as "speculative" grade bonds.

A recent phenomenon has been the rise of the high-yield or junk bond market, composed of original-issue, speculative grade bonds. Beginning from a base of just over $10 billion outstanding in 1979, the junk bond market has exploded to over $100 billion in mid-1987.[1] A principal factor in this growth has been a rethinking on the part of some investors of the risks inherent in speculative grade bonds. Although interest rate pre-

---

[1]Edward I. Altman and Scott A. Nammacher, "The Default Rate Experience on High-Yield Corporate Debt," *Financial Analysts Journal* (July–August 1985) p. 26, and *Standard & Poor's CreditWeek,* June 15, 1987, p. 1.

TABLE 5-2
Standard & Poor's Debt Rating Definitions

A Standard & Poor's corporate or municipal debt rating is a current assessment of the creditworthiness of an obligor with respect to a specific obligation. This assessment may take into consideration obligors such as guarantors, insurers, or lessees.

The debt rating is not a recommendation to purchase, sell, or hold a security, inasmuch as it does not comment as to market price or suitability for a particular investor.

The ratings are based, in varying degrees, on the following considerations:

1. Likelihood of default—capacity and willingness of the obligor as to the timely payment of interest and repayment of principal in accordance with the terms of the obligation.
2. Nature of and provisions of the obligation.
3. Protection afforded to, and relative position of, the obligation in the event of bankruptcy, reorganization, or other arrangement under the laws of bankruptcy and other laws affecting creditors' rights.

AAA   Debt rated 'AAA' has the highest rating assigned by Standard & Poor's. Capacity to pay interest and repay principal is extremely strong.

AA   Debt rated 'AA' has a very strong capacity to pay interest and repay principal and differs from the highest rated issues only in small degree.

A   Debt rated 'A' has a strong capacity to pay interest and repay principal although it is somewhat more susceptible to the adverse effects of changes in circumstances and economic conditions than debt in higher rated categories.

BBB   Debt rated 'BBB' is regarded as having an adequate capacity to pay interest and repay principal. Whereas it normally exhibits adequate protection parameters, adverse economic conditions or changing circumstances are more likely to lead to a weakened capacity to pay interest and repay principal for debt in this category than in higher rated categories.

Debt rated 'BB,' 'B,' 'CCC,' 'CC,' and 'C' is regarded as having predominantly speculative characteristics with respect to capacity to pay interest and repay principal. 'BB' indicates the least degree of speculation and 'C' the highest degree of speculation. While such debt will likely have

TABLE 5-2—*Continued*

some quality and protective characteristics, these are outweighed by large uncertainties or major risk exposures to adverse conditions.

BB Debt rated 'BB' has less near-term vulnerability to default than other speculative grade debt. However, it faces major ongoing uncertainties of exposure to adverse business, financial, or economic conditions which could lead to inadequate capacity to meet timely interest and principal payments.

B   Debt rated 'B' has a greater vulnerability to default but presently has the capacity to meet interest payments and principal repayments. Adverse business, financial, or economic conditions would likely impair capacity or willingness to pay interest and repay principal.

CCC Debt rated 'CCC' has a current identifiable vulnerability to default, and is dependent upon favorable business, financial, and economic conditions to meet timely payment of interest and repayment of principal. In the event of adverse business, financial, or economic conditions, it is not likely to have the capacity to pay interest and repay principal.

CC The rating 'CC' is typically applied to debt subordinated to senior debt which is assigned an actual or implied 'CCC' rating.

C   The rating 'C' is typically applied to debt subordinated to senior 'CCC −' debt rating.

CI The rating 'CI' is reserved for income bonds on which no interest is being paid.

D   Debt rated 'D' is in default, or is expected to default upon maturity or payment date.

Plus (+) or minus (−): The ratings from 'AA' to 'CCC' may be modified by the addition of a plus or minus sign to show relative standing within the major rating categories.

Source: *Debt Rating Criteria: Industrial Overview* (New York: Standard & Poor's, 1986), p. 10.

miums on junk bonds relative to government bonds were as high as five percentage points, accumulating evidence suggested that premiums of only one to two percentage points were sufficient to compensate for the higher default risk of junk bonds. The resulting investor interest in speculative grade bonds has been a boon to a number of midsized companies, which for the first time are finding the public debt market a viable alternative to traditional bank financing. Whether investor enthusiasm for junk bonds will weather a meaningful recession is yet to be determined.

Common Stock

Common stock is a *residual income* security. The stockholder has a claim on any income remaining after the payment of all obligations, including interest on debt. *If the firm prospers, stockholders are the chief beneficiaries; if it falters, they are the chief losers.* The amount of money a stockholder receives annually depends on the dividends the company chooses to pay. The board of directors makes this decision quarterly and is under no obligation to pay any dividend at all.

Shareholder Control. Stockholders exercise control over company decisions through their ability to elect the board of directors. In the United States, the wide distribution of share ownership and the laws governing election of the board frequently combine to reduce greatly this authority. In some companies, ownership of as little as 10 percent of the stock is sufficient to control the entire board. In many other firms, there is no dominant shareholder group, and management controls the board, even though its members may own little or none of the company.

This does not imply that managers in such companies are free to ignore shareholder interests, for they face at least two potential constraints on their actions. One is created by their need to compete in product markets. If management does not make a product or provide a service efficiently and sell it at a competitive price, the company will lose market share to more aggressive competitors and will eventually be forced out of the industry. The actions taken by managers to compete effectively in product markets are consistent with shareholder interests. Securities markets provide a second check on management discretion. If a company wants to raise debt or equity capital in future years, it must maintain its profitability in order to appeal to new investors. Moreover, if managers ignore shareholder interests, stock price will fall, and the firm may fall within a raider's sights. This is the subject of Chapter 9.

Common Stock as an Investment. A common stockholder receives a return on his investment in two forms: dividends and possible share price appreciation. If d_0 is the dividends per share during the year and P_0 and P_1 are the beginning-of-year and end-of-year stock price, the *annual income* earned by the stockholder is

$$d_0 + P_1 - P_0.$$

Dividing by the beginning-of-year stock price, the *annual return* is

$$\frac{\text{Annual}}{\text{return}} = \frac{\text{Dividend}}{\text{yield}} + \frac{\text{Percentage change}}{\text{in share price}}$$

$$= \frac{d_0}{P_0} + \frac{P_1 - P_0}{P_0}.$$

Common stocks are an ownership claim against primarily real, or productive, assets. If companies can maintain profit margins during inflation, real, inflation-adjusted profits should be relatively unaffected by inflation. For years, this reasoning led to the belief that common stocks are a hedge against inflation, but this did not prove to be the case during the recent bout of high inflation. Looking at Table 5–1 again, we see that had an investor purchased a representative portfolio of common stocks in 1926 and had he reinvested all dividends received in the same portfolio, his average annual return through 1987, over the entire 62 years, would have been 12.0 percent. However, from 1973 through 1981, a period when prices rose an average of 9.2 percent per annum, the average annual return on common stocks was only 5.2 percent.

The common stock return of 12.0 percent from 1926 through 1987 compares with a return of 4.6 percent on government bonds over the same period. The difference of 7.4 percent (12.0% − 4.6%) between the common stock return and the government bond return can be thought of as a *risk premium*. It is the extra return earned by common stockholders as compensa-

---

Do Dividends Increase Annual Return?

It may appear from the above equation that annual return rises with current dividends per share. But the world is not so simple. An increase in current dividends means one of two things: The company will have less money for investment, or it will have to raise more money from external sources to make the same investments. Either way, an increase in current dividends will reduce the stockholders' claim on future income, which will reduce share price appreciation. Depending on which effect dominates, annual returns may or may not increase as dividends rise.

---

tion for the added risks they bore. Comparing the return on common stocks to the annual percentage change in consumer prices, we see that the *real* return to common stock investors over the period was 8.8 percent (12.0% − 3.2%).

Figure 5–1 presents much the same information more dramatically. It shows an investor's wealth at year-end 1987 had she invested $1 in various assets at year-end 1925. Common stocks are the clear winners here. By 1987 the original $1 investment in the common stock of small companies would have grown to a whopping $1,202.97, while $1 invested in the common stock of companies represented in the Standard & Poor's 500 stock index would have grown to a very respectable $347.96. In contrast, a dollar invested in long-term government bonds would have been worth only $13.35 in 1987. Common stocks, however, have proved to be a much more volatile investment than bonds, as Figure 5–2 attests.

Preferred Stock

Preferred stock is a hybrid security—like debt in some ways, like equity in others. Like debt, preferred stock is a fixed-income security. It promises the investor a fixed annual dividend equal to the security's coupon rate times its par value. Like equity, the board of directors need not distribute this dividend unless it

FIGURE 5–1
Wealth Indexes of Investments in the U.S. Capital Markets, 1926–1987
(Assumed Initial Investment of $1 at Year-End 1925; Includes
Reinvestment Income)

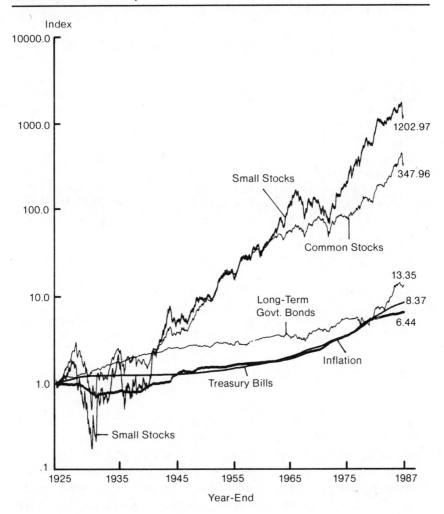

Source: Roger G. Ibbotson and Rex Sinquefield, *Stocks, Bond, Bills, and Inflation (SBBI)* (Chicago: Ibbotson Associates, 1982—updated in *SBBI 1987 Yearbook*), p. 21.

FIGURE 5–2
Volatility of Annual Returns from the U.S. Capital Markets (common stocks versus long-term government bonds)

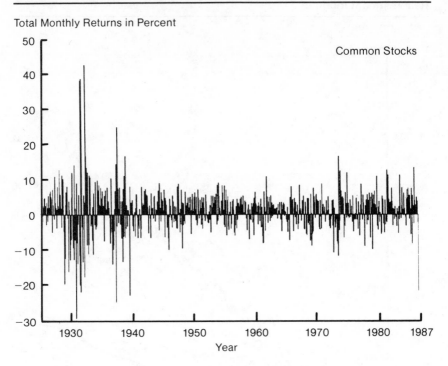

Total Monthly Returns in Percent

chooses. Also like equity, preferred dividend payments are *not* a deductible expense for corporate tax purposes. For the same coupon rate, this makes the *after-tax* cost of bonds about two-thirds that of preferred shares. Another similarity with equity is that although preferred stock may have a call option, it frequently has no maturity. The preferred shares are outstanding indefinitely unless the company chooses to call them.

Cumulative Preferred. Company boards of directors have two strong incentives to pay preferred dividends. One is

FIGURE 5–2—*Continued*

Total Monthly Returns in Percent

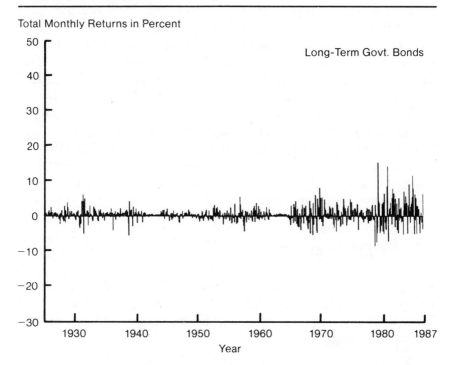

Source: *SBBI, Stocks, Bonds, Bills, and Inflation, 1988 Yearbook*, Ibbotson Associates, Chicago, p. 79.

that preferred shareholders have priority over common shareholders as to dividend payments. Common shareholders receive no dividends unless preferred holders are paid in full. Secondly, virtually all preferred stocks are *cumulative*. If a firm passes a preferred dividend, the arrearage accumulates and must be paid in full before the company can resume common dividend payments.

The control that preferred shareholders have over management decisions varies. In some instances, preferred shareholders' approval is routinely required for major decisions; in others, preferred shareholders have no voice in management unless dividend payments are in arrears.

Preferred stock is not a widely used form of financing. Some persons see preferred stock as *cheap equity*. They see that preferred stock gives management much of the flexibility regarding dividend payments and maturity dates that common equity provides. Yet because preferred shareholders have no right to participate in future growth, they see preferred stock as less expensive than equity. The majority, however, sees preferred stock as *debt with a tax disadvantage*. Because few companies would ever omit a preferred dividend payment unless absolutely forced to, the majority places little value on the flexibility of preferred stock. To them the important fact is that interest payments on bonds are tax deductible, whereas dividend payments on preferred stock are not.

FINANCIAL MARKETS

Having reviewed the basic security types, let us turn now to a look at the markets in which these securities are issued and traded. Of particular interest will be the controversial notion of market efficiency.

Private Placement or Public Issue?

Companies raise money in two broad ways: through private negotiations with banks, insurance companies, pension funds, or other financial institutions, or by selling securities to the public. The former is known as a *private placement;* the latter is a *public issue*. Although private placements of equity are rare, private debt placements account for a significant fraction of total corporate debt.

To sell securities to the public, a company must register the issue with the Securities and Exchange Commission. This is an expensive, time-consuming, cumbersome task, but unless registered, securities may not trade on public markets. This is a valuable privilege. It means that the owner of registered securities can sell them by just calling a stockbroker and placing an order. In contrast, when a financial institution wants to liquidate some of its holdings of private placements, it must find another institution willing to purchase a large block of the securities.

A company's choice of whether to raise money via private placement or public issue comes down to this: Private placements are simpler, quicker, and can be tailored more closely to the particular needs of the issuer, but because they are difficult for buyers to resell, private placements carry a higher interest rate than public issues.

Organized Exchanges and Over-the-Counter Markets

Public issues trade on two types of markets: organized exchanges and over-the-counter markets. Organized exchanges, such as the New York Stock Exchange and the American Stock Exchange, are centralized trading locations that maintain active markets in hundreds of securities. Stockbroker members of the exchange transmit clients' buy-and-sell orders to specialists on the floor of the exchange, who attempt to match buyers with sellers. Specialists may buy or sell securities for their own accounts, but more often they act as agents, pairing buyers with sellers.

Over-the-counter (OTC) markets are much more informal. Any stock brokerage house anywhere in the country can create an OTC market for a security by quoting a *bid* price at which it will buy the security and a higher *asked* price at which it will sell the security. The spread between bid and asked prices is the broker's revenue. In return, the broker must keep an inventory of the security and must frequently trade for his or her own account to maintain an active market. Most well-known equity securities trade on organized exchanges, whereas the shares of smaller, regional companies and a great many bonds trade on the OTC market.

Investment Banking

Investment bankers are the grease that keeps financial markets running smoothly. They are finance specialists who assist companies in raising money. Other activities include stock and bond brokerage, investment counseling, merger and acquisition analysis, and corporate consulting. Some investment banking companies, such as Merrill Lynch, employ thousands of brokers and have offices all over the world. Others, exemplified by Morgan Stanley and First Boston, specialize in working with companies and are consequently less in the public eye.

The responsibilities of an investment banker are many and varied—not unlike his fees. In a private placement, he or she customarily acts as an agent, bringing issuer and potential buyer together and helping them negotiate an agreement. In a public issue, the investment banker's responsibilities are much broader; they vary depending on whether the company registers the securities with the SEC in the traditional manner or uses what is known as a "shelf-registration."

Traditional Registration. In this mode, the investment banker begins working with the issuing company very early in the decision process. In most instances, the banker will have worked closely with management for some years and will have built up a working rapport. The first task is to help the company decide what type of security to sell. Then, if it is to be a public issue, the banker will help the company register the issue with the SEC. This usually takes 30–90 days. A deterrent to registration for many companies, particularly foreign firms, is the extent of the SEC disclosure requirements. Companies must disclose detailed information about their finances, officers, plans, etc.—information some managements would prefer to keep confidential.

While a traditional registration wends its way toward approval, the investment banker puts together a *selling* and an *underwriting syndicate.* A syndicate is a team of as many as 100 investment banking houses that join forces for a brief time to place the new securities. Each member of the selling syndicate accepts responsibility for selling a specified portion of the new securities to investors. Members of the underwriting syndicate act, in effect, as wholesalers, purchasing all of the securities from the company at a guaranteed price and attempting to sell them to the public at a higher price. The "Rules of Fair Practice" of the National Association of Securities Dealers prohibit underwriters from selling the securities to the public at a price above the original offer price quoted to the company. If necessary, however, the syndicate may sell at a lower price.

Given the volatility of security prices and the length of time required to go through registration, it may appear that underwriters bear significant risks when they guarantee the company a fixed price. This is not the way the world works, however. The underwriters do not commit themselves to a firm price until just hours before the sale, and if all goes as planned, the entire issue will be sold to the public on the same day. It is the company, not the underwriters, that bears the risk that the terms on which the securities can be sold will change during registration.

The life of a syndicate is a brief one. Syndicates form several months prior to an issue for the purpose of preselling and disband as soon as the securities are sold. Even on unsuccessful issues, the syndicate breaks up several weeks after the issue date, leaving each underwriter to dispose of his unsold shares on his own.

Shelf-Registration. In March 1982, after a period of experimentation, the SEC greatly simplified the registration process for larger companies by allowing what has come to be known as shelf-registration. Prior to this date, companies wishing to sell new securities to the public had to wait as long as three months before gaining the necessary SEC approval to proceed. This lengthy delay had two effects: (1) it exposed the issuer to considerable uncertainty about the eventual issue price, and (2) it gave the investment bankers ample time to put together their syndicates.

Shelf-registration eliminates this delay by allowing the issuer to file a general-purpose registration good for up to two years. Once the SEC approves the registration, and provided it is updated periodically, the company can put it on the shelf ready for use as needed. The waiting time between decision to issue and receipt of proceeds is thus cut from months to as little as 48 hours.

In addition to giving issuers much more flexibility in timing new issues, shelf-registration changes fundamentally the role of the investment banker. Even though the banker may continue working closely with the company, he no longer has the luxury of several months to put together selling and underwriting syndicates. Instead, he is apt to get a telephone call to the effect that the company wants to go to market in two days and asking if he wishes to bid on the issue.

Because two days is far too little time to throw together a syndicate, shelf-registration has fostered an increase in "bought deals" by larger investment houses, in which one bank buys the entire issue, hoping to resell it piecemeal at a profit. Some observers also believe that shelf-registration has contributed to increased industry concentration as investment houses seek the capital and distribution capabilities necessary to engage in bought deals. Finally, because shelf-registration increases the likelihood of competitive bidding among investment banks, issue costs for shelf-registrations are as much as 10 to 50 percent lower than for traditional registrations, depending on the type of security and other factors.[2]

With cost savings of this magnitude, it should not be surprising that shelf-registration has been a big hit with companies and a corresponding pain to investment banks. Its popularity is evidenced by the fact that shelf-registration accounted for almost 60 percent of the value of new bond issues in only its third year of existence. And although shelf-registration is somewhat less popular for equity issues, it still accounted for approximately one-third of all such issues by large firms in 1983.

Cost of New Issues

Financial securities impose two kinds of costs on the issuer: annual costs and issue costs. We will consider the more important annual costs later. Issue costs are the costs incurred by the issuer and its shareholders on initial sale. For a private place-

---

[2]Robert J. Rogowski and Eric H. Sorensen, "Deregulation in Investment Banking, Shelf Registrations, Structure, and Performance," *Financial Management* (Spring 1985) pp. 5–15. See also Sanjai Bhagat, M. Wayne Marr, and G. Rodney Thompson, "The Rule 415 Experiment: Equity Markets," *Journal of Finance* (December 1985) pp. 1385–1402.

ment, the only substantive cost is the fee charged by the investment banker in his or her capacity as agent. On a public issue, there are legal, accounting, and printing fees, plus those paid to the investment banker. The investment banker states his fee in the form of a *spread*. To illustrate, suppose ABC Corporation wants to sell 1 million new shares using traditional registration procedures and that its shares are presently trading at $20 on the American Stock Exchange. A few hours prior to public sale, the lead investment banker might inform ABC management that "Given the present tone of the markets we can sell the new shares at an issue price of $19 and a spread of $1.50, for a net to the company of $17.50." This means that the investment banker intends to *underprice* the issue $1 per share ($20 market price less $19 issue price) and that he is charging a fee of $1.50 per share, or $1.5 million for his services. This fee will be split among the managing underwriter, or lead bank, and the syndicate members by prior arrangement according to each bank's importance in the syndicates.

To underprice an issue means to offer the new shares for sale at a price below that prevailing for existing shares. Investment bankers often underprice on the theory that the price of the new shares must be below that of existing shares to induce investors to hold more and because it makes their own job easier. Selling something worth $20 for $19 is a lot easier than selling it for $20. Underpricing is not an out-of-pocket cost to the company, but it is a cost to shareholders. The greater the underpricing, the more new shares a company must issue to raise a given amount of money. And as the number of shares issued goes up, the percentage ownership of existing shareholders goes down.

Table 5–3 summarizes some of the issue costs of various kinds of securities as of the early 1970s. Omitted from the table are underpricing costs and payment to investment bankers in the form of warrants and stock options. Two facts are apparent from the data. First, common stock issue costs, which average 12.43 percent of the gross proceeds, are on average over eight times as high as debt issue costs. Second, issue costs fall noticeably as issue size increases. For instance, the total cost of issuing under $500,000 of bonds is 14.15 percent of the gross

TABLE 5–3
Issue Costs as Percentage of Proceeds on SEC-Registered Securities Offered General Public, 1971–1972

Size of Issue ($ millions)	Bonds, Notes, and Debentures			Preferred Stock			Common Stock		
	Underwriter's Compensation*	Other Expenses	Total Costs	Underwriter's Compensation*	Other Expenses	Total Costs	Underwriter's Compensation*	Other Expenses	Total Costs
Under .5	11.51%	2.64%	14.15%	—	—	—	13.24%	10.35%	23.59%
.5– .99	5.25	3.70	8.95	—	—	—	12.48	8.26	20.74
1.0– 1.99	12.95	4.00	16.95	8.26%	3.48%	11.74%	10.60	5.87	16.47
2.0– 4.99	4.02	2.21	6.23	—	—	—	8.19	3.71	11.90
5.0– 9.99	2.36	0.78	3.14	1.88	0.66	2.54	6.70	2.03	8.73
10.0– 19.99	1.24	0.65	1.89	1.37	0.42	1.79	5.52	1.11	6.63
20.0– 49.99	1.00	0.43	1.43	1.37	0.29	1.66	4.41	0.62	5.03
50.0– 99.99	0.89	0.28	1.17	1.35	0.20	1.55	3.94	0.31	4.25
100.0–499.99	0.83	0.19	1.02	2.25	0.18	2.43	3.03	0.16	3.19
Over 500.00	0.88	0.07	0.95	—	—	—	—	—	—
Average	1.14%	0.45%	1.59%	1.52%	0.39%	1.91%	8.41%	4.02%	12.43%

*Does not include contingent payments in form of warrants or options paid to underwriter. Such payments are common in small stock issues.

Source: Securities and Exchange Commission, *Cost of Flotation of Registered Securities, 1971–1972* (Washington, D.C.: U.S. Government Printing Office, December 1974). More recent data generally support these numbers. Wayne Mikkelson and Megan Partch present issue costs for completed public security offerings made by 360 randomly selected industrial companies on the New York and American stock exchanges in the years 1972–82. Total offering costs as a percent of proceeds were 5.5 percent, 1.0 percent, 1.6 percent, and 4.1 percent for common stock, straight debt, convertible debt, and preferred stock, respectively. Median issue sizes were $24 million, $112.5 million, $50 million and $87.5 million, respectively. See Wayne H. Mikkelson and M. Megan Partch, "Valuation Effects of Security Offerings and the Issuance Process," *Journal of Financial Economics*, January/February 1986, p. 38.

proceeds, but the same figure for issues in excess of $500 million is only 0.95 percent. Comparable figures for common stock are 23.59 percent for the smallest issues and 3.19 percent for those between $100 million and $499.99 million.

Regulatory Changes

Financial market deregulation has ignited a revolution among American financial institutions. In part, deregulation has been the outgrowth of a changing regulatory philosophy, but at least as important has been a wide array of technological and competitive innovations that have made regulation increasingly ineffective.

Prior to the depression, U.S. banks were allowed to engage in commercial and investment banking. In 1933, Congress passed the Glass-Steagall Act to eliminate perceived conflicts of interest between the two activities. Since then, commercial banks have been prohibited from engaging in most securities trading activity, while investment banks have been prohibited from acting as depository institutions. However, it has become increasingly difficult to draw a clear line defining commercial banking as opposed to investment banking; we see today a steady encroachment of each type of bank on the other's turf. This trend has prompted many observers to predict that the legal barriers separating the two activities cannot be long maintained in the face of heightening competition. In other countries, most banks, including U.S. multinational banks, are free to engage in investment and commercial banking activities.

EFFICIENT MARKETS

A recurring issue in raising new capital is that of *timing*. Companies are naturally anxious to sell new securities when prices are high. Toward this end, managers routinely devote considerable time and money to the prediction of future price trends in financial markets.

Concern for proper timing of security issues is natural, but there is a growing perception among academicians and market

professionals that an attempt to forecast future prices in financial markets will be successful only in exceptional circumstances, and that unless these circumstances exist, there is
nothing to be gained by forecasting.

Such pessimism follows from the notion of *efficient markets,*
a much debated and controversial topic in recent years. This is
not the place for a detailed discussion of efficient markets; because the implications of the topic are far-reaching and because
the concept is beginning to affect the way financial managers
think about their jobs, however, it deserves some attention. The
interested reader is referred to the recommended readings at
the end of the chapter for more detailed treatments of the topic.

Market efficiency is controversial in large part because
many proponents have overstated the evidence supporting efficiency and have misrepresented its implications. To avoid this,
let us agree on two things right now. First, market efficiency is
not a question of black or white but rather of shades of gray. A
market, rather than being efficient or inefficient, is *more* or *less*
efficient. Moreover, the degree of efficiency is an empirical question that can be answered only by studying a particular market.
Second, market efficiency depends on one's perspective. The
New York Stock Exchange can be efficient to a dentist in Des
Moines who doesn't know an underwriter from an undertaker;
and at the same time, it can be highly *in*efficient to a specialist
on the floor of the exchange who has detailed information about
buyers and sellers of each stock and up-to-the-second prices.

What Is an Efficient Market?

Market efficiency is a description of how prices in competitive
markets respond to new information. The arrival of new information in a competitive market can be likened to the arrival of
a lamb chop in a school of flesh-eating piranha, where investors
are—plausibly enough—the piranha. The instant the lamb chop
hits the water, there is turmoil as the fish devour the meat. Very
soon the meat is gone, leaving only the worthless bone behind,
and the water returns to normal. Similarly, when new information reaches a competitive market there is much turmoil as
investors buy and sell securities in response to the news, caus-

How Rapidly Do Stock Prices Adjust to New Information?

The following graph, Figure 5–3, gives an indication of the speed with which common stock prices adjust to new information. It is a result of what is known as an "event study." In this instance the researcher is studying the impact of acquisition offers on the stock price of the target firm. It is easiest to think of the graph initially as a plot of the daily prices of the target firm's stock from a period beginning 40 days before the announcement of the acquisition offer and ending 40 days after. An acquisition offer is invariably good news to the target firm's shareholders because the offer is made at a price well above the prevailing market price of the firm's shares, so we expect to see the target company's stock price rise after the announcement. The question is, How rapidly? The answer evident from the graph is, Very rapidly. We see that the stock price drifts upward prior to the announcement, shoots up dramatically on the announcement day, and then drifts without much direction after the announcement. Clearly, if you read about the announcement in the evening paper and buy the stock the next morning, you will miss out on the major price move. The market will already have responded to the new information.

The upward drift in stock price prior to the announcement is consistent with three possible explanations: (1) insiders are buying the stock in anticipation of the announcement, (2) security analysts are very good at anticipating which firms will be acquisition targets and when the offer will be made, or (3) acquiring firms tend to announce offers after the price of the target firm's stock has increased for several weeks. I have my own views, but will leave it to you to decide which explanation is more plausible.

An old Jewish proverb says, "For example is no proof." If the price pattern illustrated by the graph were for just one firm, it would only be a curiosity. To avoid this problem, the researcher has studied the price patterns of 161 target firms involving successful acquisitions that occurred during 15 years ending in 1977. The prices you see are an index composed of the prices of the 161 firms, and the time scale is in "event time," not calendar time. Here the event is the acquisition announcement, defined as day 0, and all other dates are expressed relative to this event date. The pattern observed, therefore, describes general experience, not an isolated event.

In recent years, academicians have performed a number of event studies involving different markets and events, and the preponderance of these studies indicates that financial markets in the United States respond to new, publicly available information within one day or less.

FIGURE 5–3
**Time Series of the Mean Price Index of the Shares of 161 Target Firms
Involved in Successful Tender Offers**

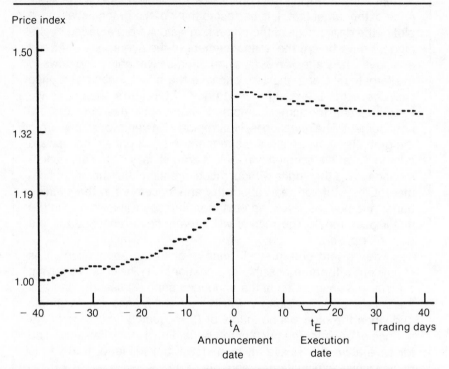

Source: Michael Bradley, "Interfirm Tender Offers and the Market for Corporate Control," *Journal of Business* 53, no. 4 (1980).

ing prices to change. Once prices adjust, all that is left of the information is the worthless bone. No amount of gnawing on the bone will yield any more meat, and no further study of old information will yield any more valuable intelligence.

An efficient market, then, is one in which prices adjust rapidly to new information and in which current prices fully reflect available information about the assets traded. "Fully reflect" means that investors rapidly pounce on new information, analyze it, revise their expectations and buy or sell securities accordingly. They continue to buy or sell securities until price changes eliminate the incentive for further trades. In such an environment, current prices reflect the cumulative judgment of investors. They *fully reflect* available information.

The degree of efficiency displayed by a particular market depends on the speed with which prices adjust to news and the type of news to which prices respond. It is common to speak of three levels of informational efficiency:

A market is *weak-form* efficient if current prices fully reflect all information about past prices.

A market is *semistrong-form* efficient if current prices fully reflect all publicly available information.

A market is *strong-form* efficient if current prices fully reflect all information, public or private.

Extensive tests of many financial markets suggest that with limited exceptions most financial markets are semistrong-form efficient, but not strong-form efficient. This statement needs to be qualified in two respects. First, there is the issue of perspective. The above statement applies to the typical investor, subject to brokerage fees and without special information-gathering equipment. It does *not* apply to market makers. Second, it is impossible to test every possible type and combination of public information for efficiency. All we can say is that the most plausible types of information, tested with the most sophisticated techniques available, indicate efficiency. This does not preclude the possibility that a market may be inefficient with respect to some as-yet-untested information source.

Implications of Efficiency

If financial markets are semistrong-form efficient, the following are true:

Publicly available information is not helpful in forecasting future prices.

In the absence of private information, the best forecast of future price is current price, perhaps adjusted for a long-run trend.

Without private information, a company cannot improve

the terms on which it sells securities by trying to select the optimal time to sell.

Individuals without private information have two choices. They can reconcile themselves to efficiency and quit trying to forecast security prices, or they can attempt to make the market inefficient from their perspective. This involves becoming a market insider by acquiring the best available information-gathering system in hopes of learning about events before others. A variation—usually illegal—on this theme is to seek inside information. Advance knowledge that Carl Icahn will attempt to acquire TWA, for example, would undoubtedly be useful in forecasting TWA's future stock price. A third strategy used by some is to purchase the forecasts of prestigious consulting firms, the chief virtue of which appears to be that there will be someone to blame if things go wrong.

As the above comments suggest, market efficiency is a subtle and provocative notion with a number of important implications for investors as well as companies. Our treatment of the topic here has been necessarily brief, but it should be sufficient to suggest that unless executives have inside information or superior information-gathering and analysis systems, there may be little to be gained from trying to forecast prices in financial markets. This conclusion applies to many markets in which companies participate, including those for government and corporate securities, foreign currencies, and commodities.

APPENDIX

OPTIONS AND CONVERTIBLE SECURITIES

An option is a document entitling the holder to either buy or sell a security at a specified price and for a specified time. To illustrate, on January 14, 1988, Chrysler Corporation common stock closed at $24 per share. On this same date for $550, you could have purchased a *call option* on Chrysler stock giving you the right to purchase 100 shares for $20 per share at any time through March 31. $20 is the option's *striking price* and March 31, 1988, is its maturity date.

The value of this option depends quite obviously on the price of Chrysler's stock prior to the maturity date. Because Chrysler stock is presently trading well above the striking price, the option is said to be "in the money" and is clearly valuable. At a minimum it is worth $399 because you could immediately combine it with $2,000 and buy 100 shares of Chrysler common worth $2,400. However, even if the stock is trading below the $20 striking price, investors will still buy the options, hoping the price will rise above $20 prior to maturity. Unexercised options beyond their maturity date are worthless.

There are four basic types of options: *Puts* and *calls* are options written by investors on existing securities and traded on exchanges, *stock options* are granted by companies to managers as part of their compensation, *preemptive rights* are granted by companies to existing shareholders as part of an equity issue, and *warrants* are issued by companies to outside investors. A distinguishing feature of stock options and warrants is their longevity, which can be many years. Preemptive rights tend to have maturities of a month or less, and the longest maturity of puts and calls is nine months.

Convertible Securities

A convertible security is a fixed-income security with an option attached. To illustrate, convertible bonds of the XYZ Company might be convertible into XYZ common stock and have the following terms: a par value of $1,000, a coupon rate of 10 percent, a maturity of 20 years, and a *conversion ratio* of 100 to 1. The 100-to-1 conversion ratio means that, at any time, the holder can trade his or her bonds into the company in exchange for common stock in the ratio of 100 common shares for each bond.

Conversion Value and Investment Value. It is appropriate to speak of two values for convertible securities. One is the security's *conversion value,* which is the current value of the common stock a holder would receive upon conversion. In our example, if XYZ common stock were trading at $8 per share, the conversion value of the company's convertible bonds would be $800 per bond ($8 per share × 100 shares). The security's other value is its *investment value.* The investment value of a convertible security is the price at which the convertible would trade if the conversion option were removed. It is the value ignoring the conversion option and viewing the instrument as a conventional fixed-income security.

The market price of a convertible security can never be lower than its conversion value or its investment value. Let us see why this is true. If the security's price were below its conversion value, speculators could earn riskless profits by purchasing the convertible, converting to common stock, and immediately selling the stock. For example, if XYZ's convertible was selling for $700 when its common stock was selling for $8, a speculator could purchase one convertible bond for $700, exchange it for $800 worth of stock, and sell the stock for a riskless and immediate profit of $100. In the process, the speculator would bid up the price of the convertible and would bid down the price of the stock, until the convertible's price once again equaled or exceeded its conversion value.

If a convertible security's price were less than its investment value, the convertible would offer investors a higher return than similar quality and maturity securities that did not possess the conversion option. Resulting demand for the convertible would raise its price until it once again exceeded the security's investment value.

Forcing Conversion. Virtually all convertible securities give the issuer the right to redeem, or call, the securities for cash at a fixed price. This call price does not put a ceiling on the market price of a convertible security, however, because even after the company has issued its call, investors have a grace period in which to decide whether to accept cash or to convert into common shares. The company can easily predict what investors will do when they issue a call, for if conversion value exceeds the call price, investors will convert; otherwise they will redeem their shares for cash. For example, suppose the XYZ convertible has a call price of $1,050 per bond. If the conversion value is $800 when XYZ calls the securities, holders have the option of receiving $1,050 in cash or $800 worth of common stock, so investors will redeem their bonds for cash. However, if the conversion value is $1,200 on the call date, investors will convert to common stock rather than settle for $1,050 in cash.

Calling a convertible security when its conversion value exceeds its call price is known as *forcing conversion*. In the absence of such a call, few investors will voluntarily convert; first, because the annual income from a convertible usually exceeds the dividend income from the common stock received on conversion, and second, because a convertible security provides *downside protection*. Even if the price of the company's common stock falls to very low levels, the investment value of the convertible will create a floor under the price of the convertible, preventing it from sinking to comparable levels.

Why Issue a Convertible? Historically, a principal use of convertibles has been as *delayed equity financing*. A growing company needs additional equity financing, but feels its stock price will be higher in a few years; so it issues a convertible security, hoping to force conversion in the near future. The presumed advantage of this strategy is that it enables the firm to secure needed equity on more favorable terms. To illustrate, suppose XYZ Company needs $10 million in new equity. If its current stock price is $8 per share, it would need to sell 1.25 million new shares today to raise the needed funds ($10 million/$8 = 1.25 million). But suppose instead it sells 10,000 convertible bonds with a conversion ratio of 100 to 1 at $1,000 per bond. Then, in a few years, when its stock price is above $10 per share, it can issue a call and force conversion. After conversion, only 1 million new common shares will be outstanding, a 20 percent reduction in shares issued (10,000 bonds × 100 shares per bond = 1 million shares).

There are at least two problems with this logic. One is that a company can achieve much the same result by just issuing debt and then refinancing with equity in a few years. A second problem is that despite the best of expectations, the issuing firm's stock price may not rise. In this case, the company will have a *frozen,* or *hung,* convertible; and more importantly, it will have $10 million of debt when it really needs equity. As discussed in the next chapter, this can prove to be a risky proposition.

The investor appeal of convertible securities and fixed-income securities with attached warrants varies with the inflation rate. Investors have learned that long-term, fixed-income securities are risky investments during times of volatile inflation, and they are reluctant to hold them without "equity kickers" in the form of conversion options or warrants.

CHAPTER SUMMARY

1. This chapter has examined financial instruments and markets. When raising capital, the financial manager

acts much like a marketing manager. The product is claims on the firm's assets and income, and the manager's goal is to package and sell these claims in a manner that yields the highest price to the company.

2. Companies are *not* greatly restricted by law or regulation in their ability to select or design a security. The key questions in designing a new security are: What does the investor want, and what meets the company's needs?

3. Fixed-income securities, such as bonds and most preferred stock, receive a comparatively safe income stream but do not participate in the growth of the firm. As an investment over the last 50-odd years, corporate bonds have done little more than keep up with inflation.

4. Common stock is a residual income security with claim on all income after payment of prior fixed claims. Common stockholders are the principal beneficiaries of company growth. They receive income as dividends and share price appreciation. Since 1926, the average *real* return on common stocks has been about 8.8 percent per year.

5. Private placement of new securities with a small group of knowledgeable institutions is usually faster and more flexible than a public issue; because private placements are illiquid, they customarily carry a higher interest rate.

6. Recent procedural changes in the registration and sale of public securities, introducing what is known as shelf-registration, appear to have reduced issue costs substantially. Moreover, many observers feel these changes are a catalyst promoting a significant restructuring of the investment banking industry.

7. A sizable body of empirical evidence suggests that financial markets in the United States are quite efficient. To earn above-average returns, an investor in these markets must have access to private information, or must be among the first to act upon newly available public information.

ADDITIONAL READING

Brealey, Richard, and Stewart Myers. *Principles of Corporate Finance.* 2d ed. New York: McGraw-Hill, 1984. 847 pages.
    A leading graduate-level text. Lively, well-written. Particularly strong on recent developments in the field. Chapter 13, Corporate Financing and the Six Lessons of Market Efficiency, is especially good.

Smith, Clifford W. "Investment Banking and the Capital Acquisition Process," *Journal of Financial Economics* (January/February 1986): 3–29.
    A concise, well-written summary of the role of investment banks in the raising of corporate capital. Authoritative discussion of recent academic research and regulatory issues.

Van Horne, James C. *Financial Market Rates and Flows.* 2d ed. Englewood Cliffs, N.J.: Prentice-Hall, 1984. 311 pages.
    A well-written, informative look at the function of financial markets, the flow of funds through markets, market efficiency, interest rates, and interest rate differentials. Excellent review of empirical studies of financial markets. Intended as a supplement for courses in financial markets and for practitioners interested in issuing or investing in fixed-income securities.

CHAPTER PROBLEMS

1. If the stock market in the United States is efficient, how do you explain the fact that corporate insiders (company managers and directors) tend to earn abnormally high returns on common stock investments involving their own companies?

2. If the stock market in the United States is efficient, how do you explain the fact that some people make very high returns? Would it be more difficult to reconcile very high returns with efficient markets if the same people made extraordinary returns year after year?

3. At the end of fiscal year 1986, Tektronix, Inc.'s stock price was $30.75. A year later it was $34.88. Per share dividends

over the year were $0.55, while earnings per share were $1.33.

   a. What rate of return did the common-stock owners earn in fiscal year 1987?

   b. What was the dividend yield? What was the percentage change in share price?

   c. What proportion of the return earned by shareholders was received in the form of dividends and what proportion was in the form of share price appreciation?

4. *a.* Why are the expected returns on most bonds less than the expected returns on most stocks?

   b. Why buy a bond if it has a lower expected return than a stock?

   c. If your answer to *b* is "stocks are riskier," can you avoid this risk by purchasing a diversified portfolio of stocks?

   d. How would you respond to the following comment? "Since it is a virtual certainty that stocks will yield a higher return than bonds over the long run, the best investment strategy is to buy stocks and give them time to outperform bonds."

   e. Could the bonds of a company have a higher expected return to investors than the common stock of the same company?

   f. If a company's bonds have a lower expected return to investors than its common stock, does this mean that bonds are less costly from the company's perspective? If so, why would a company ever sell equity?

5. Mader Manufacturing's current stock price is $22 per share. The company wants to raise $150 million by selling newly issued common stock. Mader's investment banker indicates that such a sale would require 5 percent underpricing and a 6 percent spread.

   a. Assuming Mader's stock price does not change, how many shares must the company sell and at what price to the public?

   b. How much does the investment banker stand to earn on the sale?

6. **Note: You may find this problem more challenging than**

the others. On the day before Appleton Century Industries will distribute its $1.00 per share dividend, its stock price is $40 per share.

a. What do you think will happen to ACI's stock price immediately after the dividend is distributed?

b. Ignoring taxes, suppose ACI's stock price falls from $40 to $39.50 as the dividend is distributed. Can you think of a simple stock trading strategy to benefit from this price change?

c. If you and many others pursue the strategy identified in *b,* what will happen to ACI's stock price as it distributes a dividend?

d. Continuing to ignore taxes, what does your answer to *c* imply about the impact of dividends on the rates of return earned by common stock investors? What does this suggest about investor preferences for dividends versus share price appreciation?

e. Would your answer to *d* change if personal taxes were included?

Chapter 6
The Financing Decision

*Equity Capital: The least amount of money
owners can invest in a business
and still obtain credit.*

Michael Sperry

We began our inquiry into the raising of external capital in the last chapter by looking at financial instruments and the markets in which they trade. We continue here by examining the proper choice of a financing instrument by the company.

Selecting the proper financing instrument is a two-step process. The first is to decide how much external capital is required. Frequently, this is the straightforward outcome of the forecasting and budgeting process described in Chapter 3. Management estimates sales growth, the need for new assets, and the money available internally. Any remaining monetary needs must come from outside sources. Increasingly, however, this is only the first stage in the process. There follows a careful consideration of financial markets and the terms on which the company can raise capital. If management does not believe it can raise the required sums on agreeable terms, a modification of operating plans to bring them within budgetary constraints is initiated.

Once the amount of external capital to be raised has been determined, the second step is to select—or, more accurately, design—the instrument to be sold. This is the heart of the financing decision. As indicated in the last chapter, the company can choose from a tremendous variety of financial securities. The proper choice will provide the company with needed cash on attractive terms. An improper one will result in an excessive cost of funds, undue risk, or an inability to sell the securities.

For simplicity in this chapter, we will frequently consider a single financing choice: The XYZ Company needs to raise $200 million this year; should it sell bonds or stock? But do not let this focus obscure the complexity of the topic. First, bonds and stocks are just extreme examples of a whole spectrum of possible security types. Fortunately, the conclusions drawn regarding these extremes will apply in modified degree to other instruments along the spectrum. Second, and more important, financing decisions are never one-time events. Instead, the raising of money at any point in time is just one event in an evolving financial strategy. Yes, XYZ Company needs $200 million today but will likely need $150 million in two years and an undetermined amount in future years. Consequently, a major element of XYZ's present financing decision is the effect today's choice will have on the company's future ability to raise capital. Ultimately then, a company's financing strategy relates closely to its long-run competitive goals and to the way it intends to manage growth.

This chapter begins by considering a central topic in finance known as OPM: other people's money. We will look at the advantages and disadvantages of OPM in financing operations and will examine how the choice of a financing strategy affects company performance. This will involve a close look at *financial leverage* and at techniques for evaluating alternative financing options. The chapter will conclude by considering financing decisions in light of a company's growth objectives and its access to financial markets. We will see that smaller companies and those that are unable or unwilling to sell new equity view financial leverage in a perspective different from that of other firms. The appendix to the chapter takes up the related topic of the financing decision and firm value.

FINANCIAL LEVERAGE

In physics, a lever is a device to increase force. In business OPM, or what is commonly called financial leverage, is a device to increase owners' returns. It involves the prudent substitution of fixed-cost debt financing for owners' equity in the *hope* of increasing equity returns. The word *hope* is important here because leverage does not always have the intended effect. If operating profits are below a critical value, financial leverage will reduce, not increase, equity returns. If we think of the increased variability in the return to owners as an increase in risk, we can say that financial leverage is the proverbial two-edged sword: It increases the return to owners in most instances, but it also increases their risk.

To see these effects more clearly, let's look at the influence of financial leverage on ROE. Recall from Chapter 2 that, despite some problems, ROE is the most widely used single measure of financial performance. It is defined as

$$ROE = \frac{\text{Profit after tax}}{\text{Equity}}.$$

In Chapter 2 we said that an increase in financial leverage usually increases ROE. Here, we want to explore this linkage more closely. To begin, write profit after tax as

$$\text{Profit after tax} = (\text{EBIT} - jD)(1 - t),$$

where EBIT is earnings before interest and tax, j is the interest rate, D is debt outstanding, and t is the firm's tax rate. This equation reflects the steps an accountant goes through to calculate profit after tax from EBIT.

Then using some basic algebra,[1] we can rewrite ROE as

----

[1]
$$ROE = \frac{(\text{EBIT} - jD)(1 - t)}{E} = \frac{\text{EBIT}(1 - t)}{E} - \frac{jD(1 - t)}{E}$$
$$= r \times \frac{D + E}{E} - i\frac{D}{E} = r + (r - i)\frac{D}{E}$$

$$ROE = r + (r - i)D/E,$$

where r is the company's *operating return on assets,* defined as

$$r = \text{Operating return on assets} = \frac{\text{EBIT}\,(1 - t)}{\text{Assets}},$$

i is the aftertax interest rate, defined as

$$i = \text{Aftertax interest rate} = j(1 - t),$$

and E is the firm's equity. Operating return on assets, r, is very similar to ROIC, defined in Chapter 2. It is the return on assets of an all-equity company; you can think of it as the return earned by the company before the effects of financial leverage are considered. Looking at i, recall that because interest is a tax-deductible expense, a company's tax bill declines whenever its interest expense rises; i takes this relationship into account.

The revised expression for ROE is a revealing one. It shows clearly that the impact of financial leverage on ROE depends on the size of r relative to i. If r exceeds i, financial leverage—as measured by D/E—increases ROE. The reverse is also true, however; if r is less than i, leverage reduces ROE. Leverage improves financial performance when things are going well but worsens it when things are going poorly.

Figure 6–1 says the same thing graphically. It shows how ROE changes with leverage for three values of r, corresponding to a boom of 18 percent, an expected outcome of 12 percent, and a bust of zero percent. The aftertax interest rate is assumed to be six percent. Increasing leverage has two obvious effects: It increases expected ROE *and* it increases the range of possible ROEs.

For at least two reasons, it is appropriate to think of the range of possible ROEs as a measure of risk. One is that a greater range of possible outcomes means more uncertainty about what ROE the company will earn and more variability in ROE over time. The second reason is that a greater range of possible ROEs means a greater chance of bankruptcy. Look at the bust line. With zero leverage, the worst the company will do is earn an ROE of zero, but with a debt-to-equity ratio of 4.00, the same level of operating income generates a *loss* of 24 percent on equity. In this situation operating income is not sufficient to

FIGURE 6–1
Leverage Increases Expected Return and Risk

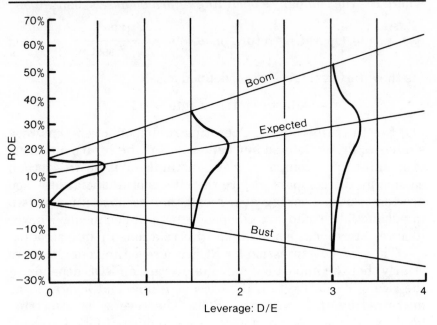

cover interest expense, and a loss results. If the loss is large enough or persistent enough, bankruptcy can occur.

To summarize, *financial leverage increases expected return to shareholders and risk.* The trick is to balance one against the other.

TECHNIQUES FOR EVALUATING FINANCING ALTERNATIVES

If management knew the value of r, the financing decision would be easy: Whenever r exceeds i, pile on the debt; whenever r is less than i, finance with equity. What makes life exciting, of course, is that future values of r are unknown and frequently subject to considerable uncertainty. The financing decision therefore comes down to a comparison of the possible benefits of leverage against the possible costs.

Ideally we would like to be able to calculate precisely what degree of financial leverage would yield a company the greatest net benefit, but this is not presently possible. Instead, the best we can do is to measure in a rough way the increased returns and risks created by debt financing and to offer some broad generalizations about what should be paramount in management's mind when selecting a financing instrument.

For a practical look at the measurement of the risks and returns of debt financing, consider the problem faced by Clark Thompson, vice president (finance) of Harbridge Fabrics, in early 1989. Harbridge Fabrics, a manufacturer of quality cotton and wool fabrics, was trying to decide how to raise $30 million to finance acquisition of a Spanish manufacturer of cotton materials. After considerable negotiation, a price of $35 million cash had been agreed to. Thompson had determined that $5 million could be financed internally, leaving $30 million to be financed from outside sources. Harbridge's investment bankers indicated that the following two options were possible:

1. Sell 1.5 million new shares of common stock at a net price of $20 per share.
2. Sell $30 million, par value, bonds at an interest rate of 12 percent. The maturity would be 20 years, and the bonds would carry an annual sinking fund of $1.5 million.

Looking to the future, Mr. Thompson expected that the addition of the Spanish manufacturer would increase Harbridge's earnings before interest and taxes (EBIT) to $30 million in 1989. Past EBIT levels had been as follows:

	1982	1983	1984	1985	1986	1987	1988
EBIT ($ millions)	$15	$10	$30	$26	$5	$15	$24

TABLE 6–1
HARBRIDGE FABRICS
Income Statement
1988
($ millions)

Sales......................................	$200
Cost of goods sold.......................	144
Gross profit..............................	56
General and administrative expenses.........	35
Interest expense..........................	4
Earnings before tax	17
Tax at 34%	6
Earnings after tax........................	11
Preferred dividends	1
Available for common	$10
Number of shares outstanding	5 million
Earnings per share.......................	$2.00

Mr. Thompson anticipated that Harbridge's need for outside capital in coming years would be substantial, ranging from $5 to $20 million annually. The company had paid annual dividends of 50 cents per share in recent years, and Mr. Thompson believed it was management's intention to continue doing so. Tables 6–1 and 6–2 present Harbridge's recent financial statements.

Range-of-Earnings Chart

Mr. Thompson's first step in analyzing the financing options available to Harbridge should be to measure the effect of the decision on Harbridge's return to shareholders. This could be done by calculating the company's ROE under alternative financing plans. Instead, the common practice is to simplify the procedure somewhat by looking at the decision's effect on earnings per share (EPS) rather than ROE. Because the analysis is virtually the same either way, we will adhere to this convention.

TABLE 6–2
HARBRIDGE FABRICS
Balance Sheet
1988
($ millions)

Assets	
Cash and securities......................	$ 14
Accounts receivable	32
Inventories	22
Total current assets....................	68
Net fixed assets	70
Total assets............................	$138

Liabilities and owners' equity	
Accrued expenses.......................	$ 15
Accounts payable	21
Short-term debt	2
Current portion long-term debt	4
Total current liabilities.................	42
Long-term debt*.........................	34
Preferred stock†	8
Common stock..........................	13
Retained earnings	41
Total liabilities and owners' equity...........	$138

*Average interest rate on debt in 1988 was 10%; annual sinking fund requirements were $4 million. Both of these numbers will stay at this level through 1994.
†Dividend rate on preferred stock is 12%; there are no principal repayment requirements on the preferred.

To see the effect of financial leverage on Harbridge's EPS we need to look at the company's income statement under the two financing plans. We can save considerable work in doing this by noting that all of the income statement entries from sales down through EBIT are unaffected by the way a company is financed. Consequently, we can ignore these items and begin with EBIT. The figures below show the bottom portion of a 1989 pro forma income statement for Harbridge under bust and boom

HARBRIDGE FABRICS
Partial Pro Forma Income Statement
1989
($ million except EPS)

	Bust		Boom	
	Bonds	Stock	Bonds	Stock
EBIT	$10.0	$10.0	$40.0	$40.0
Interest expense	7.2	3.6	7.2	3.6
Earnings before tax	2.8	6.4	32.8	36.4
Tax at 34%	1.0	2.2	11.2	12.4
Earnings after tax	1.8	4.2	21.6	24.0
Preferred dividends	1.0	1.0	1.0	1.0
Available for common	0.8	3.2	20.6	23.0
Number of shares (millions)	5.0	6.5	5.0	6.5
EPS	$0.17	$0.50	$4.13	$3.54

conditions. Bust corresponds to a recessionary EBIT of only $10 million, while boom represents a very healthy EBIT of $40 million.

The accounting here is straightforward. Interest expense under the stock financing alternative is 10 percent of the debt outstanding in 1989. Debt outstanding in 1989 equals present short- and long-term debt of $40 million, less the $4 million sinking fund due during 1989, or $36 million. Interest expense under the bond alternative is higher by an amount equal to the interest on the new bonds. Preferred dividends are an aftertax expense, so they are subtracted from earnings after tax. Finally, selling stock increases the number of shares outstanding from 5 to 6.5 million.

Several noteworthy observations emerge from these figures. One involves the tax advantage of debt financing. Provided only that Harbridge has sufficient taxable income, its tax liability is always $1.2 million lower under bond financing than under stock financing. This figure equals 34 percent of the added interest expense of the debt financing option over stock financing.

In effect, the government pays companies a subsidy, in the form of reduced taxes, to encourage the use of debt financing. Letting t be the company's tax rate, and I its interest expense, the subsidy can be expressed as tI. Frequently known as the *interest tax shield* from debt financing, this subsidy is thought by many to be the chief benefit of debt financing.

A second observation is that common stock financing produces higher earnings after tax simply because it involves no additional interest expense. The most important thing to observe, however, is the effect of the financing decision on EPS. Looking at the boom conditions, we see the expected impact of leverage: EPS with debt financing is a healthy 17 percent higher than with equity financing. Under bust conditions, the reverse is true; stock financing produces a significantly higher EPS. This corresponds to our earlier example when r was less than i.

To display this information more informatively, it is useful to construct a *range-of-earnings chart*. To do so, we need only plot the EBIT-EPS pairs calculated above on a graph and connect the appropriate points with straight lines. Figure 6–2 shows the resulting range-of-earnings chart for Harbridge. It presents the EPS Harbridge will report for any level of EBIT under the two financing plans. Note that the bond financing line passes through an EPS of $4.13 at $40 million EBIT and $0.17 at $10 million EBIT, whereas the corresponding figures for stock financing are $3.54 and $.50, respectively.

Mr. Thompson will be particularly interested in two aspects of the range-of-earnings chart. One is the increase in EPS Harbridge will report at the expected EBIT level if the company selects bond financing instead of stock financing. As shown on the graph, this increase will be 11 percent at an expected EBIT of $30 million. Thompson also will observe that in addition to an immediate increase in EPS, bond financing also puts Harbridge on a faster growth trajectory. This is represented by the steeper slope of the bond financing line. For each dollar Harbridge adds to EBIT, EPS will rise more with bond financing than with equity financing. Unfortunately, the reverse is also true; for each dollar EBIT declines, EPS will fall more with bond financing than with equity financing.

FIGURE 6–2
Range-of-Earnings Chart for Harbridge Fabrics

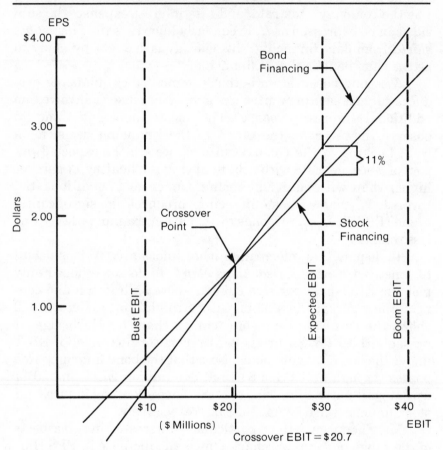

The second aspect of the range-of-earnings chart that will catch Mr. Thompson's eye is that bond financing does not yield a higher EPS at all EBIT levels. In particular, if Harbridge's EBIT should fall below a critical crossover value of $20.7 million, EPS will actually be higher with stock financing than with bond financing. Harbridge's expected EBIT is well above the crossover value, but the historical record presented earlier indicates that EBIT has been quite volatile in past years. In fact, it has been below $20.7 million in four of the seven years for which we have data. A higher EPS with bond financing is clearly not assured.

Coverage Ratios

The primary use of a range-of-earnings chart is to examine the return dimension of financial leverage: What EPS, or ROE, can a company anticipate at expected levels of operating income for the various financing plans under consideration? The risk dimension of leverage is best considered by calculating coverage ratios. Because coverage ratios were treated in Chapter 2, our discussion here will be brief.

The before- and after-tax burdens of Harbridge Fabrics' financial obligations appear below. Recall that because we wish to compare these financial obligations to the company's EBIT, it is necessary to calculate the *before*-tax numbers. Since Harbridge is in the 34 percent tax bracket, the before-tax burden is about one and one-half times the aftertax burden for all obligations except interest, which is a tax-deductible expense ($[1/(1-.34)] = 1.5$).

Financial Obligations ($ million)

	Bonds		Stock	
	Aftertax	Before-tax	Aftertax	Before-tax
Interest expense		$7.2		$3.6
Principal payment	$5.5	8.3	4	6.1
Preferred dividends. . . . . :	1	1.5	1	1.5
Common dividends.	2.5	3.8	3.3	4.9

Four coverage ratios, corresponding to the progressive addition of each of these financial obligations, appear below for an assumed EBIT of $30 million. To illustrate calculation of these ratios, "times common covered" equals $30 million EBIT divided by the sum of all four financial burdens in before-tax dollars. [For bonds, 1.44 = 30 / (7.2 + 8.3 + 1.5 + 3.8).]

Coverage Ratios

	Bonds		Stock	
	Coverage	Percent EBIT Can Fall	Coverage	Percent EBIT Can Fall
Times interest earned	4.17	76%	8.33	88%
Times burden covered.	1.94	48	3.09	68
Times preferred covered	1.76	43	2.68	63
Times common covered	1.44	31	1.86	46

The column headed "Percent EBIT Can Fall" presents a second way to interpret coverage ratios. It is the percentage amount EBIT can decline from its expected level before coverage equals 1.0. For example, interest expense with bond financing is $7.2 million; hence, EBIT can fall from $30 million to $7.2 million, or 76 percent, before times interest earned for bond financing equals 1.0. A coverage of 1.0 is critical in the sense that a lower coverage indicates the financial burden under examination cannot be covered out of operating income and another source of cash must be available.

Harbridge's coverage ratios clearly illustrate the added risks implied by debt financing. For each ratio, coverage is significantly worse with bond financing than with stock financing. Given the instability of Harbridge's operating income over past years, debt financing implies a worrisome increase in the likelihood of default.

To put Harbridge's numbers into perspective and to see how coverage has changed in recent years, Table 6–3 presents times-interest-earned ratios and debt-to-total-asset ratios for companies comprising the Standard & Poor's 400 industrial stock averages, and for selected industries over the period 1981–86. Note the general decline in coverage and increase in indebtedness over these years. Table 6–4 shows the variation in key performance ratios across Standard & Poor's rating categories in the 1984–86 period. Observe that the median times-interest-earned ratio falls steadily from 12.63 for AAA corporations down to 1.83 for B corporations.

TABLE 6–3
Times Interest Earned Has Generally Declined and Debt to Total Assets Has Generally Increased Over the Years 1981–1986 (Numbers in parentheses are the number of companies in industry)

	1981	1982	1983	1984	1985	1986
Standard & Poor's 400 Industrials:						
Debt to total assets (%)	23	24	23	25	26	27
Times interest earned	5.0	4.0	4.6	4.8	4.2	3.6
Aerospace Defense (10):						
Debt to total assets (%)	10	14	8	10	10	13
Times interest earned	6.9	5.6	8.8	5.7	6.4	6.6
Broadcast Media (6):						
Debt to total assets (%)	16	17	18	20	43	43
Times interest earned	8.4	7.5	7.7	6.7	3.2	2.5
Cosmetics (5):						
Debt to total assets (%)	17	18	22	27	34	33
Times interest earned	7.8	5.6	5.6	4.7	3.1	4.4
Hospital Management (4):						
Debt to total assets (%)	51	47	45	45	45	49
Times interest earned	2.8	2.8	3.2	3.2	2.8	1.3
Household Furnishings and Appliances (7):						
Debt to total assets (%)	13	16	12	13	14	15
Times interest earned	14.3	5.0	11.1	11.1	7.3	9.5
Textile Apparel Manufacturers (5):						
Debt to total assets (%)	19	16	16	21	19	26
Times interest earned	5.7	6.8	11.1	9.4	15.1	16.2

Source: *Standard & Poor's Analysts Handbook: Official Series,* 1987 Annual Edition. Companies in selected industries are those firms represented in the Standard & Poor's 400 industrial stock averages. Generally, they are among the largest companies in the industry.

SELECTING THE APPROPRIATE FINANCING INSTRUMENT

Thompson now has quantitative indicators of the risk and the return to Harbridge from each financing option. The next question is how best to use this information to pick the most appropriate financing instrument. Unfortunately, the state of the art does not allow very specific answers to this question, so we must be content with some rather general advice. Let us begin by placing Harbridge's decision in the proper time frame.

TABLE 6–4
Averages of Key Ratios by Standard & Poor's Rating Category
(Industrial Long-Term Debt, Three-Year Median Figures, 1984–1986)

	AAA	AA	A	BBB	BB	B
Times interest earned	12.63	9.06	5.24	3.19	2.49	1.83
Times interest and rental expense earned	7.39	4.62	3.02	2.32	1.83	1.54
Cash flow/Total debt (%)	135.22	90.32	54.63	40.45	24.64	16.43
Pretax return on average long-term capital (%)	24.80	21.38	18.16	13.30	12.75	11.40
Operating income/ Sales (%)	20.63	14.85	12.21	10.91	11.44	10.55
Long-term debt/ Capitalization* (%)	11.31	17.67	26.85	31.61	43.10	53.15

*Capitalization = All long-term sources of capital = Total assets − Short-term liabilities.
Note: These figures are not meant to be minimum standards.

Source: "Credit Comment," *Standard & Poor's CreditWeek,* September 7, 1987, p. 15.

Financial Flexibility

Up to now, we have looked at the financing decision as if it were a one-time event. Should Harbridge Fabrics raise $30 million today by selling bonds or stock? Realistically, such individual decisions are part of a longer-run financing strategy shaped in large part by the firm's access to capital markets over time.

At one extreme, if Harbridge has the rare luxury of always being able to raise debt or equity capital on acceptable terms, the decision is straightforward. Thompson can simply select a target capital structure based on long-run risk-return considerations and then base specific debt-equity choices on transitory market conditions and on the proximity of the company's present capital structure to its target.

In the more realistic case, when continuing access to capital markets is not assured, the decision becomes more complex. For now Thompson must worry about how today's decision affects Harbridge's future access to capital markets. This is the notion of *financial flexibility:* the concern that today's decision not jeopardize future financing options or growth opportunities.

Looking at Harbridge, we know that the company anticipates tapping the markets for $5 to $20 million annually in coming years. And given the company's volatile past earnings and comparatively low coverage ratios, it is possible that selling bonds now will "close off the top," meaning that over the next few years Harbridge may be unable to raise meaningful amounts of additional debt without a proportional increase in equity. ("Top" as used here refers to the top portion of the liabilities side of the balance sheet.) Having thus reached its debt capacity, Harbridge could become dependent on the equity market over the next few years for any additional external capital. This is a precarious position, for if equity could not be sold on reasonable terms when needed, Harbridge would be forced to forgo attractive investment opportunities for lack of funds. This could prove very expensive, because the inability to make competitively necessary investments can result in a permanent loss of market position. Consequently, a concern for financing future growth would suggest that Harbridge issue equity now while it is available, thereby maintaining financial flexibility to meet future contingencies.

Market Signaling

Concern for future financial flexibility customarily favors equity financing. A persuasive argument in opposition to equity, however, is the stock market's likely response. Mention was made in Chapter 4 that on balance U.S. corporations do not make extensive use of new equity financing, and several possible explanations of this apparent bias were suggested. It is time now to discuss another.

Recently academic researchers have begun to explore the stock market's reaction to various company announcements regarding future financing. And although the results must still be considered preliminary, they make fascinating reading. In one study, Paul Asquith and David Mullins of Harvard were interested in what happens to a company's stock price when it announces a new equity sale.[2] To find out, they performed an event

---

[2]Paul Asquith and David W. Mullins, Jr., "Equity Issues and Offering Dilution," *Journal of Financial Economics* (January/February, 1986) pp. 61–89.

study, similar to the one described in the last chapter, on 531 common stock offerings over the period 1963–81. Defining the event date as the day of first public announcement, Asquith and Mullins found that *over 80 percent* of the industrial firms sampled experienced a decline in stock price on the event date, and that for the sample as a whole, the decline could not reasonably be attributed to random chance. Moreover, the observed decline did not appear to be recouped in subsequent trading, but rather remained as a permanent wealth loss to existing owners.

The size of the announcement loss was startling, averaging *over 30 percent* of the size of the new issue. To put this number into perspective, a 30 percent loss means that Harbridge Fabrics could expect to suffer a permanent loss of about $9 million in equity value the day it announced a $30 million equity issue.

To complete the picture, similar studies of debt announcements have *not* observed the adverse price reactions found for equity financing. Further, it appears that equity announcements work both ways. That is, a company's announcement of its intention to repurchase some of its shares is greeted by a significant *increase* in stock price.

Why do these price reactions occur? No one is yet certain, but several tentative explanations exist. One, suggested most often by executives and market professionals, attributes the observed price reactions to dilution. According to this reasoning, a new equity issue slices the corporate pie into more pieces and reduces the portion of the pie owned by existing shareholders. It is natural, therefore, that the shares owned by existing shareholders will be worth less. Conversely, when a company repurchases its shares each remaining share represents ownership of a larger portion of the company and hence is worth more. Other observers, including yours truly, remain unconvinced by this reasoning, pointing out that while an equity issue may be analogous to slicing a pie into more pieces, the pie is also larger by virtue of the equity issue. And there is no reason to expect that a smaller slice of a larger pie is necessarily worth less. Nor is there any reason to expect remaining shareholders necessarily to gain from a share repurchase. True, each post-repurchase share represents a larger percentage ownership claim, but the repurchase also reduces the size of the company.

A more intriguing explanation involves what is known as market signaling. Suppose, plausibly enough, that Harbridge Fabrics' top management knows much more about their company than do outside investors, and consider again Harbridge's range-of-earnings chart, Figure 6–2. Begin by reflecting on which financing option you would recommend if, as Harbridge's vice president (finance) you were highly optimistic about the company's future. After thorough analysis of the market for Harbridge's products and those of its competitors, you were confident that EBIT could only grow over the next decade, most likely at a rapid pace. If you have been awake the last few pages, you would obviously recommend debt financing. It yields the higher EPS today, and it puts the company on the steeper growth trajectory.

Now reverse the exercise and consider which financing option you would recommend if you were concerned about Harbridge's prospects, fearing that future EBIT might well decline. In this scenario, equity financing is the clear winner because of its superior coverage and higher EPS at low operating levels.

But if those who are best informed about a company finance with debt when the future looks bright, and with equity when it looks grim, what does an equity announcement tell investors? Right. It signals the market that management is concerned about the future and has opted for the safe financing choice. Is it any wonder then that stock price falls on the announcement and that many companies are consequently reluctant to even mention the E-word, much less to sell it?

The market signal conveyed by a share repurchase announcement is just the reverse. Top management is optimistic about the company's future prospects and perceives that current stock price is inexplicably low, so low that share repurchase constitutes an irresistible bargain. A repurchase announcement, therefore, signals good news to investors and stock price rises.

I find market signaling stories such as these highly plausible, but whether they will stand up to further inquiry, only time can tell. Nonetheless, regardless of what explanation one favors, it does appear that the stock price reaction to new equity announcements is usually large and negative.

The Financing Decision and Sustainable Growth

When selecting a financing instrument, we have suggested so far that management should be cognizant of the need to maintain financial flexibility and of the decision's effect on stock price. Concern for financial flexibility customarily weighs in favor of equity financing, while concern for stock price favors debt. How then does management strike a balance between these opposing concerns? The answer for many companies is to place the financing decision within the broader context of managing growth.

Recall from Chapter 4 that when a company is unable or unwilling to sell new equity, its sustainable growth rate is

$$g^* = PRAT,$$

where P, R, A, and T are profit margin, retention ratio, asset turnover, and financial leverage, respectively. P and A in this equation are determined on the operating side of the business, and the financial challenge is to develop dividend, financing, and growth strategies that enable the firm to expand at the target rate without resorting to common stock financing. For these companies, the chief appeal of leverage is not increased ROE, but an increased sustainable growth rate, while the principal disadvantages are the risk of closing off the top and the heightened chance of bankruptcy. Managements in these firms do not view the financing choice as a stand-alone decision, but rather as one aspect of the broader issue of managing growth.

SELECTING A MATURITY STRUCTURE

When a company elects to raise debt capital, the next question is what maturity should the debt have? Should the company take out a one-year loan, sell seven-year notes, or market 30-year bonds? Looking at the firm's entire capital structure, *the minimum-risk maturity structure occurs when the maturity of liabilities equals or exceeds that of assets* because, in this configuration, cash generated from operations over coming years

---

Academic Views of the Debt-Equity Choice

Rather than study the influence of financial leverage on company risk and return as we have done, the usual academic practice has been to examine the effect of leverage on the market value of the firm. Fundamentally, these are not conflicting approaches because a capital structure that effectively balances risk against return in the long-run interests of the company should also increase firm value.

Academicians usually begin by demonstrating that in properly functioning markets with no taxes and no bankruptcy costs, the increased risk to equity from debt financing just counterbalances the increased expected return, so that leverage has no effect on firm value. They then relax the no-taxes, no-bankruptcy assumptions to demonstrate that the capital structure decision ultimately involves a prudent balancing of the tax advantage of debt financing against the increased chance of bankruptcy. At low levels of indebtedness, the tax advantage of debt financing predominates, so that increases in leverage produce higher market values. But beyond some prudent range, the increasing probability of bankruptcy begins to outweigh the tax advantage, and firm value falls with further increases in leverage.

To date, academic research has yielded two benefits: it has greatly clarified our thinking about the financing decision, and it has proved useful in understanding and interpreting the recent rise in major financial restructuring. However, it has been of only modest help to financial executives in developing practical financing strategies. The principal difficulty has been that by assuming the continuous availability of debt and equity capital to firms, academicians have assumed away a major part of the problem as it really exists. As a result, academic treatments of the topic tend to involve one-time debt-equity choices without consideration for future financing flexibility. See the appendix to this chapter for more on the ties between the financing decision and firm value, and Chapter 9 for a look at corporate restructuring.

---

should be sufficient to repay existing liabilities as they mature. In other words, the liabilities will be self-liquidating. If the maturity of liabilities is less than that of assets, the company incurs a refinancing risk because some maturing liabilities will have to be paid off from the proceeds of newly raised capital.

And as noted in an earlier chapter, the rollover of maturing debt is not an automatic feature of capital markets. When the maturity of liabilities is greater than that of assets, cash provided by operations should be more than sufficient to repay existing liabilities as they mature. This provides an extra margin of safety, but it also means that the firm may have excess cash in some periods.

If maturity matching is minimum-risk, why do anything else? Why allow the maturity of liabilities to be less than that of assets? Companies mismatch either because long-term debt is unavailable on acceptable terms or because management anticipates that mismatching will reduce total borrowing costs. For example, if management believes that interest rates will decline in the future, an obvious strategy is to use short-term debt now and hope to roll it over into longer-term debt at lower rates in the future. Of course, advocates of efficient markets criticize this strategy on the grounds that management has no reason to believe it can forecast future interest rates in an efficient market.

Inflation, Taxes, and Borrowing Costs

A related consideration involves taxes. Although much of the interest rate during inflation is really compensation to the creditor for the declining principal value of the loan, the tax authorities nonetheless allow all the interest as a tax-deductible expense. This works to the borrower's benefit. Because the lender must declare the entire interest receipt as income, however, it works to the lender's disadvantage. If borrower and lender were in the same tax bracket, we would expect interest rates to increase to the point where the real, aftertax cost of borrowing was unaffected by inflation. However, if a borrower in a high tax bracket can find a lender in a low tax bracket, this need not happen. And inflation can result in lower real borrowing costs to the company and higher real returns to the lender. In this case, only the Internal Revenue Service loses in the form of reduced tax receipts.

INFLATION AND FINANCING STRATEGY

An old saying in finance is that it's good to be a borrower during inflation because the borrower repays the loan with depreciated dollars. It is important to understand, however, that this saying is correct only when the inflation is *unexpected*. When creditors expect inflation, the interest rate they charge rises to compensate them for the expected decline in the purchasing power of the loan principal. This means that it is not necessarily advantageous to borrow during inflation. In fact, if inflation unexpectedly declines during the life of a loan, inflation can work to the disadvantage of the borrower.

APPENDIX

THE FINANCING DECISION
AND FIRM VALUE

Our purpose here is to study the relation between a company's capital structure and its market value. As noted in Chapter 2, many academicians and consultants recommend that managers work to increase the market value of their firm. With this in mind, we are interested in whether financial leverage affects firm value, and if so, what capital structure maximizes value.

Our strategy will be to begin with an idealized world of no taxes and no bankruptcy. Once this foundation is firmly established, we will add progressive doses of reality by first introducing taxes and then bankruptcy. While other potentially influential forces might also be considered, taxes and bankruptcy are thought to be among the more pervasive, and their review will provide a useful overview of the subject.[3] Although this line of inquiry will not enable us to specify precisely how much debt a particular company should have, it will enable us to identify several important factors management should consider when making financial decisions.

---

[3]See Thomas E. Copeland and J. Fred Weston, *Financial Theory and Corporate Policy,* 3d edition, Reading, Mass.: Addison-Wesley (1988) chapters 13 and 14 for a more complete review of the possible links between capital structure and firm value.

No Taxes or Bankruptcy

When once asked how many slices he would like his pizza cut into, Yogi Berra is said to have replied, "You'd better make it six; I don't think I'm hungry enough to eat eight." Absent taxes and bankruptcy, a company's financing decision can be likened to slicing Yogi's pizza; for no matter how you slice up claims to the firm's earnings, it is still the same firm with the same earning power, and hence, the same market value. In this world, the return benefits to shareholders from increased leverage are precisely offset by the increased risks, so that market value is unaffected by leverage.

Here is an analytical demonstration of this apparently extreme position. Imagine two companies, U and L, identical in all respects except that U is unlevered and L is levered. Because U has no debt, the market value of its equity equals the market value of the entire firm, V_U. The market value of L, on the other hand, is

$$V_L = E_L + D_L,$$

where V_L is the market value of the firm, and E_L and D_L are the market value of its equity and debt, respectively. We want to know how V_U compares to V_L. Because U and L differ only in their use of debt financing, any difference we observe between V_U and V_L must be due to differences in leverage.

To see how the two values compare, consider an investor contemplating two possible investment strategies: (1) buy 1 percent of U's equity, or (2) buy 1 percent of L's equity and 1 percent of its debt. The costs and incomes for these strategies are as follows:

	Cost	Income
Strategy 1:	$.01V_U$	$.01EBIT$
Strategy 2:	$.01E_L$ $+.01D_L$ $.01V_L$	$.01(EBIT - I)$ $+.01I$ $.01EBIT$

For strategy 1, because U has no debt, 1 percent of U's equity is also 1 percent of its value. The income from this strategy equals 1 percent of EBIT, which by assumption is the same for both companies. Looking at strategy 2, the income to equity portion of the investment equals 1 percent of EBIT less interest expense, represented by I, while the income to the debt portion of the investment is just 1 percent of interest expense.

The rest is simple. Because the two strategies yield precisely the same income, they must sell for the same price; that is $V_U = V_L$. If this were not so, investors would clearly sell the higher priced company and buy the lower priced one until the two prices equaled one another. In fact, some clever investors might buy a portion of the lower priced company, repackage claims to its income to look like those of the higher priced firm, and resell them for a profit. Such arbitrage would quickly drive prices of the two firms together.

Here is a more intuitive way to say the same thing. Companies typically own physical assets, like trucks and buildings, and owe paper assets, like stocks and bonds. Our argument is essentially that a company's physical assets are the real creators of value and that simply reshuffling paper claims to the income produced by these assets does not add value. The only exception would be if the reshuffling also increased income, and in the absence of taxes and bankruptcy, this does not occur. Firm value is, therefore, independent of financial leverage.

Corporate Taxes But Still No Bankruptcy

Let us now repeat the exercise in the presence of corporate taxes. Below are the costs and the incomes for our two investment strategies when the corporate tax rate is t.

	Cost	Income
Strategy 1:	$.01V_U$	$.01\text{EBIT}(1 - t)$
Strategy 2:	$.01E_L$	$.01(\text{EBIT} - I)(1 - t)$
	$+.01D_L$	$+.01I$
	$.01V_L$	$.01\text{EBIT}(1 - t) + tI$

Note that companies U and L must now both pay taxes on earnings to equity, so their income after tax is $(1 - t)$ times before-tax income. However, because interest is a before-tax expense, no corporate tax is applied to interest payments to creditors.

The key observation here is that the two income streams are no longer identical, but differ by the amount tI, defined earlier in the chapter as the *interest tax shield* from debt financing. Because interest expense is deductible for tax purposes, the aftertax income to owners *and* creditors generated by the levered firm is $\$tI$ higher each year than that of the unlevered firm. Consequently, L is now worth more than U, a fact we can represent as follows:

$$V_L = V_U + \text{Value } \{tI\}$$

where Value $\{tI\}$ represents the value today of all future interest tax shields. In the next chapter we will refer to this term as the *present value* of future tax shields.

The value of the levered firm now exceeds that of the unlevered firm, implying that value is maximized at 100 percent debt financing. Fortunately, there is more to our story.

But before proceeding, it is worth reflecting for a moment on the implications of the above equation for company financing. The equation tells us that not all companies can benefit from interest tax shields. Certainly if a company is losing money, it has no taxable income to shield and hence sees no benefit from debt financing. Similarly, a company in danger of incurring losses over the life of the debt financing will find the tax benefits of leverage less appealing than will a company with robust profits. A similarly disposed group of companies are those that although profitable, are already shielding all or most of their income from taxes through the use of various tax credits, accelerated depreciation, and other legitimate tax reduction or deferral techniques. We should thus expect companies such as these to use less debt financing than other enterprises facing predictable future tax liabilities.

Taxes and Bankruptcy

We have seen that the tax deductibility of interest increases aftertax income to owners and creditors, and thereby increases firm value. Corporate bankruptcy creates a second link between the financing decision and income that works in opposition to interest tax shields.

A number of events can push a company into bankruptcy. For present purposes, let us agree that a company is bankrupt when its market value is equal to or less than its liabilities, or equivalently, when the market value of its equity falls to zero. Once in bankruptcy, the courts determine whether a company is worth more to its creditors dead or alive. If dead, the company is liquidated and the proceeds are

---

Personal Taxes

To test your understanding of the taxes argument, try your hand at demonstrating that the inclusion of personal taxes in the example above reduces, but does not eliminate, the tax shield benefits of debt financing. To keep things simple, suppose all earnings are distributed as dividends and all investors are taxed at the same rate, T_p.

Answer: You should be able to demonstrate that $V_L = V_U +$ Value $\{(1 - T_p)tl\}$.

---

distributed to creditors. If alive, the company is reorganized and continues in business. In either case, owners of a bankrupt firm can expect to come away with little or nothing, and senior management can expect to be polishing their resumes.

The Probability of Bankruptcy. The expected cost of bankruptcy to a company depends on two things: the probability that bankruptcy will occur, and the cost if it does occur. Looking first at the probability of occurrence, it should come as no surprise to hear that raising financial leverage increases the probability of bankruptcy. To illustrate, suppose some unforeseen economic event causes the market value of a company to fall from $10 billion to $5 billion. If the firm has $4 billion of debt outstanding, it will avoid bankruptcy, but with a greatly diminished equity, while if it has $6 billion in debt, bankruptcy awaits.

Because companies in volatile, unpredictable economic environments are more likely to suffer such unforeseen declines in firm value, one obvious conclusion from this example is that companies operating in such environments are wise to use less debt financing than companies in more stable operating environments. This is one reason Tektronix and many of its competitors employ comparatively little debt financing, while public utilities use much more.

The Cost of Bankruptcy. To some companies, bankruptcy is little more than a pothole along the road of corporate life, while to others it is a complete disaster. A key factor determining the cost of

---

Changing Attitudes Toward Bankruptcy

Although not entirely relevant to the topic at hand, it is interesting to note that attitudes toward bankruptcy have changed dramatically in recent years. Bankruptcy used to be seen as a black hole where companies were clumsily dismembered for the benefit of creditors, and shareholders lost everything. Partly because of a liberalization of the law, bankruptcy today is seen increasingly as a quiet refuge where the courts keep creditors at bay while management works on its problems. Manville Corporation was the first company to see the virtues of bankruptcy in August 1982, when, although solvent by any conventional definition, it declared bankruptcy in anticipation of massive product liability suits involving asbestos. Continental Airlines followed in September 1983, using bankruptcy protection to abrogate what it considered ruinous labor contracts. And more recently, A. H. Robbins and Texaco have found bankruptcy an inviting haven while wrestling with product liability suits and a crushing legal judgment, respectively. In all of these instances, the companies expect to emerge from bankruptcy healthier and more valuable than when they entered. Because financial leverage plays no part in these dramas, however, we will focus attention on the costs of bankruptcy rather than any possible benefits.

---

bankruptcy to an individual company is what can be called "the resale value" of its assets. Two simple examples will illustrate the concept. Suppose ACE Corporation's principal asset is an apartment complex, and that because of local overbuilding and overly aggressive use of debt financing, ACE has been forced into bankruptcy. Because apartment complexes are readily salable, the likely outcome will be sale of the complex to a new owner and distribution of the proceeds to creditors. The cost of bankruptcy in this instance will be correspondingly modest, consisting of the obvious legal, appraisal, and court costs, plus whatever price concessions are necessary to sell the apartments. In substance, because bankruptcy has little influence on operating income generated by the apartment complex, bankruptcy costs are modest.

Note that the cost of bankruptcy does *not* include the difference between what ACE and its creditors originally thought the apartments were worth and their value just prior to bankruptcy. This loss is due to overbuilding, not bankruptcy, and is incurred by the firm regardless of how it is financed or whether it declares bankruptcy. Even all-equity financing, while it may avoid bankruptcy, will not eliminate this loss.

At the other extreme, consider Moletek, a genetic engineering firm, whose chief assets are a brilliant research team and attractive growth opportunities. If Moletek stumbles into bankruptcy, the costs are likely to be very high. Selling the company's assets individually in a liquidation will generate little cash because most of the assets are intangible. It will also be difficult to realize value by keeping the company intact, either as an independent company or in the hands of a new owner. For in such an unsettled environment, it will be hard to retain key employees and to raise funds necessary to exploit growth opportunities. In essence, because bankruptcy adversely affects Moletek's operating income, bankruptcy costs are likely to be large.

In addition to bankruptcy costs themselves, companies may also incur costs of *financial distress* as the probability of bankruptcy increases. Internally, these costs include lost profit opportunities as the company cuts back investment, research and development, and advertising to conserve cash. Externally, they include lost sales as potential customers become concerned about future availability of parts and service, and increased costs as suppliers become reluctant to make long-run commitments and to provide trade credit.

In sum, our brief review of bankruptcy costs suggests that they vary with the nature of a company's assets. If the resale value of the assets is high either in liquidation or when sold intact to new owners, bankruptcy costs are correspondingly modest. Such firms should be expected to make liberal use of debt financing. Conversely, when resale value is low because the assets are largely intangible and would be difficult to sell intact, bankruptcy costs are comparatively high. Companies matching this profile should use more conservative financing.

Concluding Comments

Figure 6A–1 summarizes the results of our musings about debt financing and firm value. It shows the value of a typical firm as a function of financial leverage, denoted by the ratio of debt to firm value. At modest debt levels, the tax shield benefits outweigh the expected cost of bankruptcy, and value rises with leverage. But at higher debt levels, bankruptcy costs predominate, and value declines with further increases in leverage. The object of the exercise is to position the firm at the optimal capital structure, (D/V)*, where value is maximized.

The appendix also suggests that managers consider the following three firm-specific issues when making financing choices:

1. The ability of the company to utilize additional interest tax shields over the life of the debt;
2. The increased risk of bankruptcy created by added leverage; and
3. The cost to the firm if bankruptcy were to occur.

A final observation: The viewpoint throughout this appendix has been that of shareholders; yet it is ultimately management, not shareholders, who make financing decisions. This distinction is an important one because there is reason to believe that the costs and benefits

FIGURE 6A–1

The Market Value of a Company Increases and then Decreases as Financial Leverage Rises

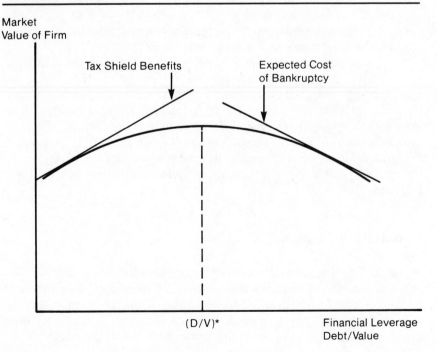

of leverage to managers differ systematically from those to shareholders. In particular, managers appear to incur much higher costs in bankruptcy, in the form of disrupted lives and careers, than do shareholders, while the chief managerial benefit of leverage may well be increased sustainable growth. As a result, unless burdened by sustainable-growth problems, managers may be much more conservative in their use of debt financing than shareholders would prefer.

CHAPTER SUMMARY

1. The intent of this chapter has been to study the corporate financing decision and, in particular, to look at the advantages and disadvantages of financial leverage.
2. For businesses that are unable or unwilling to raise new equity, debt financing increases growth. It enables the business to acquire assets that are otherwise unattainable, and it increases the firm's sustainable growth rate. For businesses with access to new equity, the chief benefit of debt financing is that it increases the expected return on equity.
3. The principal disadvantages of debt financing are increased variability of income and of return on equity and increased bankruptcy risk.
4. Coverage ratios are useful for evaluating the added risk of debt financing, while a range-of-earnings chart is useful for looking at the return dimensions of the decision.
5. Because money from external sources is not always available on agreeable terms, a major concern in most financial decisions is the impact of today's choice on tomorrow's options. Decisions that constrain a company's future ability to raise capital reduce financial flexibility.
6. When management announces a new equity issue, it appears to signal investors that it is concerned about the company's future prospects. In most instances, this results in a stock price decline equal to about 30 percent of the new issue. Repurchase announcements have a positive effect of stock price, and debt announcements have little or no impact.

ADDITIONAL READING

Asquith, Paul, and David W. Williams, Jr. "Signaling with Dividends, Stock Repurchases, and Equity Issues." *Financial Management* (Autumn 1986): 27–44.

A well-written summary of recent empirical work on measuring the capital market's reaction to major equity-related decisions. An excellent introduction – overview of market signaling.

Myers, Stewart C. "The Search for Optimal Capital Structure." *Midland Corporate Finance Journal* (Spring 1983): 6–16.

A nontechnical review of what we think we know about the impact of financial leverage on firm value and its implications for corporate decision making, written by one of the leading contributors to the topic.

Donaldson, Gordon. "New Framework for Corporate Debt Capacity." *Harvard Business Review* (March–April 1962): 117–31.

Old, but still one of the best practical discussions of the financial decision.

Piper, Thomas R., and Wolf A. Weinhold. "How Much Debt Is Right for Your Company?" *Harvard Business Review* (July–August 1982): 106–14.

A practical, well-balanced look at the financing decision with particular emphasis on flexibility.

CHAPTER PROBLEMS

1. Suppose there is an equal chance that a company's operating return on assets [EBIT(1 – tax rate)/assets] next year will be either 30 percent or 5 percent.

   a. If the company's debt-to-equity ratio, in book value terms, is 80 percent, the interest rate on borrowed funds is 12 percent, and the tax rate is 34 percent, what will the company's return on equity be?

   b. How does your answer to a change if the debt-to-equity ratio rises to 200 percent?

2. In general do you think debt tends to be more expensive than equity or less? Why?

3. This chapter considered the financing decision of Harbridge Fabrics. Looking at Harbridge's coverage ratios and range-

of-earnings chart, explain how each of the following changes would affect these ratios and the range-of-earnings chart. Which changes would make equity more attractive? Which would make debt more attractive?

a. An increase in the interest rate on the new debt.

b. An increase in Harbridge's stock price.

c. Increased uncertainty about Harbridge's future earnings.

d. Increased common stock dividends.

4. Valley Computer has the opportunity to invest $200 million in a project promising an annual EBIT of $60 million. The firm's investment bankers indicate that the markets would not be receptive to an equity issue at this time, and recommend instead a debt issue at a 15 percent interest rate. Without the investment, the company's EBIT next year is expected to be $300 million; its interest expense will be $100 million. The tax rate is 34 percent, and there are 20 million shares outstanding.

a. Calculate expected EPS with and without the new investment.

b. Calculate the company's times interest earned ratio with and without the investment.

5. Vermont Mining wants to raise $150 million in new capital. The company can sell equity at $10 per share, or it can sell bonds at par with a 14 percent coupon rate. Vermont Mining currently has an interest expense of $50 million and pays $10 million in preferred dividends. The company has 80 million common shares outstanding and is in the 34 percent tax bracket.

a. Draw a range-of-earnings chart for the company.

b. Can you calculate the value of EBIT at the crossover point?

Part IV

Evaluating Investment Opportunities

Chapter 7
Discounted Cash Flow Techniques

A nearby penny is worth a distant dollar.

Anonymous

The chief determinant of what a company will become is the investments it undertakes today. The generation and evaluation of creative investment proposals is too critical a task to be left to finance specialists; instead it is the ongoing responsibility of all managers throughout the organization. In well-managed companies the process starts at a strategic level, when senior management specifies the businesses in which the company will compete and determines the means of competition. Operating managers then translate these strategic goals into concrete action plans involving specific investment proposals. A key aspect of this process is the financial evaluation of investment proposals, or what is frequently called *capital budgeting*. The achievement of an objective requires the outlay of money today in expectation of future income. And it is necessary to decide, first, whether the anticipated future income is large enough, given the risks, to justify the current expenditure, and second, whether the proposed investment is the most cost-effective way to achieve the objective. This and the following chapter address these questions.

FIGURES OF MERIT

The financial evaluation of any investment opportunity can be broken down into three discrete steps:

1. Estimate the relevant cash flows.
2. Calculate a figure of merit for the investment.
3. Compare the figure of merit to an acceptance criterion.

A figure of merit is a number summarizing an investment's economic worth. A common figure of merit is the rate of return. Like the other figures of merit to be discussed, the rate of return translates the complicated cash inflows and outflows associated with an investment into a single number summarizing its economic worth. An acceptance criterion, on the other hand, is a standard of comparison that helps the analyst determine whether an investment's figure of merit is attractive enough to warrant acceptance. It's like a fisherman who must throw back all fish shorter than 10 inches. To the fisherman, the length of the fish is the relevant figure of merit, and 10 inches is the acceptance criterion.

Although figures of merit and acceptance criteria may appear difficult on first exposure, the first step, estimating the relevant cash flows, is the most challenging in practice. Difficulties include the proper treatment of depreciation, financing costs, and working capital investments, as well as sunk costs, shared resources, and excess capacity. Another pervasive problem is that many important costs and benefits frequently cannot be stated in monetary terms and must be treated qualitatively.

The plan in this chapter is initially to set aside questions of relevant cash flows and acceptance criteria in order to concentrate on figures of merit. Later in the chapter, we will return to the estimation of relevant cash flows. Acceptance criteria will be addressed in the following chapter under the general heading, "Risk Analysis in Investment Decisions."

To begin our discussion of figures of merit, let's consider a simple numerical example. Pacific Rim Resources, Inc., is contemplating construction of a container loading pier in Seattle. The company's best estimate of the cash flows associated with constructing and operating the pier for a 10-year period appear in Table 7–1.

Figure 7–1 presents the same information in the form of a *cash flow diagram,* which is nothing more than a graphical display of the pier's costs and benefits distributed along a time line. Despite its simplicity, I find that many common mistakes can be avoided by preparing such a diagram for even the simplest investment opportunities. We see that the pier will cost $40 million to construct and is expected to generate cash inflows of $7.5 million annually for 10 years. In addition, the company expects to salvage the pier for $9.5 million at the end of its useful life, bringing the 10th year cash flow to $17 million.

The Payback Period and the Accounting Rate of Return

Pacific's management wants to know whether the anticipated benefits from the pier justify the $40 million cost. As we will see shortly, a proper answer to this question must reflect *the time value of money.* But before addressing this topic, let's consider two commonly used, back-of-the-envelope type figures of merit that despite their popularity suffer from some glaring weaknesses. One, known as the *payback period,* is defined as the time the company must wait before recouping its original invest-

TABLE 7–1
Cash Flows for Container Loading Pier ($ millions)

Year	0	1	2	3	4	5	6	7	8	9	10
Cash flow	(40)	7.5	7.5	7.5	7.5	7.5	7.5	7.5	7.5	7.5	17

FIGURE 7–1
Cash Flow Diagram for Container Loading Pier

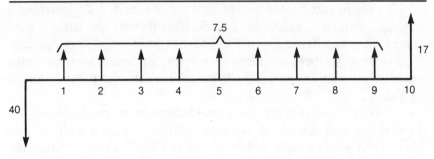

ment. For an investment with a single cash outflow followed by uniform annual inflows:

$$\text{Payback period} = \frac{\text{Investment}}{\text{Annual cash inflow}}.$$

The pier's payback period is thus 5⅓ years, meaning the company will have to wait this long to recoup its original investment (5⅓ = 40/7.5).

The second widely used, but nonetheless deficient, figure of merit is the accounting rate of return, defined as

$$\text{Accounting rate of return} = \frac{\text{Average annual cash inflow}}{\text{Total cash outflow}}.$$

The pier's accounting rate of return is 21.1 percent [(7.5 × 9 + 17)/10 / 40].

The problem with the accounting rate of return is its insensitivity to the timing of cash flows. For example, a postponement of all of the cash inflows from Pacific's container loading pier to year 10 obviously reduces the value of the investment but does not affect the accounting rate of return. In addition to ignoring the timing of cash flows, the payback period is also insensitive to all cash flows occurring beyond the payback date. Thus an increase in the salvage value of the pier from $9.5 million to $90.5 million clearly makes the investment more attractive. Yet, it has no effect on the payback period; nor does any other change in cash flows in years 6 through 10.

In fairness to the payback period, I should add that although it is clearly an inadequate figure of investment merit, it has proved to be useful as a rough measure of investment risk. For in most settings, the longer it takes to recoup an original investment, the greater the risk. This is especially true in high-technology environments, where management can only forecast a few years into the future. Under these circumstances an investment that does not promise to pay back within the forecasting horizon is equivalent to a night in Las Vegas without the floor show.

The Time Value of Money

An accurate figure of merit must reflect the fact that a dollar today is worth more than a dollar in the future. This is the notion of the time value of money, and it exists for at least three reasons. One is that inflation reduces the purchasing power of future dollars relative to current ones; another is that in most instances the uncertainty surrounding the receipt of a dollar increases as the date of receipt recedes into the future. Thus the promise of $1 in 30 days is usually worth more than the promise of $1 in 30 months, simply because it is likely to be more certain.

A third reason money has a time value involves the notion of *opportunity costs*. By definition, the opportunity cost of any investment is the return one could earn on the next best alternative. A dollar today is worth more than a dollar in one year because the dollar today can be productively invested and will grow into more than a dollar in one year. Waiting to receive the dollar until next year carries an opportunity cost equal to the return on the forgone investment.

Compounding and Discounting. Because money has a time value, we cannot simply combine cash flows occurring at different dates, as is done in calculating the payback period and the accounting rate of return. To adjust investment cash flows for their differing time value, we need to use the ideas of compounding and discounting. Everyone who has ever had a bank account knows intuitively what compounding is. Suppose you have a bank account paying 10 percent annual interest, and you deposit $1 at the start of the year; what will it be worth at the end of the year? Obviously, $1.10. Now, suppose you leave the dollar in the account for two years, what will it be worth then? This is a little harder, but most of us realize that, because you earn interest on your interest, the answer is $1.21. Compounding is the process of determining the future value of a present sum. The simple cash flow diagrams below summarize the exercise.

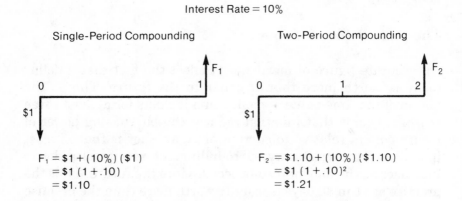

Discounting is just compounding turned on its head: It is the process of finding the present value of a future sum. Yet despite the obvious similarities, many persons find discounting somehow mysterious. And as luck would have it, the convention has become to use discounting rather than compounding to analyze investment opportunities.

Here is how discounting works. Suppose you can invest money to earn a 10 percent annual return and that you are promised $1 in one year; what is the value of this promise today? Clearly, it is worth less than $1, but the exact figure is probably not something that pops immediately to mind. In fact, the answer is $0.909. This is the *present value* of $1 to be received in one year because if you had $0.909 today, you could invest it at 10 percent interest, and it would grow into $1 in one year [$1.00 = 0.909 (1 + .10)].

Now, if we complicate matters further and ask the value of one dollar to be received in two years, intuition fails most of us completely. We know the answer must be less than $0.909, but beyond that things are a fog. In fact, the answer is $0.826. This sum, invested for two years at 10 percent interest will grow, or compound, into $1 in two years. The following cash flow diagrams illustrate these discounting problems. Note the formal similarity to compounding. The only difference is that in compounding we know the present amount and we seek the future sum; whereas in discounting we know the future sum and seek the present amount.

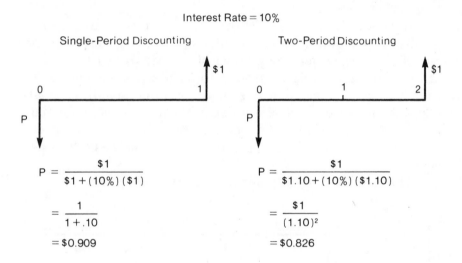

Present Value Tables. How did I know the answers to the discounting problems? I could have used the formulas appearing below the cash flow diagrams, or I could have used one of several brands of pocket calculators, or a computer spreadsheet, but I did none of these. I looked up the answers in Appendix A at the end of the book. Appendix A, known as a present value table, shows the present value of $1 to be received at the end of any number—from 1 to 50 periods—hence, and at interest rates ranging from 1 to 50 percent per period. The present values appearing in the table are generated from repeated application of the above formulas for differing time periods and interest rates. It might be useful to consult Appendix A for a moment to confirm the present values mentioned above.

As a matter of semantics, the interest rate in present value calculations is frequently called the *discount rate*. It can be interpreted in two ways. If a company already has cash in hand, the discount rate is the rate of return that could be earned on alternative investments. In other words, it is the company's *opportunity cost of the capital*. If a firm must raise the cash by selling securities, the discount rate is the rate of return expected by buyers of the securities. In other words, it is the investors' *opportunity cost of capital*. As we will see in the next chapter, the discount rate is frequently used to adjust the investment cash flows for risk and is hence also known as a *risk-adjusted* discount rate.

Appendix B at the end of the book is a close cousin to Appendix A. It shows the present value of $1 to be received at the end of *each period* for any number of periods from 1 to 50, and at discount rates ranging from 1 to 50 percent per period. To illustrate both appendixes, suppose a professional baseball player signs a contract to receive $500,000 per year for four years. Let us calculate what the contract is worth today if the ballplayer has investment opportunities yielding 15 percent per year.

The cash flow diagram for the contract is as follows.

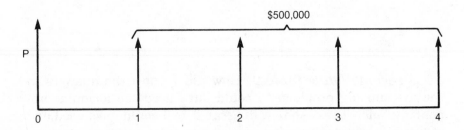

To find the present value, P, using Appendix A, we must find the present value at 15 percent of each individual payment. The arithmetic is:

Present value of contract $= .870 \times \$500,000 + .756 \times \$500,000$
$+ .658 \times \$500,000 + .572 \times \$500,000$
$= \$1,428,000.$

A much simpler approach is to recognize that since the dollar amount is the same each year, Appendix B can be used. Consulting Appendix B, we learn that the present value of $1 per period for four periods at a 15 percent discount rate is $2.855. Thus, the present value of $500,000 per period is

$$\frac{\text{Present value}}{\text{of contract}} = 2.855 \times \$500,000 = \$1,428,000.$$

Although the baseball player will receive a total of $2 million over the next four years, the present value of these payments is barely over $1.4 million. Such is the power of compound interest.

Equivalence

The important fact about the present value of future cash flows is that the present sum is *equivalent* in value to the future cash flows. It is equivalent because if you had the present value today, you could transform it into the future cash flows simply by investing it at the discount rate. To confirm this important fact, the table below shows the cash flows involved in transforming $1,428,000 today into the baseball player's contract salary. We begin by investing the present value at 15 percent interest. At the end of the first year, the investment has grown to over $1.6 million, but the first $500,000 salary payment reduces the principal to just over $1.1 million. In the second year the investment grows to over $1.3 million, but the second salary installment brings the principal down to just over $800,000. And so it goes until at the end of four years the $500,000 salary payments just exhaust the account. Hence, from the baseball player's perspective, $1,428,000 today is equivalent in value to $500,000 per year for four years because he can readily convert the former into the latter by investing it at 15 percent.

Year	Beginning-of-Period Principal	Interest at 15 percent	End-of Period Principal	Withdrawal
1	$1,428,000	$214,200	$1,642,200	$500,000
2	1,142,200	171,330	1,313,530	500,000
3	813,530	122,030	935,560	500,000
4	435,560	65,334	500,894	500,000

The Net Present Value

Now that you have mastered compounding, discounting, and equivalence, let's use these concepts to analyze the container pier investment. More specifically, let us use Appendixes A and B to replace the future cash flows appearing in Figure 7–1 with a single cash flow of equivalent worth occurring today. Because all cash flows will then be in current dollars, we will have eliminated the time dimension from the decision and can proceed to a direct comparison of present value cash inflows against present value outflows.

Here is how it works in practice. Assuming Pacific has other investment opportunities yielding 10 percent, the present value of the cash inflows for the pier investment is as follows:

$$\frac{\text{Present value}}{\text{of cash inflows}} = 5.759 \times \$7.5 + .386 \times \$17$$
$$= \$49.755 \text{ million.}$$

In this calculation, 5.759 is the present value of $1 per year for nine years at a discount rate of 10 percent, and .386 is the present value of $1 in year 10 at the same discount rate.

The cash flow diagrams below provide a schematic representation of this calculation. The present value calculation transforms the messy original cash flows into two cash flows of equivalent worth, each occurring at time zero. And our decision becomes elementary. Should Pacific invest $40 million today for a stream of future cash flows with a value today of $49.755 million? Yes, obviously. Paying $40 million for something worth $49.755 million makes sense.

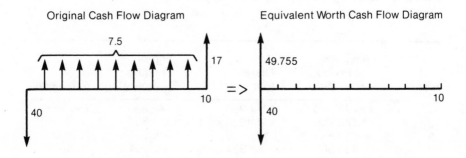

What we have just done is calculate the pier's *net present value,* or NPV, an important figure of investment merit.

$$\text{NPV} = \begin{array}{c}\text{Present value of}\\ \text{cash inflows}\end{array} - \begin{array}{c}\text{Present value of}\\ \text{cash outflows}\end{array}.$$

The NPV for the container pier is $9.755 million.

The declaration that an investment's NPV is $9.755 million may not generate a lot of enthusiasm around the water cooler, so it might be informative to offer a more intuitive definition of the concept. Specifically, an investment's NPV measures how much richer you will become by undertaking the investment. Thus Pacific's wealth rises $9.755 million when it builds the pier because it pays $40 million for an asset worth $49.755 million. Because most of us prefer more wealth to less, it is safe to conclude that all investments with a positive NPV are attractive because they increase wealth; all investments with a negative NPV are unattractive because they destroy wealth; and all investments with a zero NPV are marginal because they leave wealth unchanged.

In symbols, when

NPV > 0, accept the investment;
NPV < 0, reject the investment; and
NPV = 0, the investment is marginal.

The Profitability Index

The net present value is a perfectly respectable figure of investment merit, and if all you want is one way to analyze investment opportunities, feel free to skip ahead to "determining relevant cash flows." On the other hand, if you want to be able to communicate with people who use different, but equally acceptable, figures of merit, and if you want to reduce the work involved in analyzing certain types of investments, you will need to slog through a few more pages.

A second time-adjusted figure of investment merit popular in government circles is the *profitability index* (PI), or what is sometimes called the *benefit-cost ratio,* defined as

$$\text{PI} = \frac{\text{Present value of cash inflows}}{\text{Present value of cash outflows}}.$$

The container pier's PI is 1.24 ($49.755/$40). Obviously, an investment is attractive when its PI exceeds 1.0 and is unattractive when its PI is less than 1.0.

The Internal Rate of Return

Without doubt the most popular figure of merit among executives is a close cousin to the NPV known as the investment's *internal rate of return* or IRR. To illustrate the IRR and to show its relation to the NPV, let's follow the fanciful exploits of the Seattle area manager of Pacific Rim Resources as he tries to win approval for the container pier investment. After determining that the pier's NPV is positive at a 10 percent discount rate, the manager forwards his analysis to the company treasurer with a request for approval. The treasurer responds that he is favorably impressed with the manager's methodology, but that in today's high interest rate environment, he feels a discount rate of 12 percent is more appropriate. So the Seattle manager calculates a second NPV at a 12 percent discount rate and finds it to be $5.434 million, still positive but considerably lower than the original $9.7 million ($5.434 million = 5.328 × $7.5 million + 0.322 × $17 million − $40 million). Confronted with this evidence, the treasurer reluctantly agrees that the project is acceptable and forwards the proposal to the vice president (finance). (That the NPV falls as the discount rises here should come as no surprise, for all of the pier's cash inflows would occur in the future, and a higher discount rate reduces the present value of future flows.)

The vice president (finance), being even more conservative than the treasurer, also praises the methodology but argues that with all the risks involved and the difficulty raising money, an 18 percent discount rate is called for. Doing his calculations a third time, the dejected Seattle manager now finds that at an 18 percent discount rate the NPV is −$4.481 million. Because the NPV is now negative, the vice president (finance), betraying his former career as a bank loan officer, gleefully rejects the proposal. The manager's efforts prove unproductive, but in the process he has helped us to understand the IRR.

TABLE 7–2
NPV of Container Pier at Differing Discount Rates

Discount Rate	NPV
10%	$ 9.755 million
12	5.434
	⟵———— IRR = 15%
18	− 4.481

Table 7–2 summarizes the manager's calculations. From these figures, it is apparent that something critical happens to the investment merit of the container pier as the discount rate increases from 12 to 18 percent. Somewhere within this range the NPV changes from positive to negative, and the investment changes from acceptable to unacceptable. The critical discount rate at which this change occurs is the investment's IRR.

Formally, an investment's IRR is defined as

> IRR = Discount rate at which the investment's
>   NPV equals zero.

The IRR is yet another figure of merit. The corresponding acceptance criterion against which to compare the IRR is the opportunity cost of capital to the firm. If the investment's IRR exceeds the opportunity cost of capital, the investment is attractive, and vice versa. If the IRR equals the cost of capital, the investment is marginal.

In symbols, if K is the percentage cost of capital, then

> $IRR > K$, accept investment;
> $IRR < K$, reject investment;
> $IRR = K$, investment is marginal.

You will be relieved to learn that in most, but regrettably not all, instances the IRR and the NPV yield the same investment recommendations. That is, in most instances, if an investment is attractive based on its IRR, it will also have a positive NPV, and vice versa. Figure 7–2 illustrates the relation between the container pier's NPV and its IRR by plotting the information in Table 7–2. Note that the pier's NPV equals zero at a discount rate of about 15 percent; so this by definition is the project's IRR. At capital costs below 15 percent, the NPV is positive and the IRR also exceeds the cost of capital; so the investment is acceptable on both counts. When the cost of capital exceeds 15 percent, the reverse is true, and the investment is unacceptable according to both criteria.

Figure 7–2 suggests several informative ways to interpret an investment's IRR. One is that the IRR is a type of break-even return in the sense that at capital costs below the IRR the investment is attractive, but at capital costs greater than the IRR it is unattractive. A second, more important interpretation is that the IRR is the rate at which money remaining in an investment grows, or compounds. As such, an IRR is comparable in

FIGURE 7–2
NPV of Container Pier at Different Discount Rates

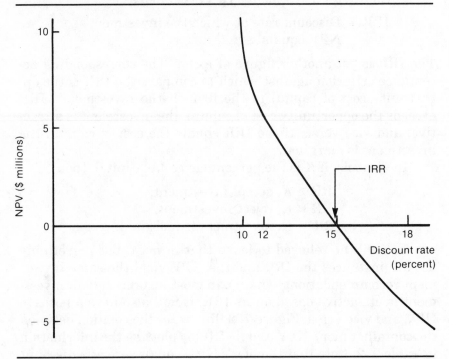

all respects to the interest rate on a bank loan or a savings deposit. This means you can compare the IRR of an investment directly to the cost of the capital to be invested. We cannot say the same thing about other simpler measures of return, such as the accounting rate of return, because they do not properly incorporate the time value of money.

Calculating an Investment's IRR. The IRR has considerably more intuitive appeal to most executives than the NPV or the PI. The statement that an investment's IRR is 45 percent is more likely to get the juices flowing than one indicating the investment's NPV is $12 million, or that its PI is 1.41. The IRR is, however, usually harder to calculate; for it is frequently necessary to search for the IRR by trial and error or, as the computer people would say, iteratively.

The first step in this trial-and-error process is to pick a likely IRR, selected in any fashion you like, and to test it by calculating the investment's NPV at the chosen rate. If the resulting NPV is zero, you're through. If it is positive, this is usually a signal that you need to try a higher discount rate. Conversely, if the NPV is negative you need to try a lower one. This trial-and-error process continues until you find a discount rate for which the NPV equals zero.

To see how this works in practice, let's calculate the container pier's IRR. From Table 7–2 and Figure 7–2 we know that the IRR must be somewhere between 12 and 18 percent, because 12 percent yields a positive NPV and 18 percent a negative one. So let's try 15 percent. Using Appendixes A and B:

$$\text{NPV} = 4.772 \times \$7.5 + .247 \times \$17 - \$40 \stackrel{?}{=} 0$$
$$- 0.01 \stackrel{?}{=} 0$$

For practical purposes, the NPV is zero at a discount rate of 15 percent, therefore this is the project's IRR. Further, if Pacific's opportunity cost of capital is less than 15 percent, we know the pier is acceptable; otherwise, it is not. The need to solve for an investment's IRR iteratively was a meaningful limitation before the advent of computers and pocket calculators, but this is no longer a significant barrier to its use.

Bond Valuation

Investors regularly use discounted cash flow techniques to value bond investments. Here is an example. Suppose ABC Corporation bonds have an 8 percent coupon rate paid annually, a par value of $1,000, and nine years to maturity. What is the most an investor should pay for an ABC bond if she wants a return of at least 14 percent on her investment? The cash flow diagram is as follows.

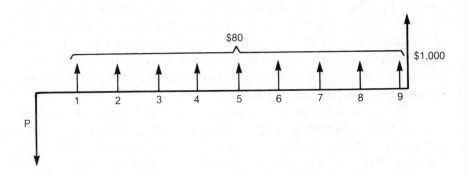

We want to find P such that it is equivalent in value to the future cash receipts discounted at 14 percent. Taking the present value of the receipts:

$$P = \$80\,(4.946) + \$1,000\,(.308)$$
$$= \$703.68.$$

Thus we know that when the investor pays $703.68 for the bond, her return over nine years will be 14 percent. When she pays more, her return will fall below 14 percent.

Suppose now that we know a bond's price and want to learn the return we will earn by holding the bond to maturity. In the jargon of the trade, we want to know the bond's *yield to maturity*. To illustrate, suppose a $1,000 par value bond pays a 10 percent annual coupon, matures in seven years, and is selling presently for $639.54. What is its yield to maturity or, equivalently, its IRR? Let's begin by trying a discount rate of 12 percent.

$$NPV = 4.564 \times \$100 + .452 \times \$1,000 - \$639.54 \stackrel{?}{=} 0$$
$$268.85 \neq 0$$

The IRR of a Perpetuity

A perpetuity is an annuity that lasts forever. Many preferred stocks are annuities, as are some British and French government bonds. They have no maturity date and promise the holder a constant annual dividend or interest payment forever. Let us use Appendix B to calculate the approximate present value of a perpetuity yielding $1 per year forever. Begin by noting that at a discount rate of say 15 percent, the present value of $1 per year for 50 years is $6.661. Think of it; although the holder will receive a total of $50, the present value of this stream is less than $7. Why? Because if the investor put $6.661 in a bank account today yielding 15 percent per year, he could withdraw approximately $1 in interest each year *forever* without touching the principal. (15% × $6.661 = $0.999). Consequently, $6.661 today is approximately equivalent in value to $1 per year forever.

This suggests the following formula for the present value of a perpetuity. Letting A equal the annual receipt, r the discount rate, and P the present value,

$$P = \frac{A}{r}$$

and

$$r = \frac{A}{P}.$$

As an example, suppose a share of preferred stock sells for $480 and promises an annual dividend of $82 forever. Then its IRR is 17.1 percent (82/480). Because the equation is so simple, perpetuities are often used to value long-lived assets.

Clearly, 12 percent is too low a discount rate. Suppose we try 25 percent.

$$NPV = 3.161 \times \$100 + .210 \times \$1,000 - \$639.54 \stackrel{?}{=} 0$$
$$-113.44 \neq 0$$

The NPV is now negative, so 25 percent is too high. Let's try 20 percent.

$$NPV = 3.605 \times \$100 + .279 \times \$1,000 - \$639.54 \overset{?}{=} 0$$
$$- 0.04 = 0$$

Because NPV is approximately zero, we know the bond's yield to maturity, or IRR, is approximately 20 percent.

Mutually Exclusive Alternatives and Capital Rationing

Before turning to the determination of relevant cash flows in investment analysis, we should consider briefly two common occurrences that often complicate investment selection. We begin by looking at mutually exclusive alternatives.

Frequently there is more than one way to accomplish an objective, and the investment problem is to select the best alternative. In this case, the investments are said to be mutually exclusive. Examples of mutually exclusive alternatives include the choice of whether to build a concrete structure or a wooden one, whether to drive to work or take the bus, and whether to build a 40-story building or a 30-story one. Even though each option gets the job done and may be attractive individually, it does not make economic sense to exercise more than one. If you decide to take the bus to work, also driving to work could prove a difficult feat. When confronted with mutually exclusive alternatives, then, it is not enough to decide whether each option is attractive individually: you must determine which is best. Mutually exclusive investments stand in contrast to independent investments where the capital budgeting problem is simply to accept or reject a single investment.

When investments are independent, all three of the figures of merit introduced above will yield the same investment decision, but this is no longer true when the investments are mutually exclusive. In all of the examples above we have implicitly assumed independence.

A second complicating factor in many investment appraisals is known as capital rationing. In the preceding discussion we have implicitly assumed that sufficient money is available to enable the company to undertake all investments promising an IRR greater than the opportunity cost of capital. In contrast, under capital rationing the decision maker has a fixed investment budget that he may not exceed. A limit on investment capital may be imposed externally by investors' unwillingness to supply more money, or it may be imposed internally as part of the company's budgeting-control system. In either case, the investment decision under capital rationing requires the analyst to rank the opportunities according to their investment merit and to accept only the best.

Both mutually exclusive alternatives and capital rationing require a ranking of investments, but here the similarity ends. With mutually exclusive investments, money is available but for technological reasons only certain investments can be accepted, whereas under capital rationing, a lack of money is the complicating factor. Moreover, even the criteria used to rank the investments differ in the two cases, so that the best investment among mutually exclusive alternatives need not be best under conditions of capital rationing. The appendix to this chapter discusses these technicalities, and indicates which figures of merit are appropriate under which conditions.

DETERMINING THE RELEVANT CASH FLOWS

Calculating a figure of merit requires an understanding of the time value of money and equivalence, and it necessitates a modicum of algebra. But these difficulties pale to insignificance compared to those arising in the estimation of an investment's relevant cash flows. For the former require only technical competence, whereas the latter calls for the exercise of judgment and perspective.

Two principles govern the determination of relevant cash flows. Both are obvious when stated in the abstract but can be very difficult to apply in practice. They are—

The cash flow principle: Because money has a time value, record investment cash flows when they actually occur, not when the accountant using accrual concepts says they occur.

The with-without principle: Imagine two worlds, one in which the investment is made and one in which it is rejected. All cash flows that are different in these two worlds are relevant to the decision, and all those that are the same are irrelevant.

The following examples illustrate the practical application of these principles to commonly recurring cash flow estimation problems.

Depreciation

Depreciation is a noncash charge and, according to the cash flow principle, is therefore not a relevant cash flow. Depreciation does influence the determination of income taxes, however, and taxes are a relevant cash flow. So we need to use the following two-step procedure: (1) Use standard accrual accounting techniques, including the treatment of depreciation as a cost, to calculate taxes due, then (2) add depreciation back to income after tax to calculate the investment's aftertax cash flow (ATCF). ATCF is the correct measure of an investment's operating cash flow. To illustrate, assume that the container loading pier considered earlier in the chapter will generate an annual income before depreciation and taxes of $9.8 million, that annual depreciation will be $3 million, and that Pacific Rim Resources is in the 34 percent tax bracket. Then, aftertax cash flow is $7.5 million, as shown in the table below.

Operating income	$9.8 million
Less: Depreciation	3.0
Earnings before tax	6.8
Less: Tax at 34%	2.3
Earnings after tax	4.5
Plus: Depreciation	3.0
Aftertax cash flow	$7.5 million

Another way to say the same thing is:

$$\text{Aftertax cash flow} = \text{Operating income} - \text{Taxes}$$
$$\$7.5 = \$9.8 - \$2.3.$$

This formulation shows clearly that aftertax cash flow treats depreciation as irrelevant except for its role in determining taxes.

Note that our treatment of depreciation here is not equivalent to saying that depreciation is irrelevant. The physical deterioration of assets over time is an economic fact of life that is relevant in investment evaluation. We include depreciation in our analysis, however, whenever an asset's salvage value is estimated to be below its original cost. To also subtract an annual amount from operating income would be double-counting.

Working Capital

In addition to increases in fixed assets, many investments, especially those for new products, require increases in working capital items, such as inventories and receivables. According to the with-without principle, changes in working capital that are the result of an investment decision are relevant to the decision. In some instances they are the largest cash flows involved.

There are two unique features of working capital investments. One is that such investments are reversible in the sense that at the end of the project's life, the liquidation of working capital generates cash inflows. The second unique feature is that many investments requiring increases in working capital also generate *spontaneous sources of cash* in the form of increased trade credit and the like, which partially offset the working capital investment. The proper treatment of these spontaneous sources is to subtract them from the increases in current assets when calculating the project's working capital investment.

To illustrate, suppose XYZ Corporation is considering a new product investment that, in addition to an increase in plant and equipment, will require a $3 million investment in inventories and accounts receivable. Partially offsetting this buildup in current assets, management also anticipates that accounts payable, accrued wages, and accrued taxes will rise by $1 million as a result of the new product. So the net increase in working capital is $2 million. Management has agreed to analyze the proposed investment over a 10-year horizon and feels that all of the working capital investment will be recovered at the end of 10 years as the company sells off inventory, collects receivables, and pays off trade creditors. The cash flow associated only with the working capital portion of this investment is shown in the following diagram.

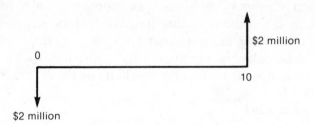

If money had no time value, these offsetting cash flows would cancel one another out, but because money does have a time value, we need to include them in our analysis.

Allocated Costs

According to the with-without principle, those cash flows that do not change as a result of an investment are irrelevant for the decision. For example, many companies allocate overhead costs to departments or divisions in proportion to the amount of direct labor expense incurred by the departments. Suppose a department manager in such an environment has the opportunity to invest in a laborsaving asset. From the department's narrow perspective, there are two benefits to such an asset: (1) a reduction in direct labor expense and (2) a reduction in the overhead costs allocated to the department. Yet from the total company perspective and from the correct economic perspective, only the reduction in direct labor is a benefit because the overhead costs are unaffected by the decision. They are just reallocated from one cost center to another.

Let us consider a subtler example involving a new product investment. Suppose a company is considering a new product investment that if undertaken will increase sales by 5 percent over the next 10 years. The point at issue is whether allocated costs that are not directly associated with the new product, such as the president's salary, legal department expenses, and accounting department expenses, are relevant to the decision. A narrow interpretation of the with-without principle suggests that if the president's salary does not change as a result of the investment, it is not relevant. Yet we observe that over time, as companies grow, presidents' salaries tend to increase; and we observe that presidents of large companies tend to have higher salaries than those of small companies. This suggests that although we are unable to see a direct cause-effect tie between such costs and increasing sales, there is a longer-run relation between the two. Consequently, such costs may well be relevant to the decision.

Sunk Costs

A sunk cost is one that has already been incurred and that according to the with-without principle is not relevant for present decisions. This seems easy enough, but consider some examples. Suppose you purchased some common stock a year ago at $100 per share and that it is presently trading for $70 per share. Even though you believe the stock is fairly priced at $70, would you be prepared to admit your mistake and sell it now, or would you be tempted to hold it in hopes of recouping your original investment? The with-without principle says the $100 price is sunk and hence irrelevant, except for possible tax effects.

Suppose the R&D department of a company has devoted 10 years and $10 million to perfecting a new, long-lasting light bulb. Their original estimate was a development time of two years at a cost of $1 million, and every year since they have progressively extended the development time and increased the cost. Now they are estimating only one more year and an added expenditure of only $1 million. Since the present value of the benefits from such a light bulb is only $4 million, there is considerable feeling in the company that the project should be killed and whoever had been approving the budget increases throughout the years should be fired.

In retrospect, it is clear the company should never have begun work on the light bulb. Even if successful, the cost will be well in excess of the benefits. Yet at any point along the development process, including the current decision, it may have been perfectly rational to continue work. Past expenditures are sunk, so that the only question at issue is whether the anticipated benefits exceed the *remaining* costs required to complete development. Past expenditures are relevant only to the extent that they influence one's assessment of whether the remaining costs are properly estimated.

Excess Capacity

For technological reasons, it is frequently necessary to acquire more capacity than required to accomplish an objective, and a question arises of how to handle the excess. For example, suppose a company is considering the acquisition of a hydrofoil boat to provide passenger service across a lake, but that effective use of the hydrofoil will require construction of two very expensive special purpose piers. Each pier will be capable of handling 10 hydrofoils, and for technical reasons it is impractical to construct smaller piers. If the full cost of the two piers must be borne by the one boat presently under consideration, the boat's NPV will be large and negative; yet if only one-tenth of the pier costs is assigned to the boat, its NPV will be positive. How should the pier costs be treated?

The proper treatment of the pier costs depends on the company's future plans. If the company does not anticipate acquiring any additional hydrofoils in the future, the full cost of the piers is relevant for the present decision. On the other hand, if this boat is but the first of a contemplated fleet of hydrofoils, then it is appropriate to consider only a fraction of the pier's costs. More generally, the problem faced by the company is that of defining the investment. The relevant question is not whether the company should acquire a boat, but whether it should enter the hydrofoil transportation business. The broader question forces the company to look at the investment over a longer time span.

The reverse situation also arises. A company has excess capacity of some sort and is considering an investment that will utilize the unused resources. In this case, the question is what cost, if any, to assign to the excess capacity. As an example, a

prominent producer of canned foods was considering the addition of a new product line that would utilize some presently
underemployed canning facilities. Some company executives argued that since the facilities had already been paid for, their
cost was sunk and consequently irrelevant. Others argued that
the canning capacity was a scarce resource and should be assigned a cost. What cost should be assigned to the excess
capacity?

The answer again depends upon future plans. If there are
no alternative uses for the canning facilities now or in the future, no costs are involved in its use. On the other hand, if the
company is likely to have need for the facilities in the future,
there is an opportunity cost associated with their use by the
new product line.

Financing Costs

Financing costs are relevant in investment evaluation. Care
must be taken, however, not to double-count them. As the next
chapter will clarify, the most common discount rate used in
calculating any of the recommended figures of merit equals the
annual percentage cost of capital to the company. It would obviously be double-counting to subtract financing costs from an
investment's annual cash inflows *and* to expect an investment
to generate a return greater than the cost of the capital. The
standard procedure, therefore, is to reflect the cost of money in
the discount rate and to ignore all financing costs when estimating an investment's cash flows.

APPENDIX

MUTUALLY EXCLUSIVE ALTERNATIVES
AND CAPITAL RATIONING

We noted briefly in the chapter that the presence of mutually exclusive
alternatives or capital rationing complicates investment analysis. The
purpose of this appendix is to demonstrate how investments should be
analyzed in these cases.

Two investments are mutually exclusive if accepting one precludes further consideration of the other. The choices between building a steel or a concrete bridge, between laying a 12-inch pipeline or an 8-inch one, or between driving to Boston or flying are all mutually exclusive alternatives. In each case, there is more than one way to accomplish a task, and the objective is to choose the best. Mutually exclusive investments stand in contrast to independent investments where each opportunity can be analyzed on its own without regard to other investments.

When investments are independent and the decision is simply to accept or reject, the NPV, the PI, and the IRR are equally satisfactory figures of merit. You will reach the same investment decision regardless of the figure of merit used. When investments are mutually exclusive, the world is not so simple. Let's consider an example. Suppose Petro Oil and Gas Company is considering two alternative designs for new service stations and wants to evaluate them using a 10 percent discount rate. As shown in the cash flow diagrams in Figure 7A–1, the inexpensive option involves a present investment of $522,000 in return for an anticipated $100,000 per year for 10 years; the expensive option costs $1.1 million, but because of its greater customer appeal, is expected to return $195,000 per year for 10 years.

Table 7A–1 presents the three figures of merit for each investment. All of the figures of merit signal that both options are attractive, the NPVs are positive, the PIs are greater than 1.0, and the IRRs exceed Petro's opportunity cost of capital. If it were possible, Petro should make both investments but because they are mutually exclusive, this does not make technological sense. So rather than just accepting or rejecting the investments, Petro must rank them and select

FIGURE 7A–1
Cash Flow Diagrams for Alternative Service Station Designs

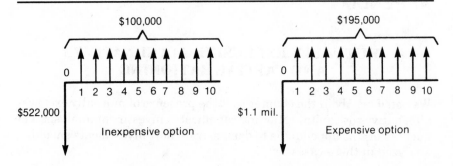

Inexpensive option · Expensive option

TABLE 7A–1
Figures of Merit for Service Station Designs

	NPV at 10 Percent	PI at 10 Percent	IRR
Inexpensive option	$92,500	1.18	14%
Expensive option	98,275	1.09	12%

the best. When it comes to ranking the alternatives, however, the three figures of merit no longer give the same signal, for although the inexpensive option has a higher PI and a higher IRR, it has a lower NPV than the expensive one.

To decide which figure of merit is appropriate for mutually exclusive alternatives, we need only remember that the NPV is a direct measure of the anticipated increase in wealth created by the investment. Since the expensive option will increase wealth by $98,275, as opposed to only $92,500 for the inexpensive option, the expensive option is clearly superior.

The problem with the PI and the IRR for mutually exclusive alternatives is basically that they are insensitive to the scale of the investment. As an extreme example, would you rather have an 80 percent return on a $1 investment or a 50 percent return on a $1 million investment? Clearly, when investments are mutually exclusive, scale is relevant, and this leads to the use of the NPV as the appropriate figure of merit.

What Happened to the Other $578,000? Some persons feel the above reasoning is incomplete because we have said nothing about what Petro can do with the $578,000 it would save by choosing the inexpensive option. It would seem that if this saving could be invested at a sufficiently attractive return, the inexpensive option might prove to be superior after all. We will address this concern in the section titled Capital Rationing. For now, it is sufficient to say that the problem arises only when there are fixed limits on the amount of money Petro has available for investment. When the company can raise sufficient money to make all investments promising IRRs greater than its opportunity cost of capital, this concern is not an important one.

Unequal Lines. The Petro Oil and Gas example conveniently assumed that both service station options had the same 10-year life.

Frequently, mutually exclusive alternatives have different service lives. When this occurs, a simple comparison of NPVs is usually inappropriate. Consider the following example of a company trying to decide whether to build a wooden bridge or a steel bridge.

The wooden bridge has an initial cost of $125,000, requires annual maintenance expenditures of $15,000, and will last 10 years. The steel bridge costs $200,000, requires $5,000 annual maintenance, and will last 40 years.

At, say, a 15 percent discount rate, the present value cost of the wooden bridge over its expected life of 10 years is $150,190 ($125,000 + 5.019 × $15,000). This compares to a figure for the steel bridge over its 40-year life expectancy of $233,210 ($200,000 + 6.642 × $5,000). So if the object is to minimize the cost of the bridge, a simple comparison of present values would suggest that the wooden structure is a clear winner. However, this obviously overlooks the difference in the life expectancy of the two bridges.

When comparing mutually exclusive alternatives having differing service lives, it is necessary to examine each over the same *common investment horizon*. For example, suppose the company in the above example believes it will need a bridge for 20 years, that because of inflation, the wooden bridge will cost $200,000 to reconstruct at the end of 10 years, and that the salvage value of the steel bridge in 20 years will be $90,000. The cash flow diagrams for the two options are as follows.

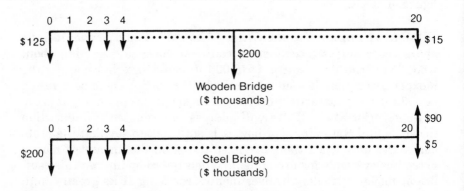

Now the present value cost of the wooden bridge is $268,285 ($125,000 + 6.259 × $15,000 + .247 × $200,000), and that of the steel bridge is $225,805 ($200,000 + 6.259 × $5,000 − .061 × $90,000). Compared over a common 20-year horizon, the steel bridge has the lower present value cost.

Capital Rationing. Implicit in our discussion to this point has been the assumption that investment capital is readily available to companies at a cost equal to the discount rate. The other extreme is *capital rationing*. Under capital rationing, the company has a fixed investment budget, which it may not exceed. As was true with mutually exclusive alternatives, capital rationing requires us to rank investments rather than simply to accept or reject them. Despite this similarity, however, you should understand that the two conditions are fundamentally different. With mutually exclusive alternatives, the money is available, but for technological reasons, the firm cannot make all investments. Under capital rationing, it may be technologically possible to make all investments, but there is not enough money. This difference is more than semantic, for as the following example illustrates, the nature of the ranking process differs fundamentally in the two cases.

Suppose Sullivan Electronics Company has a limited investment budget of $200,000 and that management has identified the four independent investment opportunities appearing in Table 7A–2. According to the three figures of merit, all investments should be undertaken, but this is impossible because the total cost of the four investments exceeds Sullivan's budget. Looking at the investment rankings, the NPV criterion ranks A as the best investment, followed by B, C, and D in that order, while the PI and IRR rank C best, followed by D, B, and A. So we know that A is either the best investment or the worst.

To make sense of these rankings, we need to remember that the underlying economic objective in evaluating investment opportunities is to increase wealth. Under capital rationing, this means the company

Table 7A–2
Four Independent Investment Opportunities under Capital Rationing
(Capital Budget = $200,000)

Investment	Initial Cost	NPV at 12 Percent	PI at 12 Percent	IRR
A	$200,000	$10,000	1.05	14.4%
B	120,000	8,000	1.07	15.1
C	50,000	6,000	1.12	17.6
D	80,000	6,000	1.08	15.5

should undertake that *bundle* of investments that generates the highest *total* NPV. How is this to be done? One way is to look at every possible bundle of investments that has a total cost less than the budget constraint and to select the bundle with the highest *total* NPV. A short cut is to rank the investments by their PI and work down the list, accepting investments until either the money runs out or the PI drops below 1.0. This suggests that Sullivan should accept projects C, D, and 7/12 of B, for a total NPV of $16,670 [6,000 + 6,000 + 7/12 × 8,000]. Only 7/12 of B should be undertaken because the company only has $70,000 remaining after accepting C and D.

Why is it incorrect to rank investments by their NPV under capital rationing? Because under capital rationing, we are interested in the payoff per dollar invested, not simply in the payoff itself. The Sullivan example illustrates the point. Investment A has the largest NPV, equal to $10,000, but it has the smallest NPV per dollar invested. Since investment dollars are limited under capital rationing, we must look at the benefit per dollar invested when ranking investments. This is what the PI does.

Two other details warrant mention. In the above example, the IRR provides the same ranking as the PI, and although this is usually the case, it is not always so. It turns out that when the two rankings differ, the PI ranking is the correct one. The explanations of why the rankings differ and why PI is superior are not worth explaining here. It is sufficient to remember that if you rank by IRR rather than PI, you might occasionally be in error, but that in the grand sweep of life, it probably won't matter much. A second detail is that when fractional investments are not possible—when it does not make sense for Sullivan Electronics to invest in 7/12 of project B—then rankings according to any figure of merit are unreliable, and one must resort to the tedious method of looking at each possible bundle of investments in search of the highest total NPV.

The Problem of Future Opportunities. Implicit in the above discussion is the assumption that as long as an investment has a positive NPV, it is better to make the investment than to let the money sit idle. However, under capital rationing, this may not be true. To illustrate, suppose that the financial executive of Sullivan Electronics believes that within six months company scientists will develop a new product costing $200,000 and having an NPV of $60,000. In this event, the company's best strategy is to forgo all of the investments presently under consideration and to save its money for the new product.

As illustrated, investment evaluation under capital rationing involves more than a simple appraisal of current opportunities; it also involves a comparison between current opportunities and future prospects. The difficulty with this comparison, at a practical level, is that it is unreasonable to expect a manager to have anything more than a vague impression of what investments are likely to arise in the future. Consequently, it is impossible to decide with any assurance whether it is better to invest in current projects or to wait for brighter future opportunities. This means that practical investment evaluation under capital rationing necessarily involves a large degree of subjective judgment.

A Decision Tree

Mutually exclusive investment alternatives and capital rationing complicate an already confusing topic. To provide a summary and overview, Figure 7A–2 presents a capital budgeting decision tree. It

FIGURE 7A–2
Capital Budgeting Decision Tree

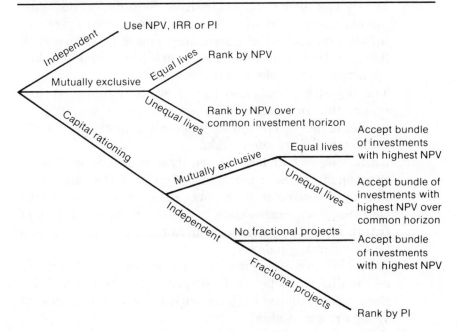

indicates the figure or figures of merit that are appropriate under the various conditions discussed in the chapter. For example, following the lowest branch in the tree, we see that when evaluating investments under capital rationing that are independent and that can be acquired fractionally, ranking by the PI is the appropriate technique. To review your understanding of the material, see if you can explain why the recommended figures of merit are appropriate under the various conditions indicated whereas the others are not.

CHAPTER SUMMARY

1. This chapter has examined the use of discounted cash flow techniques in investment appraisal.

2. The three steps in financial evaluation of investment opportunities are: *(a)* estimate the relevant cash flows, *(b)* calculate a figure of merit, and *(c)* compare this figure with an acceptance criterion. The first step is the hardest in practice.

3. Money has a time value for three reasons: *(a)* risk customarily increases with the remoteness of an event, *(b)* inflation reduces the purchasing power of future cash flows, and *(c)* waiting for future cash flows involves a lost opportunity to make interim investments.

4. The payback period and the accounting rate of return ignore the time value of money and, hence, are inferior figures of merit. The payback period, however, is a useful indicator of investment risk.

5. Cash flows at two dates are equivalent if it is possible to transform the near-term cash flow into the later cash flow by investing it at the prevailing interest rate. Discounting uses equivalence to convert a messy stream of future receipts and disbursements into equal-value cash flows occurring today.

6. A valid figure of merit is the net present value, defined as the difference between the present values of cash inflows and outflows. Projects with a positive net present value are acceptable.

7. A second popular, valid figure of merit is the internal rate of return, defined as the discount rate that makes

the investment's NPV equal zero. It is also the rate at which money left in a project is compounding and is therefore comparable to the interest rate on a bank loan. Investments with an internal rate of return greater than the cost of capital are acceptable.

8. The guiding principles in deciding what cash flows are relevant for an investment decision are the with-without principle and the cash flow principle.

9. Recurring problems in determining relevant cash flows involve depreciation, working capital changes, allocated costs, sunk costs, temporarily excess capacity, and financing costs.

ADDITIONAL READING

Bierman, Harold, Jr., and Seymour Smidt. *The Capital Budgeting Decision*. 6th ed. New York: MacMillan, 1984. 544 pages.

This textbook has more of a finance orientation than *Principles of Engineering Economy* and is somewhat harder to follow.

Grant, Eugene L., Grant Ireson, and Richard S. Leavenworth. *Principles of Engineering Economy*. 7th ed. New York: Ronald Press, 1982. 624 pages.

Everything you ever wanted to know about discounted cash flow techniques and more. A very solid, understandable treatment containing many practical examples.

CHAPTER PROBLEMS

1. Answer the following questions assuming the interest rate is 10 percent. (Answers to alternate questions appear at the end of this problem.)

    a. What is the present value of $100 in 6 years?

    b. What is the present value of $100 in 10 years? Why does the present value fall as the number of years increases?

    c. How much would you pay to receive a 15-year bond with a par value of $1,000 and a 12 percent coupon rate? Assume interest is paid annually.

    e. What will be the value in 10 years of $5 invested today? [**Hint:** Present value = PVF × future value, where PVF is the present value factor from the tables for the appropriate interest rate and time period. So, future value = (1/PVF) × present value.]

    f. About how long will it take for a $10 investment to double in value?

    g. What will be the value in 10 years of $5 invested at the end of each year for the next 10 years?

    h. A couple wishes to save $100,000 over the next 15 years for their child's college education. What uniform annual amount must they deposit at the end of each year to accomplish their objective?

    (**Answers to alternate problems:** *a.* $56.40, *c.* $1,151.72, *e.* $12.95, *g.* $79.60.)

2. An investment costing $50,000 promises an aftertax cash flow of $18,000 per year for 6 years.

    a. Find the investment's accounting rate of return and its payback period.

    b. Find the investment's net present value at a 15 percent discount rate.

    c. Find the investment's profitability index at a 15 percent discount rate.

    d. Find the investment's internal rate of return.

    e. Assuming that the required rate of return on the investment is 15 percent, which of the above figures of merit indicate the investment is attractive? Which indicate it is unattractive?

3. A $1,000 par value, 10 percent coupon bond matures in 20 years. If the price of the bond is $1,196.80, what is the yield to maturity on the bond? Assume interest is paid annually.

4. Consider the following investment opportunity.

Initial cost	$850,000
Annual revenues	$500,000
Annual operating costs,	
exclusive of depreciation	$200,000
Expected life	20 years
Salvage value after taxes	$ 40,000
Annual depreciation	
for tax purposes	$ 25,000
Tax rate	34%

What is the rate of return on this investment? Assuming the investor wants to earn at least 12 percent, is this investment an attractive one?

The following problems are best analyzed using a business calculator or a computer.

5. In 1987, Vincent Van Gogh's painting of sunflowers (not reputed to be one of his best) sold at auction, net of fees, for $36 million. In 1889, 98 years earlier, the same painting sold for $125. Calculate the rate of return to the seller on this investment. What does this suggest about the merits of fine art as an investment?

6. Given the following information about three bonds, answer the questions below.

Bond	A	B	C
Par value	$1,000	$1,000	$1,000
Coupon rate	6%	6%	6% .
Time to maturity	1 yr.	5 yrs.	20 yrs.

   a. Calculate the prices of the bonds at an 11 percent interest rate.

   b. Calculate the prices of the bonds at a 12 percent interest rate.

   c. Looking at your answers to *a* and *b,* do bond prices vary directly or inversely with interest rates?

   d. Does it appear that bond prices become more or less sensitive to interest rate changes as time to maturity increases? Does this suggest that short-term bonds are riskier or less risky than long-term bonds?

Chapter 8

Risk Analysis in Investment Decisions

A man's gotta make at least one bet a day,
else he could be walking around lucky
and never know it.

Jimmy Jones, horse trainer

All interesting financial decisions involve considerations of risk as well as return. By their nature, business investments require the expenditure of a known sum of money today in anticipation of uncertain future benefits. Consequently, if the discounted cash flow techniques discussed in the last chapter are to be useful in evaluating such investments, we must incorporate risk effects into the analysis. Two such effects are important: At the practical level, risk increases the difficulty of estimating relevant cash flows, while at the conceptual level, risk itself enters as an important determinant of investment value. A simple example will illustrate the latter point. If two investments promise the same return but have differing risks, most of us will prefer the lower-risk alternative. In the jargon of economics, we are risk-averse.

Risk aversion among individuals and corporations creates the recognizable pattern of investment risk and return shown in Figure 8–1. For low-risk investments, such as government securities, the figure shows that the anticipated return is modest, but as risk increases, so too must the anticipated return. I say "must" here because the risk-return pattern shown is more than wishful thinking. Unless higher-risk investments promise higher returns, you and I as risk-averse investors will never hold them.

This risk-return trade-off is fundamental to much of finance. Over the past two decades, researchers have demonstrated that under idealized conditions, and with risk defined in a specific way, the risk-return trade-off is a straight-line relationship, as depicted in the figure. The line is known as the Market Line and represents the combinations of risk and return one can expect in a properly functioning economy.

The details of the Market Line need not detain us here. What is important is the realization that knowledge of an investment's anticipated return is not enough to determine its worth. Instead, investment evaluation is a two-dimensional task involving a balancing of risk against return. The appropriate question when evaluating investment opportunities is not, "What's the rate of return?" but rather "Is the return sufficient to justify the risk?" The investments represented by points A and B in Figure 8–1 illustrate this point. Investment A has a higher expected return than B; nonetheless, B is the better investment. Despite its modest return, B lies above the Market Line, meaning that it promises a higher return for its risk than available alternatives, whereas investment A lies below the Market Line, meaning that alternative investments are available that promise a higher return for the same risk.

This chapter examines the incorporation of risk into investment evaluation with particular emphasis on risk-adjusted discount rates and the cost of capital. After defining terms, we will estimate the cost of capital to Tektronix, Inc., the high-technology company discussed in earlier chapters, and we will examine the limitations of the cost of capital as a risk-adjustment mechanism. The chapter concludes with a look at two important pitfalls to avoid when evaluating investments. An appendix

FIGURE 8–1
The Risk-Return Trade-Off

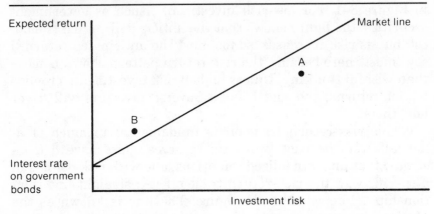

considers diversification and what is known as β-risk as they affect investment appraisal.

You should know at the outset that the topics in this chapter are not simple, for the addition of a whole second dimension to investment analysis in the form of risk introduces a number of complexities and ambiguities. The results of the chapter, therefore, will be a general road map for how to proceed and an appreciation of available techniques rather than a detailed set of answers. But look on the bright side. If investment decisions were simple, there would be less demand for well-educated managers and aspiring financial writers.

RISK DEFINED

Intuitively, investment risk is concerned with the range of possible outcomes from an investment; the greater this range, the greater the risk. Figure 8–2 extends this intuitive notion. It shows the possible rates of return that might be earned on two investments in the form of bell-shaped curves. According to the figure, the expected return on investment A is about 12 percent, and the corresponding figure for investment B is about 22 percent.

FIGURE 8–2
**Illustration of Investment Risk: Investment A Has a Lower Expected
Return and a Lower Risk than B**

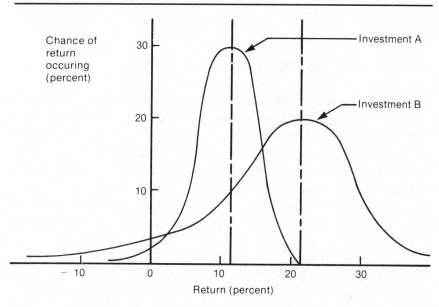

A statistician would define "expected return" as the probability-weighted average of possible returns. To take a simple
example, if three returns are possible—8, 12, and 18 percent—
and if the chance of each occurring is 40, 30, and 30 percent,
respectively, the investment's expected return is

$$\text{Expected return} = .40 \times 8\% + .30 \times 12\% + .30 \times 18\% = 12.2\%.$$

Risk refers to the bunching of possible returns about an
investment's expected return. If there is considerable bunching,
as with investment A, the investment is low-risk. With investment B there is considerably less clustering of returns about the
expected return, so it has higher risk. Borrowing again from
statistics, one way to measure this clustering tendency is to
calculate a probability-weighted average of the deviations of
possible returns from the expected return. One such average is
the standard deviation of returns. The details of calculating an

investment's standard deviation of returns need not concern us here.[1] It is sufficient to know that risk corresponds to the dispersion in possible outcomes, and that there exist techniques to measure this dispersion.

ESTIMATING INVESTMENT RISK

Having now defined risk in at least a general way, let us next consider how we might estimate the amount of risk present in a particular investment opportunity. In some business situations an investment's risk can be calculated objectively from scientific or historical evidence. This is true, for instance, of oil and gas development wells. Once an exploration company has found a field and mapped out its general configuration, the probability that a development well drilled within the boundaries of the field will be commercially successful can be determined with reasonable accuracy.

Sometimes history can be a guide. A company that has opened 500 fast-food restaurants across the country should have a good idea about the expected return and risk of opening the

---

[1]To illustrate calculation of the standard deviation of returns, the difference between the possible returns and the expected return in the above example are (8% − 12.2%), (12% − 12.2%), and (18% − 12.2%). Because some of these differences are positive and others negative, they would tend to cancel one another out if we added them directly. So we square them to assure the same sign, calculate the probability-weighted average of the squared deviations, and then find the square root.

$$\text{Standard deviation} = [.4(8\% - 12.2\%)^2 + .3(12\% - 12.2\%)^2 + .3(18\% - 12.2\%)^2]^{1/2}$$
$$= 4.1\%.$$

The probability-weighted average difference between the investment's possible returns and its expected return is 4.1 percentage points. In symbols,

$$\sigma_i = \left[\sum_{i=1}^{n} p_i(r_i - \bar{r})^2 \right]^{1/2},$$

where σ_i is the investment's standard deviation of returns, p_i is the probability the ith return will occur, r_i is ith return, $\bar{r}$ is the expected return, n is the number of different returns which might occur, and Σ indicates the n squared deviations should be added together.

501st. Similarly, if you are thinking about buying IBM stock, the historical record of annual returns to IBM shareholders and the variability of these returns is an important starting point when estimating future risk and return on IBM shares.

These are the easy situations. More often, business ventures are one-of-a-kind investments for which the estimation of risk must be largely subjective. When a company is contemplating a new product investment, for example, there is frequently little technical or historical experience on which to base an estimate of investment risk. In this situation, risk appraisal depends on the perceptions of the managers participating in the decision, on their knowledge of the economics of the industry, and their understanding of the investment's ramifications.

Sensitivity Analysis and Simulation

Two previously mentioned techniques, sensitivity analysis and simulation, are useful when investment risk must be estimated subjectively. Although neither technique provides an objective measure of investment risk, both help the executive to think systematically about the sources of risk and their effect on project return. Reviewing briefly, an investment's IRR or NPV depends upon a number of economic factors, such as selling price, quantity sold, useful life, and so on, many of which are not known with certainty. Sensitivity analysis involves a determination of how the investment's figure of merit varies with changes in one of these uncertain factors. One commonly used approach is to calculate three returns corresponding to an optimistic, a pessimistic, and a most likely forecast of the uncertain factor. This provides some indication of the range of possible outcomes.

Simulation is an extension of sensitivity analysis in which the analyst assigns a probability distribution to each uncertain factor, specifies any interdependence among the factors, and asks a computer repeatedly to select values for the factors according to their probability of occurring. For each set of values chosen, the computer calculates the investment's return. The result is a graph, such as Figure 8–2, plotting project return against frequency of occurrence. The chief benefits of sensitivity

---

An Example of Sensitivity Analysis

A number of software programs are commercially available for analyzing investment opportunities on a personal computer. A standard option on many is the ability to analyze the sensitivity of the results to changes in key assumptions. Below is representative output from such an analysis.

Relative Influence of Key Variables on Net Present Value
(Investment NPV = $212,597)

A 1% Increase in:	Increases NPV by:	% Increase
Sales growth rate	$2,240	1.33
Operating profit margin	3,462	2.05
Capital investment	−1,249	−0.74
Working capital investment	−1,143	−0.68
Discount rate	−4,996	−2.96

---

analysis and simulation are that they force the analyst to think systematically about the individual economic determinants of investment risk, they indicate the sensitivity of the investment's return to each of these determinants, and they provide information about the range of possible returns.

INCLUDING RISK IN INVESTMENT EVALUATION

Once you have an idea of the amount of risk inherent in an investment, the final step is to incorporate this information into your evaluation of the opportunity. Speaking broadly, there are two ways to do this: by fiddling with the investment's cash flows, or by fiddling with its discount rate. The former uses what are known as *certainty equivalents*.

A certainty equivalent is a risk-free, or certain, sum of money that has the same value to the analyst as a risky cash flow. If you would just as soon receive $10 as a lottery ticket offering a 50-50 chance at $25 or nothing, $10 is your certainty equivalent of the lottery ticket.

To evaluate risky investments using certainty equivalents, the first step is to replace each risky cash flow with its certainty equivalent. Having thus accounted for risk, the second step is to evaluate the investment as if it were risk-free. This means using a risk-free discount rate, such as the government borrowing rate, to calculate the investment's NPV or PI. Or if the IRR is used, it means comparing the certainty equivalent IRR to a risk-free interest rate to determine the investment's acceptability.

Certainty equivalents seldom are used in industry, primarily because there is no practical, objective way to estimate them. When you are making personal investment decisions, it might be possible to estimate certainty equivalents based on your own subjective feelings about risk. But when an executive analyzes an investment on behalf of his company, there is no practical way to determine what certainty equivalents are appropriate. This makes risk assessment almost entirely a matter of personal opinion.

Risk-Adjusted Discount Rates

The more common way to incorporate risk into investment appraisal is to adjust the discount rate. Instead of replacing risky cash flows with their certainty equivalents, the analyst discounts the expected value of the risky cash flows at a discount rate that includes a premium for risk. Alternatively, the analyst compares an investment's IRR, based on expected cash flows, to a required rate of return that again includes a risk premium. The size of the premium naturally increases with the perceived risk of the investment.

To illustrate the use of risk-adjusted discount rates, consider a $10 million investment promising risky cash flows having an expected value of $2 million annually for 10 years. What is the investment's NPV when the risk-free interest rate is 8 percent and management has decided to use a 6 percent risk premium to compensate for the uncertainty of the cash flows?

The cash flow diagram for the investment appears below. At a 14 percent risk-adjusted discount rate, the project's NPV is

$$NPV = -\$10 \text{ million} + \$2 \text{ million } (5.216)$$
$$= \$432{,}000,$$

where 5.216, from Appendix B, equals the present value of $1 per year for 10 years at 14 percent interest. Because the investment's NPV is positive, it is attractive even after adjusting for risk. An equivalent approach is to calculate the investment's IRR, using expected cash flows, and compare it to the risk-adjusted rate. Because the project's IRR of 15.1 percent exceeds 14 percent, we again conclude the investment is attractive despite its risk.

Note how the risk-adjusted discount rate reduces the investment's appeal. If the investment were riskless, its NPV at an 8 percent discount rate would be $3.4 million, but because a higher risk-adjusted rate is deemed appropriate, NPV falls by almost $3 million.

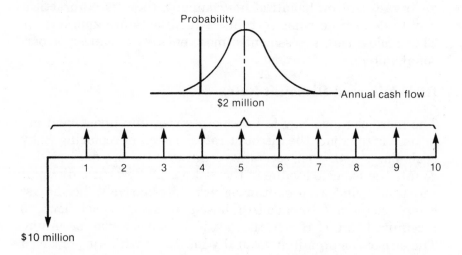

Two things make risk-adjusted discount rates superior to certainty equivalents in practical application. One is that most executives have at least a rough idea of how an investment's required rate of return should vary with risk. Stated differently, they have a basic idea of the position of the Market Line in Figure 8–1. For example, they know from the historical data in Table 5–1 that over many years common stocks have yielded an average annual return about 7.4 percent higher than the return on government bonds. If the present return on government bonds is 8.8 percent, then it is plausible to expect an investment that is about as risky as common stocks to yield a return of about 16.2 percent. Similarly, executives know if an investment promises a return of 40 percent, that unless the risk is extremely high, the investment is likely to be attractive. Granted, such reasoning is imprecise; nonetheless, it does lend some objectivity to risk assessment.

THE COST OF CAPITAL

The second attraction of risk-adjusted discount rates involves the cost of capital. When creditors and owners invest money in a company, they incur an opportunity cost equal to the return they could have earned on alternative investments. This opportunity cost is the firm's cost of capital; it is the minimum rate of return the company can earn on existing assets and still meet the expectations of its capital providers. The cost of capital is a risk-adjusted discount rate, and because we can at least estimate the cost of capital for individual companies, it introduces a welcome degree of objectivity into the risk-adjustment process. In following paragraphs we will define the cost of capital more precisely, estimate the cost of capital to Tektronix, Inc., and discuss its use as a risk-adjustment factor.

The Cost of Capital Defined

Suppose we want to estimate the cost of capital to the XYZ Corporation. We know the tax rate is 50 percent, and we have the following information:

	XYZ Liabilities and Owners' Equity	Opportunity Cost of Capital
Debt	$100	10%
Equity	$200	20%

We will discuss the origins of the opportunity costs of capital in a few pages. For now just assume we know that, given alternative investment opportunities, creditors expect to earn at least 10 percent on their loans and shareholders expect to earn at least 20 percent on their ownership of XYZ shares. With this information, we need answer only two simple questions to calculate XYZ's cost of capital:

1. How much money must XYZ earn annually on existing assets to meet the expectations of creditors and owners?
    The creditors expect a 10 percent return on their $100 loan, or $10. However, because interest payments are tax deductible, the effective aftertax cost to a profitable company in the 50 percent tax bracket is only $5. The owners expect 20 percent on their $200 investment, or $40. So in total, XYZ must earn $45 [$45 = (1 − .5)(10%) $100 + (20%) $200].

2. What rate of return must the company earn on existing assets to meet the expectations of creditors and owners?
    There is a total of $300 invested in XYZ on which the company must earn $45, so the required rate of return is 15 percent ($45/$300). This is XYZ's cost of capital.

Let's repeat the above reasoning, using symbols. The money XYZ must earn annually on existing capital is

$$(1 - t)K_D D + K_E E,$$

where t is the tax rate, K_D is the expected return on debt, or the cost of debt, D is the amount of debt in XYZ's capital structure, K_E is the expected return on equity, or the cost of equity, and E is the amount of equity in XYZ's capital structure. Similarly, the annual return XYZ must earn on existing capital is

$$K_W = \frac{(1 - t)K_D D + K_E E}{D + E}, \tag{8-1}$$

where K_W is the cost of capital.
    From the above example,

$$15\% = \frac{(1 - 50\%) \times 10\% \times \$100 + 20\% \times \$200}{\$100 + \$200}.$$

In words, a company's cost of capital is the cost of the individual sources of capital, weighted according to their importance in the firm's capital structure. The subscript W appears in the cost of capital expression to denote that the cost of capital is a weighted-average cost. To demonstrate, one third of XYZ's capital is debt and two thirds is equity, so its cost of capital is one third the cost of debt plus two thirds the cost of equity:

$$15\% = \frac{1}{3} \times 5\% + \frac{2}{3} \times 20\%.$$

The Cost of Capital and Stock Price. An important tie exists between a company's cost of capital and its stock price. To see the linkage ask yourself what happens when XYZ Corporation earns a return on existing assets greater than its cost of capital. Because the return to creditors is fixed by contract, the excess return accrues entirely to shareholders. And because the company can earn more than shareholders' opportunity cost of capital, XYZ's stock price will rise as new investors are attracted by the excess return. Conversely, if XYZ earns a return below its cost of capital, shareholders will not receive their expected return, and stock price will fall. Another definition of the cost of capital, therefore, is the return a firm must earn on existing assets to keep its stock price constant. Finally, from the perspective of creating shareholder value we can say that management creates value when it earns returns above its cost of capital and destroys value when it earns returns below its cost of capital.

TEK's Cost of Capital

To use the cost of capital as a risk-adjusted discount rate in investment evaluation, we must be able to measure it. This involves assigning values to the quantities on the right-hand side of Equation 8–1. To illustrate the process, let's estimate Tektronix, Inc.'s cost of capital at fiscal year-end 1987.

The Weights. We begin by measuring the weights, D and E. There are two common ways to do this, only one of which is correct: Use the *book values* of debt and equity appearing on the company's balance sheet, or use the *market values*. By *market value,* I mean the price of the company's bonds and common shares in securities markets multiplied by the number of each

TABLE 8–1
Book and Market Values of Tektronix's Debt and Equity (May 30, 1987)

	Book Value		Market Value	
Source	Amount ($ million)	Percent of Total	Amount ($ million)	Percent of Total
Debt	54	6.1	50	3.9
Equity	838	93.9	1,291	96.1
Total	892	100.0%	1,341	100.0%

security type outstanding. As shown in Table 8–1, the book values of TEK's debt and equity at the end of fiscal year 1987 were $54 million and $838 million, respectively. The figure for debt includes only interest-bearing debt because other liabilities are spontaneous sources, which are treated as part of working capital in the investment's cash flows. The table also indicates that the market values of TEK's debt and equity on the same date were $50 million and $1,291 million, respectively.

The market value of TEK's debt is below its book value because interest rates rose after the debt was issued; and we know that as interest rates rise, the market value of debt falls. TEK's debt is not publicly traded, so $50 million is my estimate of the price at which it would have traded given its quality, coupon rate, and maturity. The market value of TEK's equity is its price per share at fiscal year-end of $34.88 times 37 million common shares outstanding. The market value of equity exceeds the book value by about 50 percent because despite recent difficulties investors continue to believe TEK has unusually good growth prospects.

To decide whether book weights or market weights are appropriate for measuring the cost of capital, consider the following analogy. Suppose that 10 years ago you invested $20,000 in a portfolio of common stocks that, through no fault of your own, is now worth $50,000. After talking to stockbrokers and investment bankers, you feel that a reasonable return on the portfolio, given present market conditions, is 15 percent. Would you be satisfied with a 15 percent return on the original $20,000 cost of the portfolio, or would you expect to earn 15 percent on the current $50,000 market value? Obviously, the current market value is relevant for decision making; the original cost is sunk and therefore irrelevant. Similarly, TEK owners and creditors have investments worth $1,291 million and $50 million, respectively, on which they expect to earn competitive returns. Thus the market values of debt and equity are appropriate for measuring the cost of capital.

The Cost of Debt. This is an easy one. High-quality bonds of a maturity similar to TEK's were yielding a return of approximately 10.5 percent in May 1987, and the company's tax rate is about 45 percent. Consequently, the aftertax cost of debt to TEK was 5.8 percent [(1 − 45%) × 10.5%]. Some persons are tempted to use the coupon rate on the debt rather than the prevailing market rate in this calculation. But again the coupon rate is a sunk cost. Moreover, because we want to use the cost of capital to evaluate new investments, we want the cost of new debt.

The Cost of Equity. Estimating the cost of equity is as hard as debt was easy. With debt, or preferred stock, the company promises the holder a specified stream of future payments. Knowing these promised payments and the current price of the security, it is a simple matter to calculate the expected return. This is what we did in the last chapter when we calculated the yield to maturity on a bond. With common stock, the situation is more complex. Because the company makes no promises about future payments to shareholders, there is no simple way to calculate the return expected.

The following cash flow diagrams illustrate the problem, looking first at the cash flows to a bond investor and then to a stock investor. Finding K_D is a simple discounted cash flow problem. Finding K_E would be just as simple, but we do not know the future cash receipts expected by shareholders. This calls for some ingenuity.

Investor's Cash Flow Diagram for Bonds

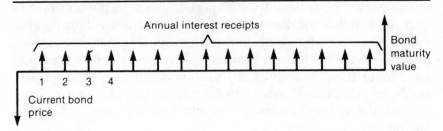

K_D = Discount rate which makes present value of cash inflows equal to current price.

Investor's Cash Flow Diagram for Common Stock

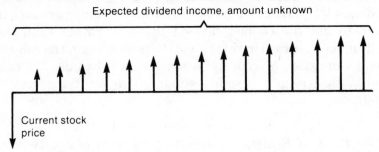

K_E = Discount rate which makes present value of unknown expected dividend income equal current price.

Assume a Perpetuity. One way out of this dilemma recalls the story of the physicist, the chemist, and the economist trapped at the bottom of a 40-foot pit. After failing with a number of schemes based on their knowledge of physics and chemistry for extracting themselves from the pit, the two scientists finally turn to the economist in desperation and ask if his professional training might suggest a method of escape. "Why, yes," he replies, "the problem is really quite elementary. Simply assume a ladder." Here our "ladder" is an assumption about the future payments shareholders expect. From this heroic beginning the problem really does become quite elementary. To illustrate, suppose equity investors expect to receive an annual dividend of d per share forever. The cash flow diagram then becomes

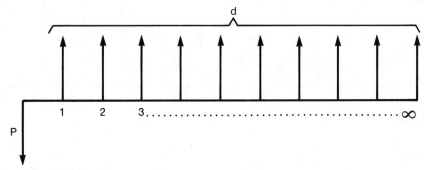

Current price of stock

Because we know P and have assumed a future payment stream, all that remains is to find the discount rate that makes the present value of the payment stream equal the current price. From the last chapter we know that the present value of such a perpetuity, at a discount rate of K_E, is

$$P = \frac{d}{K_E},$$

and, solving for the discount rate,

$$K_E = \frac{d}{P}.$$

In words, if you are willing to assume that investors expect a company's stock to behave like a perpetuity, the cost of equity capital is simply the dividend yield.

Perpetual Growth. A somewhat more plausible but still tractable assumption is that shareholders expect a per share dividend next year of d, and that they expect this dividend to grow at the rate of g percent per annum forever. In this case the case flow diagram becomes

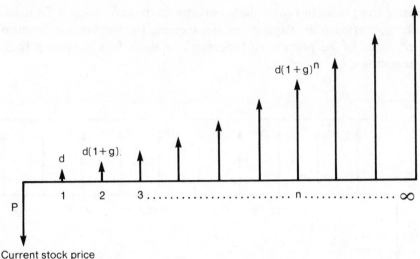

Current stock price

Fortunately, it turns out that this discounted cash flow problem also has an unusually simple solution. Without boring you with the arithmetic details, the present value of the assumed payment stream, at a discount rate of K_E, is

$$P = \frac{d}{K_E - g},$$

and, solving for the discount rate,

$$K_E = \frac{d}{P} + g.$$

This equation says that if the perpetual growth assumption is correct, the cost of equity capital equals the company's dividend yield (d/P), plus the growth rate in dividends. This is known as the perpetual growth equation for K_E.

The problem with the perpetual growth estimate of K_E is that it is only as good as the assumption on which it is based. For *mature* companies, like railroads, electric utilities, and steel mills, it may be reasonable to assume that observed growth rates will continue indefinitely. And in these cases the perpetual growth equation yields a plausible estimate of the cost of equity capital. Moreover, we can meaningfully apply the equation to the economy as a whole and say that with an average dividend yield of about 5 percent, and an average nominal dividend growth rate of 8 percent, the cost of equity capital to the typical firm is about 13 percent. The equation is clearly not applicable to TEK, however, because TEK pays almost no dividends, and because the company's growth rate is highly erratic.

Let History Be Your Guide. A second, and generally more fruitful, approach to estimating the cost of equity capital looks at the structure of expected returns on risky investments. In general, the expected return on any risky asset is composed of three factors:

$$\begin{matrix} \text{Expected return} \\ \text{on risky asset} \end{matrix} = \begin{matrix} \text{Risk-free} \\ \text{interest rate} \end{matrix} + \begin{matrix} \text{Inflation} \\ \text{premium} \end{matrix} + \begin{matrix} \text{Risk} \\ \text{premium} \end{matrix}.$$

The equation says the owner of a risky asset should expect to earn a return from three sources. The first is compensation for the opportunity cost incurred in holding the asset. This is the risk-free interest rate. The second is compensation for the declining purchasing power of his investment over time. This is the inflation premium. The third is compensation for bearing risk. This is the risk premium. Fortunately, we do not need to treat the first two terms as separate factors because together they equal the expected return on a default-free bond such as a government bond. In other words, owners of government bonds expect a return from the first two sources but not the third. Consequently,

$$\begin{matrix} \text{Expected return} \\ \text{on risky asset} \end{matrix} = \begin{matrix} \text{Interest rate} \\ \text{on government bond} \end{matrix} + \begin{matrix} \text{Risk} \\ \text{premium} \end{matrix}.$$

Since we can readily determine the government bond interest rate, the only challenge is to estimate the risk premium.

When the risky asset is a common stock, it is useful to let history be our guide and recall from Table 5–1 that on average over the period 1926 to 1987 the annual return on common stocks exceeded that on government bonds by 7.4 percent. As a reward for bearing the added risk, common stockholders earned a 7.4 percent higher annual return than government bondholders. Treating this as a risk premium, and adding it to a 1987 government bond rate of 8.8 percent, yields an estimate of 16.2 percent as the cost of equity capital for the typical company.

What is the logic of treating the 7.4 percent historical excess return as a risk premium? It is essentially that over a sufficiently lengthy period of time the return investors receive and what they expect to receive should approximate one another. For example, suppose investors expect a 20 percent excess return on common stocks but the actual keeps turning out to be 3 percent. Then two things should happen: investors should revise their expectations downward, and selling on the part of disappointed investors should increase subsequent realized returns. Eventually expectations and reality should come into rough parity.

We now have an estimate of the cost of equity capital to an average-risk company. In the appendix to this chapter, we discuss a technique for modifying this estimate to reflect the risk of a specific firm. For now, let us do this more informally. Because of the dynamic nature of its industry, TEK has considerably more business risk than most companies. Its modest use of debt financing, however, means that TEK imposes very little additional financial risk on its shareholders. Although the above-average business risk and below-average financial risk tend to offset one another, I believe that TEK is somewhat riskier than the average common stock investment. Let us, therefore, use 16.5 percent as an estimate of TEK's cost of equity capital.

Calculation of TEK's Cost of Capital. All that remains is the figure work. Table 8–2 presents our estimate of TEK's cost of capital in tabular form and in equation form. TEK's weighted-average cost of capital is 16.1 percent. This means that in 1987 TEK had to earn at least this percentage return on the market value of existing assets to meet the expectations of

TABLE 8–2
Calculation of Tektronix, Inc.'s Cost of Capital

Source	Amount ($ million)	Percent of Total	Cost After Tax	Weighted Cost
Debt	$ 50	3.9%	5.8%	0.2%
Equity	1,291	96.1	16.5	15.9
Cost of capital				16.1%

creditors and shareholders and to maintain share price. TEK's weighted-average cost of capital is quite close to its cost of equity capital because TEK has very little debt.

In equation form:

$$K_W = \frac{(1 - .45)(10.5)(\$50 \text{ million}) + (16.5\%)(\$1,291 \text{ million})}{\$50 \text{ million} + \$1,291 \text{ million}}$$

$$= 16.1\%$$

The Cost of Capital in Investment Appraisal

The fact that the cost of capital is the return a company must earn on *existing assets* to meet creditors and shareholder expectations is an interesting detail, but we are after bigger game here: We want to use the cost of capital as an acceptance criterion for *new investments*.

Are there any problems in applying a concept derived for existing assets to new investments? Not if one critical assumption holds: namely, the new investment must have the same risk as existing assets. If it does, the new investment is essentially a "carbon copy" of existing assets, and the cost of capital is the appropriate risk-adjusted discount rate. If it does not, we must proceed more carefully.

The Market Line in Figure 8–3 clearly illustrates the importance of the constant-risk assumption. It emphasizes that the rate of return anticipated by risk-averse companies and individuals rises with risk. This means, for example, that management should demand a higher expected return when introducing a new product than when replacing aged equipment because the new product is presumably riskier and, therefore, warrants a higher return. The figure also shows that a company's cost of capital is but one of many possible risk-adjusted discount rates, the one corresponding to the risk of the firm's existing assets. We conclude that the cost of capital is an appropriate acceptance criterion only when the risk of the new investment equals that of existing assets. For other investments, the cost of capital is inappropriate, but even when inappropriate itself, the cost of capital frequently serves as an important, practical touchstone about which further adjustments are made.

FIGURE 8–3
An Investment's Risk-Adjusted Discount Rate Increases with Risk

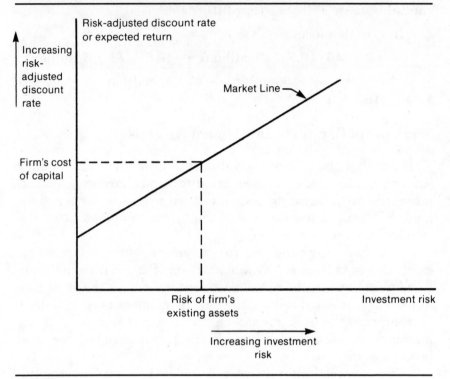

Multiple Hurdle Rates

Many companies adjust for differing levels of investment risk by using multiple hurdle rates, each rate applying to a different level of risk. For example, TEK might use the following array:

Type of Investment	Discount Rate
Replacement or repair	10.0%
Cost reduction	12.0
Expansion	16.1
New product	20.0

Investments to expand capacity in existing products are essentially carbon-copy investments, so their hurdle rate equals TEK's cost of capital. Other types of investments have a higher or lower hurdle rate, depending on their risk relative to expansion investments. Replacement or repair investments are the safest because virtually all of the cash flows are well known from past experience. Cost-reduction investments are somewhat riskier because the magnitude of potential savings is uncertain. New product investments are the riskiest type because both revenues and costs are uncertain.

The Fallacy of the Marginal Cost of Capital

Some persons look at Equation 8–1 and naively conclude that it is possible to reduce a company's weighted-average cost of capital by using more of the cheap source of financing, debt, and less of the expensive source, equity. In other words, they conclude that increasing leverage will reduce the cost of capital. This reasoning, however, evidences an incomplete understanding of leverage. As observed in Chapter 6, increasing leverage increases the risk borne by shareholders. And because they are risk-averse, shareholders react by demanding a higher return on their investment. Thus, K_E, and to a lesser extent K_D, rise as leverage increases. This means that increasing leverage affects a company's cost of capital in two opposing ways: Increasing use of cheap debt reduces K_W, but the rise in K_E and K_D that accompanies added leverage increases it.

To review this reasoning, ask yourself how you would respond to a subordinate who made the following argument in favor of an investment: "I know the company's cost of capital is 15 percent and the IRR of this carbon-copy investment is only 10 percent. But at the last directors' meeting we decided to finance this year's investments with new debt. Since new debt has a cost of only about 6 percent after tax, it is clearly in our shareholders' interest to invest 6 percent money to earn a 10 percent return."

The subordinate's reasoning is incorrect. Financing with debt means increasing leverage and increasing K_E. Adding the change in K_E to the 6 percent interest cost means the true marginal cost of the debt is well above the interest cost.

Multiple hurdle rates are consistent with risk aversion and with the Market Line, but the amount by which the hurdle rate should be adjusted for each level of risk is largely arbitrary. Whether the hurdle rate for cost-reduction investments should be three percentage points or five percentage points below TEK's cost of capital cannot be determined objectively.

Rather than assign a different discount rate to each type of investment, some multidivision companies assign a different discount rate to each division. A potential advantage of this approach is that if a division competes against one or several single-product firms, the cost of capital of these competitors can be used as the division's hurdle rate for new investment. An offsetting disadvantage of divisional hurdle rates is the implicit assumption that all investments made by the division have the same business risk.

TWO PITFALLS

Before concluding, I want to warn you about two common pitfalls in the use of discounted cash flow analysis. These pitfalls are especially dangerous because they both lead to the undervaluation of innovative, long-lived investments—precisely the kind of myopic decision making for which American executives have been criticized.

Inflation

The first pitfall involves the improper handling of inflation. Too often managers ignore inflation when estimating an investment's cash flows but inadvertently include it in their discount rate. The effect of this mismatch is to make companies overly conservative in their investment appraisal, especially with regard to long-lived assets. Table 8–3 illustrates the point. A company with a 15 percent cost of capital is considering a $10 million carbon-copy investment. The investment has a four-year life and is expected to increase production capacity by 10,000 units annually. Because the product sells for $900, the company estimates annual revenues will rise $9 million ($900 × 10,000 units), which, after subtracting production costs, yields an increase in annual aftertax cash flows of $3.3 million. The IRR of the investment is calculated to be 12.1%, which is below the firm's cost of capital.

Did you spot the error? By assuming a constant selling price and constant production costs over four years, management has implicitly estimated real, or constant dollar, cash flows, whereas the cost of capital as calculated above is a nominal one. It is nominal because both the cost of debt and the cost of equity include a premium for expected inflation.

The key to capital budgeting under inflation is always to compare like to like. When cash flows are in nominal dollars, use a nominal discount rate. When cash flows are in real, or constant, dollars, use a real discount rate. The bottom portion of Table 8–3 illustrates a proper evaluation of the investment. After including a 5 percent annual increase in selling price and in variable production costs, the expected nominal cash flows from the investment are as shown. As one would expect, the

TABLE 8–3
When Evaluating Investments Under Inflation, Always Compare Nominal Cash Flows to a Nominal Discount Rate or Real Cash Flows to a Real Discount Rate ($ millions)

A. Incorrect Investment Evaluation Comparing Real Cash Flows to a Nominal Discount Rate

	1989	1990	1991	1992	1993
Aftertax Cash Flow	($10.0)	$3.3	$3.3	$3.3	$3.3

$$IRR = 12.1\%$$
$$K_w = 15\%$$
Decision: Reject

B. Correct Investment Evaluation Comparing Nominal Cash Flows to a Nominal Discount Rate

	1989	1990	1991	1992	1993
Aftertax Cash Flow	($10.0)	$3.5	$3.8	$4.0	$4.3

$$IRR = 20.0\%$$
$$K_w = 15\%$$
Decision: Accept

TABLE 8–4
**Use of a Constant Risk-Adjusted Discount Rate Implies that Risk
Increases with the Remoteness of a Cash Flow** (Risk-Free Rate = 5%;
Risk-Adjusted Rate = 10%)

	Present Value of $1	
	Received in One Year	*Received in 10 Years*
Risk-free	.952	.614
Risk-adjusted	.909	.386
Reduction in present value due to risk	.043	.228

nominal cash flows exceed the constant dollar cash flows by a growing amount in each year. The IRR of these flows is 20%, which now exceeds the firm's cost of capital.[2]

Excessive Risk Adjustment

The second pitfall is subtler. Adding an increment to the discount rate to adjust for an investment's risk makes intuitive sense. You need to be aware, however, that as you apply this discount rate to more distant cash flows, the arithmetic of the discounting process compounds the risk adjustment. Table 8–4 illustrates the effect. It shows the present value of $1 in one year and in 10 years, first at a risk-free discount rate of 5 percent, and then at a risk-adjusted rate of 10 percent. Comparing these present values, it is apparent that addition of the risk premium knocks a modest 4.3 cents off the value of a dollar in one year, but a sizable 22.8 cents off the value of a dollar in 10 years. Clearly, use of a constant risk-adjusted discount rate is appropriate only when the risk of a cash flow grows as the cash flow recedes further into the future.

---

[2]An alternative approach would have been to calculate the firm's real cost of capital and compare it to a real IRR. But, because this approach requires more work and is fraught with potential errors, I recommend working with nominal cash flows and a nominal discount rate instead.

For many, if not most, business investments the assumption that risk increases with the remoteness of a cash flow is quite appropriate, but as shown in the following example, this is not always the case.

ABC Corporation is contemplating a high-risk investment to develop and market a new product. During the first two years, R&D costs will be $5 million annually. Management estimates there is a 40 percent chance of failure, in which case the company will receive nothing for its efforts. If ABC can successfully develop the product, however, management envisions a relatively certain aftertax cash flow of $3 million annually for the next 20 years. If ABC requires an 8 percent return on safe investments, 15 percent on moderate risk investments, and 25 percent on high-risk ones, should it undertake the project?

Too many executives would answer no. The investment's cash flow diagram, using expected cash flows, is

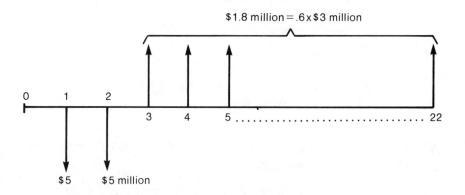

$1.8 million = .6 × $3 million

and the NPV at a 25 percent discount rate is

$$\text{NPV} = -\$5 \text{ million}(1.440) + \$1.8 \text{ million}(3.954)(0.640)$$
$$= -\$2.64 \text{ million}$$

So the investment appears to be unattractive.

However, let us think more carefully. The investment clearly involves high risk, but because most of the risk is resolved within the first two years, use of a constant risk-adjusted discount rate is overly conservative. To see the logic, divide the project into its two risk phases. Beginning with the low-risk phase, suppose we are at time 2 on the cash flow diagram, that the R&D phase has been successful, and the company is about to launch the new product. Because the product cash flows are now relatively certain, their value at time 2 is the present value of a $3 million, 20-year annuity *discounted at 8 percent,* or $29.5 million.

So as seen from the present, ABC has the opportunity to spend $5 million each of the next two years in return for a 60 percent chance at a cash flow stream worth $29.5 million. The cash flow diagram using expected cash flows is thus

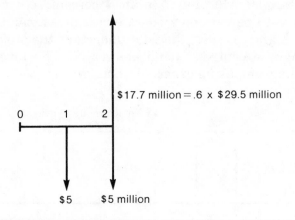

And because this phase of the investment is high-risk, the NPV at a 25 percent discount rate is

$$\text{NPV} = -\$5 \text{ million}(1.440) + \$17.7 \text{ million}(0.640)$$
$$= \$4.1 \text{ million.}$$

Seen in this light, the project has a positive NPV. Moreover, the NPV would still be positive even if we applied a certainty equivalent factor of 0.8 to the cash inflow $[-\$5$ million(1.440) + $(0.8)(\$17.7$ million$(0.640)) = \$1.9$ million$]$.

To recap, whenever you encounter an investment with two or more distinct risk phases, be careful about using a constant risk-adjusted discount rate, for although such investments are comparatively rare, they are also frequently the type of opportunities companies can ill afford to waste.

A CAUTIONARY NOTE

An always-present danger when using analytic or numerical techniques in business decision making is that the "hard facts" will assume exaggerated importance compared to more qualitative issues and that the manipulation of these facts will become a substitute for creative effort. It is important to bear in mind that numbers and theories don't get things done, people do. And the best of investments will fail unless capable workers are committed to their success. As Barbara Tuchman put it in another context, "In military as in other human affairs will is what makes things happen. There are circumstances that can modify or nullify it, but for offense or defense its presence is essential and its absence fatal."[3]

APPENDIX

DIVERSIFICATION AND β-RISK

In the chapter, we observed that the expected rate of return on a risky asset can be written as

$$\begin{matrix} \text{Expected return} \\ \text{on risky asset} \end{matrix} = \begin{matrix} \text{Interest rate on} \\ \text{government bonds} \end{matrix} + \text{Risk premium,}$$

where the interest rate on government bonds is itself the sum of a risk-free interest rate and an inflation premium. We noted too that when the risky asset in question is a typical company's common stock, one measure of the risk premium is the *excess* return earned by common shareholders relative to government bondholders over a long period. Here we want to discuss the risk premium in more detail and relate it to measures of risk, which include the effects of diversification.

We can repeat the equation above in symbols by letting i equal the prevailing interest rate on government bonds, R_m, the average annual return on a well-diversified portfolio of common stocks over a long

---

[3]Barbara W. Tuchman, *Stilwell and the American Experience in China 1911–1945* (New York: Bantam Books, 1971), pp. 561–62.

period, and i_b, the average annual return on government bonds over the same period.

$$\text{Expected return on typical company's common stock} = i + (R_m - i_b).$$

In mid-1987, the interest rate on government bonds was about 8.8 percent. From the figures in Table 5–1, the average annual return earned by investors in the 500 stocks comprising the Standard & Poor's 500 stock index over the period 1926–87 was 12.0 percent, whereas the average annual return on government bonds over the same period was 4.6 percent. This suggests a risk premium, $(R_m - i_b)$, of 7.4 percent, and an expected return on a typical company's stock, given prevailing interest rates of 16.2 percent (16.2% = 8.8% + 7.4%).

The above equation provides an estimate of a typical company's cost of equity capital, where by "typical," I mean a company having average risk.[4] However, if we want to use this equation to estimate the cost of capital of an *atypical* company, or if we want to estimate the expected return on any other kind of risky asset, we must modify the equation to reflect the particular risk of the company or asset in question. The following equation includes the necessary modification. Letting R_j equal the expected rate of return on risky asset j,

$$\text{Expected return on risky asset } j = \text{Interest rate on government bonds} + \frac{\beta\text{-risk of asset } j}{} \times \text{Risk premium}$$

$$R_j = i + \beta_j(R_m - i_b) \tag{8A-1}$$

β_j is known as the asset's beta-risk, or its *volatility*. We will talk more about the calculation of β_j in a few paragraphs. For now, think of it as

---

[4]Careful study of this topic will reveal that estimating an equity risk premium is not quite as simple as implied here. The most complete discussion of the topic of which I am aware is in Roger G. Ibbotson and Rex Sinquefield, *Stocks, Bonds, Bills, and Inflation (SBBI)* (Chicago: Ibbotson Associates, 1982—updated in *SBBI 1987 Yearbook*), chapter 10, where it is observed that 7.4 percent is an estimate of the "long-horizon" equity risk premium suitable for valuing cash flows projected over a long period. A short-horizon equity risk premium would substitute the short-term government bill rate for the long-term bond rate, yielding a premium of 8.5 percent (12.0% − 3.5%). Also, for technical reasons relating to the method used to average annual risk premiums and to the distinction between expected and realized returns on the part of bondholders, it is likely that 7.4 percent is a modest overestimate of the true risk premium. See *SBBI* for more complete details.

simply the risk of asset j relative to that of the common stock portfolio, m. Specifically,

$$\beta_j = \frac{\text{Risk of asset } j}{\text{Risk of portfolio } m}.$$

If the risk of asset j is equal to that of a typical company's common stock, $\beta_j = 1.0$, and the equation is just as before. If the asset is of above-average risk, β_j exceeds 1.0, and if it is of below-average risk, β_j is less than 1.0.

In recent years, β-risk has become an important factor in security analysis, so much so that several stock brokerage companies and investment advisors regularly publish the betas for virtually all publicly traded common stocks. Table 8A–1 presents betas for a representative sample of firms, as well as industry average betas. Recalling that a beta of 1.0 is typical, or average, note that company betas in the table range from a high of 1.90 for Apollo Computer to a low of 0.55 for Tucson Electric Power. Also note that Tektronix's beta is 1.10, indicating that TEK's common stock is of slightly above-average risk.

With knowledge of a company's beta it becomes easy to use Equation 8A–1 above to estimate a company's cost of equity capital. For example TEK's cost of equity in 1987 according to this equation was

$$R_j = i + \beta_j(R_m - i_b)$$
$$= 8.8\% + 1.10 \times (12.0\% - 4.6\%)$$
$$= 16.9\%.$$

In contrast, Apollo Computer's cost of equity is

$$8.8\% + 1.90 \times (12.0\% - 4.6\%) = 22.9\%,$$

and that of Tucson Electric is

$$8.8\% + .55 \times (12.0\% - 4.6\%) = 12.9\%.$$

At a conceptual level, Equation 8A–1 is quite important, for it tells us the rate of return we should expect on any risky asset and how that return varies with the asset's beta-risk. Looking at Figure 8–1, another way to say the same thing is that Equation 8A–1 is the equation of the Market Line. To determine the appropriate risk-adjusted discount rate for any risky asset, all we need to do is calculate the asset's beta, plug this value into Equation 8A–1, and calculate the expected return on the asset. This expected return, denoted by R_j, is the correct risk-adjusted discount rate for investment evaluation.

Diversification. To understand beta-risk more fully, we need to take a slight detour and talk about risk in general. Below is information about two very simple risky investments. For concreteness, suppose investment A is the purchase of an ice cream stand and investment B is the purchase of an umbrella shop. Further, suppose the states of nature refer to tomorrow's weather: State 1 represents sun, and state 2, rain. Investment A is clearly a risky undertaking since the investor stands to make $600 if it is sunny tomorrow but will

TABLE 8A–1
Representative Industry and Company Betas

Industry Betas		Company Betas	
Industry	Beta	Company	Beta
Aerospace defense	1.1	Amdahl	1.65
Auto—car	1.2	American Brands	1.05
Auto—tire	1.3	American Electric Power	.70
Banks—excluding NYC	1.0	Appollo Computer	1.90
Beverages—soft drinks	.9	AT&T	.80
Coal	.8	BankAmerica Corp.	1.00
Drugs	1.0	Boeing	1.00
Electronics—instruments	1.4	Burlington Northern	1.10
Electronics—semiconductors	1.3	Caterpillar	1.20
Foods	.9	Citicorp	1.25
Gold mining	.8	Coca-Cola Company	.90
Home building	1.4	Control Data	1.25
Leisure time	1.4	Detroit Edison	.70
Lodging	1.1	General Electric	1.10
Mobile homes	1.3	General Motors	1.00
Railroads	1.1	Hilton Hotels	.95
Textile—apparel	1.4	Honda Motor	1.00
Truckers	1.0	IBM	.95
Utilities—electric	.6	McDonnell Douglas	1.00
Utilities—gas distribution	.6	National Semiconductor	1.50
		Sony Corporation	.85
		St. Joseph P&L	.60
		Tektronix	1.10
		Tucson Electric Power	.55
		USX	1.00
		Westinghouse Electric	1.30
		Xerox	1.20

lose $200 if it rains. Investment B is also risky since the investor will lose $300 if tomorrow is sunny but will make $500 if it rains.

Yet despite the fact that these two investments are risky when viewed in isolation, they are not risky when viewed as members of a portfolio containing both investments.

Investment A			
State of Nature	Probability	Outcome	Weighted Outcome
1	.40	$600	$240
2	.60	− 200	− 120
		Expected outcome	$120

Investment B			
State of Nature	Probability	Outcome	Weighted Outcome
1	.40	− $300	− $120
2	.60	500	300
		Expected outcome	$180

Portfolio of A and B			
State of Nature	Probability	Outcome	Weighted Outcome
1	.40	$300	$120
2	.60	300	180
		Expected outcome	$300

In a portfolio, the losses and gains from the two investments counterbalance one another in each state of nature, so that regardless of tomorrow's weather, the outcome is a riskless $300. The expected outcome from the portfolio is the sum of the expected outcomes from each investment in the portfolio, but the risk of the portfolio is zero.

This is an extreme example, but it does illustrate an important fact. When a decision maker owns a portfolio of assets, the relevant measure of risk is not an asset's risk in isolation but rather its risk as part of the portfolio. And as the example demonstrates, the difference between these two perspectives can be substantial.

An asset's risk in isolation is greater than its portfolio risk whenever the asset's cash flows and the portfolio's cash flows are less than perfectly correlated. In this common situation, some of the asset's cash flow variability is offset by variability in the portfolio's cash flows, and the effective risk borne by the investor is reduced. Look again at the above example. The ice cream stand cash flows are highly variable, but because they are inversely correlated with those from the umbrella shop, cash flow variability for the two investments disappears. An "averaging out" process occurs when assets are added to a portfolio that reduces risk.

Because most business investments are dependent to some extent on the same underlying business cycle, it is highly unusual to find investment opportunities with perfectly inversely correlated cash flows as in the ice cream–umbrella example. However, the described diversification effect still exists. Whenever investment cash flows are less than perfectly positively correlated—whenever individual investments are unique in some respects—an investment's risk in a portfolio context is less than its risk in isolation.

Let us refer to an asset's risk in isolation as its *total risk* and to its risk as part of a portfolio as its *nondiversifiable risk*. This is the risk remaining after the rest has been diversified away in the portfolio. The part that is diversified away is known as the asset's *diversifiable risk* (surprise!). Then, for any risky asset j,

$$\begin{matrix} \text{Total risk} \\ \text{of asset } j \end{matrix} = \begin{matrix} \text{Nondiversifiable} \\ \text{risk of asset } j \end{matrix} + \begin{matrix} \text{Diversifiable} \\ \text{risk of asset } j \end{matrix}.$$

From the above discussion, we know that the portion of an asset's total risk that is nondiversifiable depends on the correlation of the returns on the asset and on the portfolio. When the correlation is high, nondiversifiable risk is a large fraction of total risk, and vice versa. To say the same thing in symbols, let σ_j equal asset j's total risk and ρ_{jm} equal a scale factor reflecting the degree to which asset j's returns correlate with those of portfolio m. Then,

$$\text{Nondiversifiable risk of asset } j = \rho_{jm}\sigma_j.$$

(ρ and σ are the lowercase Greek letters rho and sigma, respectively. They have become standard notation in the literature.)

Studying this expression, the scale factor ρ_{jm} can have any value between $+1$ and -1. At one extreme, when the returns on asset j and portfolio m are perfectly positively correlated, $\rho_{jm} = 1.00$, and nondiversifiable risk equals total risk. In this case, there are no benefits from diversification. At the other extreme, when the returns on asset j and portfolio m are perfectly negatively correlated, as in the ice cream–umbrella shop example, $\rho_{jm} = -1.00$, and nondiversifiable risk is negative. This means that addition of an appropriate amount of asset j to the portfolio will eliminate risk entirely. For most business investments, ρ_{jm} is in the range .5 to .8, meaning that 20 to 50 percent of an investment's total risk can be diversified away.

Measuring Beta.   We are now ready to reconsider beta-risk. Recall that β_j was described as the ratio of two risks and defined as

$$\beta_j = \frac{\text{Risk of asset } j}{\text{Risk of portfolio } m}.$$

When diversification is possible, we now know that the relevant measure of asset j's risk is its nondiversifiable risk. Consequently,

$$\beta_j = \frac{\rho_{jm}\sigma_j}{\rho_{mm}\sigma_m}.$$

This expression says that the beta-risk of asset j is the ratio of asset j's nondiversifiable risk to the nondiversifiable risk of the analyst's portfolio. However, a moment's reflection should convince you that ρ_{mm} equals 1 because any asset's or any portfolio's return must be perfectly positively correlated with itself. Thus,

$$\beta_j = \frac{\rho_{jm}\sigma_j}{\sigma_m}. \qquad (8A\text{--}2)$$

If you have studied a little statistics, it will come as no surprise to learn that σ_j and σ_m are commonly defined to be the *standard deviation* of returns for asset j and portfolio m, respectively, and ρ_{jm} is the *correlation coefficient* between these returns.

Using these definitions and the above equation, the betas appearing in Table 8A–1 were calculated as follows. First, for each stock calculate the monthly return to investors, including price appreciation and dividends, over the past five years. Then calculate the average monthly return and the standard deviation of returns about this average. The latter is σ_j. Second, go through the same exercise for a broad portfolio of common stocks such as the Standard & Poor's 500 stock averages. This generates σ_m. Third, calculate the correlation coefficient, ρ_{jm}, between the monthly returns for stock j and the portfolio. Fourth, plug these numbers into Equation 8A–2 to calculate the stock's beta. Or if you know a little regression analysis, just regress r_j on r_m. The slope of this line is β_j.

Using Beta in Investment Evaluation.   Beta can be used two ways in investment evaluation. As already suggested, one way is to use the beta of the company's common stock to calculate the firm's cost of equity and its weighted average cost of capital.

A more direct approach is to calculate the beta of an individual investment and plug it into Equation 8A–1 to calculate the investment's risk-adjusted discount rate. This reduces risk adjustment to a totally mechanical, objective exercise. The approach has obvious conceptual appeal, but a number of problems must be solved before it can be applied in practice. The most serious is that there is usually no objective way to estimate an investment's beta. Some researchers have experimented with using the betas of publicly traded, single-product companies engaged in the same business as the proposed investment as surrogates for the investment's beta. But this has proved to be a complicated, imprecise exercise. One difficulty is that a company's beta depends on leverage as well as business risk. So before using a company beta as a surrogate for an investment's beta, it is necessary to eliminate the effect of leverage. This can be done, but the process is complex and of unknown accuracy. A second difficulty pervading all applications is that the real object of interest is the beta that will prevail in future years. But because this is unknown, we must calculate an historical beta and assume it will hold in the future. Empirical studies of beta over time suggest this is a reasonable, but not infallible, assumption.

The bottom line in practice is that beta is useful for estimating a company's cost of equity capital. However, the calculation of project betas is still no more than a glimmer in the eyes of Ph.D. students.

Beta-Risk and Conglomerate Diversification. Some executives have seized on the idea that diversification reduces risk as a justification for conglomerate diversification. Even when merger promises no increase in profitability, it is said to be beneficial because the resulting diversification reduces the risk of company cash flows. Because shareholders are risk-averse, this reduction in risk is said to increase the value of the firm.

Such reasoning is at best incomplete. If shareholders wanted the risk-reduction benefits of such a conglomerate merger, they could have achieved them much more simply by just owning shares of the two independent companies in their own portfolios. Shareholders are not dependent on company managements for such benefits. Executives intent on acquiring other firms must look elsewhere to find a rationale for their actions.

CHAPTER SUMMARY

1. The purpose of this chapter has been to incorporate risk into investment evaluation with particular emphasis on risk-adjusted discount rates and the cost of capital.

2. Investments involve a trade-off between risk and return. The appropriate question when evaluating investment opportunities is not, What's the rate of return? but rather, Is the return sufficient to justify the risk?
3. Risk refers to the range of possible outcomes for an investment. Sometimes risk can be calculated objectively, but usually risk estimation must be subjective.
4. The most popular, practical technique for incorporating risk into investment decisions uses a risk-adjusted discount rate, in which the analyst adds a premium to the discount rate reflecting the perceived risk of the project.
5. The cost of capital is a risk-adjusted discount rate suitable for a firm's average risk, or carbon-copy, investments. It is the average cost of individual capital sources, weighted by their relative importance in the firm's capital structure. Average-risk investments yielding more than the cost of capital increase stock price.
6. Estimating the cost of equity is the most difficult step in measuring the cost of capital. For most businesses the best estimate is the current cost of government borrowing plus a risk premium, based on historical experience, of about 7.4 percent. If the equity is above or below average in risk, it is necessary to adjust the risk premium accordingly.
7. It is also necessary to raise or lower the discount rate relative to the cost of capital depending on whether a specific project is above or below average risk for the business.
8. Under inflation one must always use nominal cash flows and a nominal discount rate, or real cash flows and a real discount rate. Never mix the two.
9. A constant risk-adjusted discount rate should not be used to evaluate investments with two or more distinct risk phases. To evaluate such investments, begin with the most distant phase and use a risk-adjusted rate that is appropriate to each phase.
10. Proper technique is never a substitute for thought or leadership. People, not analysis, get things done.

ADDITIONAL READING

Brealey, Richard, and Stewart Myers. *Principles of Corporate Finance.* 2d ed. New York: McGraw-Hill, 1984. 847 pages.
   A leading graduate text. Part 3, Risk, is especially good.

Hodder, James E., and Henry E. Riggs. "Pitfalls in Evaluating Risky Projects." *Harvard Business Review* (January-February 1985) pp. 128–35.
   A thorough discussion of inflation and excessive risk adjustment in capital budgeting.

Mullins, David W., Jr. "Does the Capital Asset Pricing Model Work?" *Harvard Business Review* (January-February 1982) pp. 105–14.
   A practical look at the concepts discussed in the appendix to this chapter, including β-risk, the Market Line, and diversification.

CHAPTER PROBLEMS

1. Looking at Figure 8–1, explain why a company should reject investment opportunities lying below the Market Line and accept those lying above the Market Line.

2. What is the expected internal rate of return on the following investment opportunity?

IRR	Probability
−40%	10%
−20	5
0	10
10	5
20	60
30	10
	100%

3. A risky investment costs $10 million and has an expected, nominal, aftertax cash flow of $4 million each year for five years. The risk-free rate of interest is 6 percent including a 4 percent inflation premium.
   a. What is the net present value of the investment assuming a risk premium of 7 percentage points?

    b. By how much does the fact that the investment is risky reduce its net present value?

    c. If the certainty-equivalent of the cash flows in years one through three is $2.7 million, and the certainty-equivalent of each of the two remaining cash flows is $2 million, what is the net present value of the investment?

4. Calculate Keystone, Inc.'s weighted cost of capital given the following information: The company's tax rate is 34 percent. The opportunity cost of capital to Keystone's shareholders is 20 percent. Keystone has 10 million shares outstanding; the current price per share is $4. Using book values, the company's debt-to-equity ratio is 180 percent. Using market values, the ratio is 80 percent. Keystone's debt has a coupon rate of 6 percent and an annual principal repayment of $11 million. The yield to maturity is 12 percent.

5. For Keystone, Inc., discussed in question 4, show that if Keystone invests in a perpetuity costing $10 million with an internal rate of return equal to its weighted average cost of capital; and if Keystone finances the investment such that the debt-to-equity ratio equals 80 percent; then the company can just pay creditors and provide a return of 20 percent to its shareholders. Assuming a "carbon copy" investment, what will the impact be of such an investment on Keystone's stock price?

6. If the interest rate is 14 percent, what is the present value of a stream of cash receipts starting at $10 next year and growing 4 percent per year forever?

7. If the expected dividend of a mature company next year is $1.50 per share, and if the dividend is expected to grow 6 percent per year forever, use the perpetual growth equation to estimate the company's cost-of-equity capital when the firm's current stock price is $15.00

Chapter 9

Business Valuation and Corporate Restructuring

If you want a friend, buy a dog.

Reputed to be one of corporate raider
Carl Icahn's favorite sayings.

In late 1983, T. Boone Pickens, chief executive officer of Mesa Petroleum Company, stunned the corporate world by leading a group of investors in an attempt to take over giant Gulf Oil Corporation. One of the original "seven sisters," Gulf was a leading international integrated oil company with total 1982 revenues of $28 billion and a market value of equity equal to $6.4 billion. Mesa, on the other hand, was a small Texas oil company barely one-hundredth the size of Gulf. Although Pickens had compiled a long string of successes raiding undervalued oil companies dating back to 1969, it was all but inconceivable that he and tiny Mesa Petroleum could come up with the $10 billion and change necessary to take over Gulf. To put the matter in perspective, only four years earlier the largest contested takeover had a price tag of only $1 billion.

The Pickens group began buying Gulf stock in August for $39 a share. In the ensuing months as the Pickens bid gained legitimacy, Gulf management attempted to fend off Pickens while simultaneously soliciting more attractive suitors and attempting a management buyout. If Gulf was going to lose its independence, James Lee, chief executive officer, wanted a major say in how it happened. The drama ended in March 1984, when Standard Oil of California acquired Gulf in a friendly acquisition for $80 per share.

In seven short months, Pickens's initiative had resulted in a phenomenal $6.8 billion increase in the market value of Gulf's equity. And while the jury is still out regarding the wisdom of Standard Oil's acquisition, several clear winners are already discernible: Gulf shareholders received a Christmas present of over $6 billion in increased stock value; Pickens and his co-investors captured (I find it hard to say "earned") profits of $761 million by selling out to Standard Oil at the higher price; investment bankers Morgan Stanley, Merrill Lynch, and Salomon Brothers pocketed $63 million in fees for advising the various parties (this presumably includes overtime); and James Lee received $8.5 million for Gulf options.

If the Gulf raid were an isolated event, we might reasonably dismiss it as just another episode in what has always been a colorful industry. Evidence indicates, however, that the Gulf acquisition is but one example of a trend that is fundamentally changing corporate America. Known broadly as "corporate restructuring," this trend encompasses a number of maneuvers intended to alter fundamentally a company's asset composition, capital structure, or ownership. In addition to hostile takeover, corporate restructuring includes purchase or sale of operating units, large repurchases of common stock, major changes in financial leverage, and leveraged buyouts, or LBOs. An LBO is characterized by extensive use of the acquired company's borrowing power to help finance the acquisition.

Evidence of the growing importance of corporate restructuring is contained in the data on share repurchases in Chapter 4, Figure 4–2, and in recent merger and acquisition statistics. Over the period 1979 to 1986, the number of mergers, acquisitions, and leveraged buyouts involving U.S. companies grew almost 15 percent per year to a high of just over 4,000 in 1986. Moreover, the value of these transactions increased a whopping 28 percent per annum to over $190 billion.[1] In addition, a host of other companies not represented in these figures have initiated various other preemptive restructurings, intended at least in part to reduce the threat of hostile takeover.

Gulf Oil's cataclysmic demise and the many other corporate restructurings pose a number of important questions to harried executives, and indeed to all students of finance. In terms of the Gulf acquisition, these questions include:

1. Why did Pickens go after Gulf? Did he have reason to believe the company was worth much more than $39 a share? If so, what analysis led to this conclusion?
2. If buyers were ultimately willing to spend as much as $80 per share for Gulf stock, why was the price prior to Pickens's initiative only $39? Does the stock market misprice companies this much, or is something else at work?
3. If Gulf stock really was worth more than $39, why didn't Gulf management—who presumably knew more about their company than Pickens did—realize this fact? And if they did, why didn't they take actions to assure that the added value was reflected in Gulf's stock price?
4. How was Pickens able to get his hands on the billions of dollars necessary to make his attack credible? Why was it possible to attack such a large company in 1983 when it apparently was not possible, or at least not attempted, in prior years?
5. Could it happen to my company?

The purpose of this chapter is to answer these questions and, in the process, to examine the financial dimensions of corporate restructuring. At bottom, our story is a simple one. The market value of a company will fall below the maximum attainable value whenever management fails to run the business in the interests of owners—that is, whenever it fails to maximize shareholder value. When the divergence between actual and

---

[1] "1986 Profile," *Mergers & Acquisitions* (May/June 1987), p. 57.

attainable value becomes large, a raider can purchase controlling interest of the firm, redeploy company resources to increase value, and benefit by the difference between the new higher value and the acquisition price. Much of corporate restructuring, then, is a redeployment of company resources in pursuit of increased market value. In some highly publicized instances, the redeployment is initiated by a hostile raider; more often it is carried out by incumbent management intent on reducing the threat of takeover.

The chapter begins with a look at the techniques available for valuing all or part of a business. An important and useful topic in its own right, business valuation also sets the stage for consideration of the premium a raider might be willing to pay to gain control of a company. Attention then turns to three of the more pervasive possible benefits of restructuring, which we will consider under the headings tax shields, incentive effects, and controlling free cash flow. The chapter closes with another look at the Gulf takeover and the questions posed above.

VALUING A BUSINESS

You will be relieved to learn that in many respects business valuation is just an application of the concepts discussed in earlier chapters.

Market Value—Again

George Bernard Shaw once said that "Economists know the price of everything and the value of nothing." In a very real sense, he is correct; since to an economist the value of an asset is the price at which informed buyers and sellers are willing to trade it. The question of whether an asset has value beyond its selling price is one economists are content to leave to philosophers.

If value is synonymous with selling price, an obvious indicator of the worth of a company is its market value—the aggregate price at which its equity and debt trade in financial markets. Thus, when Boone Pickens started accumulating Gulf stock in August 1983, the market value of Gulf's equity was $39 per share times 165.3 million shares outstanding, or $6.4 billion. Adding the market value of Gulf's liabilities, similarly determined, yields the market value of the company.

The story does not end here, however, for there are many instances in which market prices are inappropriate or unavailable, and it is necessary to think about the determinants of value more carefully. These instances include:

1. The entity being valued is privately held, or a division of a public company, and market prices do not exist.
2. The company's securities are publicly traded, but so infrequently and in such modest volume that market prices are unreliable indicators of value.
3. The company's securities are actively traded, but the goal is to find bargains. By comparing an independent estimate of value against market price, the analyst hopes to discover securities that are underpriced.
4. The analyst intends to gain control of the company and to increase market value by altering the way the firm does business.

Liquidation and Going-Concern Values

If securities prices are not always appropriate or available, how else might one value a business? In broadest terms, there are two choices: to value a company in liquidation or as a going concern. *Liquidation value* is the cash generated by terminating a business and selling its assets individually, while *going-concern value* is the present worth of expected future cash flows generated by a business. In most instances we will naturally be interested in a business's going-concern value.

It will be helpful at this point to define an asset's *fair market value* (FMV) as the price at which the asset would trade between two rational individuals, each in command of all the information necessary to value the asset and neither under any pressure to trade. Estimating FMV is the first step in most valuation problems.

Usually, the FMV of a business is the *higher* of its liquidation value and its going-concern value. Figure 9–1 illustrates

FIGURE 9–1

**The Fair Market Value of a Business is Usually the Higher of Its
Liquidation and Its Going-Concern Value**

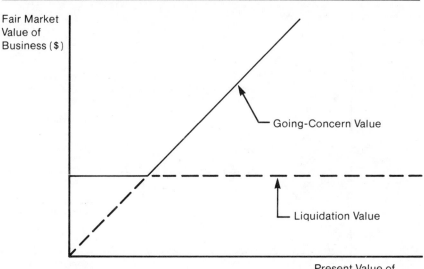

Fair Market
Value of
Business ($)

Going-Concern Value

Liquidation Value

Present Value of
Future Cash Flows ($)

the relationship. When the present value of expected future
cash flows is low, the business is worth more dead than alive,
and FMV equals the company's liquidation value. At higher
levels of expected future cash flows, liquidation value becomes
increasingly irrelevant, and FMV depends almost entirely on
going-concern value. It can also occur that some of a company's
assets, or divisions, are worth more in liquidation while others
are more valuable as going concerns. In this case, the firm's
FMV is a combination of liquidation and going-concern values
as they apply to individual assets.

An exception to Figure 9–1 occurs when the individuals
controlling the company—perhaps after reflecting on their em-
ployment alternatives and the pleasures afforded by the corporate yacht—choose not to liquidate, even though the business is
worth more dead than alive. Then, because minority investors
cannot force liquidation, FMV of the firm can fall below its
liquidation value. This is illustrated in Figure 9–2. Additional

FIGURE 9–2

When The Individuals Controlling the Business Refuse to Liquidate, Its Fair Market Value Can Fall Below Liquidation Value

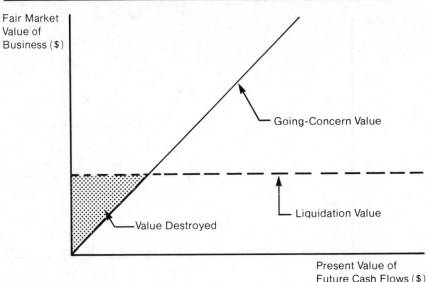

latent value exists, but because minority owners cannot get their hands on it, the value has no effect on the price they are willing to pay for the shares. As seen by minority shareholders, the individuals controlling the business are destroying value by refusing to liquidate. We will consider other instances in which price, as determined by minority investors, does not reflect full value later in the chapter.

ESTIMATING GOING-CONCERN VALUE

Having reviewed business valuation in the large, let's turn now to the more specific task of estimating a company's going-concern value. For simplicity, we will begin by considering the value of a minority interest in a privately held firm.

The most direct way to estimate going-concern value, if not always the most practical, is to think of the target company as

if it were nothing more than a large capital expenditure opportunity. Just as with any piece of capital equipment, investing in
a company requires the expenditure of money today in anticipation of future benefits. And the central issue in both cases is
whether tomorrow's benefits justify today's costs.

Valuing Equity

Building on our earlier discussion of evaluating investment opportunities in Chapters 7 and 8, we can determine whether
future benefits justify current costs, at least conceptually, by
calculating the present value of expected future cash flows to
equity. Thus,

FMV of Equity = PV{Expected Future Cash Flows to Equity}.

This formula says that the maximum price a minority investor
should pay for the equity of a business equals the present value
of expected future cash flows to the investor, discounted at an
appropriate, risk-adjusted rate. No surprises here, I trust.

Let's consider a simple (simplistic?) example. The diagram
below shows the relevant cash flows for a company that is expected to distribute common dividends of $50 million annually
for the next five years and $75 million annually during the
following five. At the end of the 10th year we assume the equity
can be sold for 20 times year-10 dividends.

Cash Flow Diagram: Expected Future Cash Flows to Equity

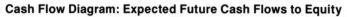

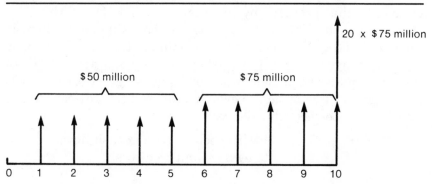

As in any other application of risk-adjusted discount rates, the discount rate employed should reflect the risk of the cash flows being discounted. Here, the cash flows are to equity investors of the target firm. So the appropriate discount rate is the target's cost of equity capital. Assuming this is 18 percent, and using the present value factors in Appendixes A and B, the estimated FMV of equity is

$$V_E = \$50 \text{ million}(3.127) + \$75 \text{ million}(3.127)(0.437)$$
$$+ \$75 \text{ million}(20)(0.191)$$
$$= \$545.34 \text{ million}$$

So, you now see how simple it is. Once you know future dividends, the cost of equity capital, and a future selling price, valuing a company's equity is almost trivial.

Valuing the Firm

One conclusion from our earlier discussion of investment analysis is that the investment decision should be separated from the financing decision whenever possible. First, decide whether the investment makes economic sense regardless of how it is financed; then decide how best to finance it. Techniques that treat the two decisions simultaneously unnecessarily complicate the issue. Unfortunately, the equity approach to business valuation does precisely this, for the cash flows to equity and the cost of equity both depend on the way the business is financed. Thus, the calculated FMV reflects both the value of the business and its financing.

A second approach to estimating going-concern value circumvents this problem by calculating the FMV of the firm rather than the FMV of equity. Once the value of the firm is known, it is then relatively easy to estimate the value of equity.

Applying the capital budgeting analogy again, the FMV of the firm equals the present value of expected aftertax cash flows available for distribution to owners *and* creditors, discounted at an appropriate risk-adjusted rate.

FMV of firm = PV{Expected aftertax cash flows
to owners and creditors},

where the term in braces can be written as

EBIT(1 − Tax rate) + Depreciation − Investment

The logic goes like this. EBIT, *earnings before interest* and *taxes*, is the income earned by the company without regard to how it is financed; so EBIT(1 − Tax rate) is income after tax excluding any effects of debt financing. Adding depreciation yields aftertax cash flow from operations. If management were prepared to run the company into the ground, it could distribute this cash flow in the form of dividends and interest payments. In the conventional case, however, where some income is retained to make new investments, only the difference between operating cash flow and investment is available for distribution.

Because the cash flow being discounted here accrues to the firm, not to equity, the appropriate risk-adjusted discount rate in the above formula is the target firm's *weighted-average* cost of capital. As with capital expenditure analysis, this approach reflects the benefits of the particular means of financing employed by the firm in the discount rate, not the cash flows.

Once the FMV of the firm is known, the FMV of equity can be deduced by recalling that

Value of equity = Value of firm − Value of liabilities.

Fortunately, the value of a company's liabilities is usually relatively easy to estimate and depends on the nature of the liabilities and the change in interest rates since the liabilities were incurred. In fact, if the liabilities are reasonably short-term and interest rates have not changed dramatically, a plausible estimate of the FMV of liabilities might be just their book value.

Here is another simple example. A 10 percent interest in the equity of AT&P Railroad is available, and it is necessary to determine a fair price. Railroading, at least as practiced by AT&P, appears to be a declining business, for although the company has large annual depreciation charges, investment is quite modest. You believe this situation will continue for the next six years as shown in Table 9–1. At the end of this period, you believe management will have to raise investment to equal annual depreciation charges, and that income will grow at two

TABLE 9–1
Free Cash Flow for AT&P Railroad ($ millions)

Year	EBIT	EBIT (1 − t)	+ Depreciation	− Investment	=	Free Cash Flow
1	100	64	160	50		174
2	98	63	170	50		183
3	96	61	170	60		171
4	95	61	160	70		151
5	96	61	150	90		121
6	95	61	140	110		91
				Present Value @ 12%	=	$634

percent per year thereafter. Finally, the company's weighted-average cost of capital appears to be about 12 percent.

The perpetual growth equation described in the last chapter says that the present value of a perpetually growing stream of receipts can be written as $R/(K − g)$, where R equals next year's receipts, K is the discount rate, and g is the growth rate. Applying this formula, the estimated value of AT&P as of year six is thus $622 million ($61 million × 1.02/[.12 − .02]). And the present worth of this amount at time zero is $315 million (0.507 × $622 million).

Adding the present value in Table 9–1 to this amount, we conclude that the FMV of AT&P is $949 million ($315 million + $634 million). Assuming the market value of AT&P's liabilities is $500 million, the fair market value of equity is $449 million. Therefore, a 10 percent interest in the company is worth $44.9 million.

Free Cash Flow. A fundamental conclusion from our discussion of investment analysis in earlier chapters was that companies should undertake only those investments promising returns in excess of capital costs. When a firm follows this optimal investment strategy, the cash flow in the firm valuation formula above is known as *free cash flow*. It is the cash flow available after financing all worthwhile investments. Free cash flow will figure prominently later in the chapter, when attention turns to corporate restructuring.

Problems with Present Value
Approaches to Valuation

If you are a little hesitant at this point about your ability to apply these discounted cash flow techniques to anything but contrived textbook examples, welcome to the club. For while DCF approaches to business valuation are conceptually correct, and even rather elegant, they are devilishly difficult to apply in practice. Valuing a business may be conceptually equivalent to

---

The Problem of Growth and Long Life

In many investment decisions involving long-lived assets, it is common to circumvent the problem of forecasting far-distant cash flows by ignoring all flows beyond some remote horizon. The justification for this practice is that the present value of far-distant cash flows will be quite small. However, when the cash flow stream is a growing one, growth offsets the discounting effect, and even far-distant cash flows can contribute significantly to present value. Consider the following problem.

At a discount rate of 10 percent, the present value of $1 per year for 20 years is $8.51. Using the perpetuity equation, the present value of $1 per year forever, at the same discount rate is $10 ($1/.10). Hence, ignoring all cash flows occurring after 20 years reduces the calculated present value of this perpetuity by only about 15 percent.

The present value, at a 10 percent discount rate, of $1 per year, growing at the rate of 6 percent per annum, for 20 years is $13.08. Use the perpetual growth equation to calculate the present value under the same conditions when growth continues forever. In the case of growing cash flows, what is the effect of ignoring flows occurring after year 20?

Answer: The present value of the perpetually growing cash flow stream is $25 ($1/[.10 − .06]). Ignoring cash flows beyond the 20th year in this case reduces the present value by 48 percent ([$25 − $13.08]/$25).

The Sensitivity Problem

Use the perpetual growth equation and a 10 percent discount rate to calculate the fair market value of a company with free cash flows next year of $1 million, growing at 5 percent per year indefinitely.

Assuming the discount rate and the growth rate could each be in error by as much as one percentage point, what are the maximum and minimum possible FMV's for the company? What does this suggest about the accuracy of present value approaches to valuation?

Answer: FMV at a 10 percent discount rate and a 5 percent growth rate is $20 million ($1 million/[.10 − .05]). The maximum is $33.3 million ($1 million/[.09 − .06]) and the minimum is $14.3 million ($1 million/[.11 − .04]). No one can charge very high fees to advise a client that a business is worth somewhere between $14.3 and $33.3 million.

---

any other capital expenditure decision, but there are several fundamental differences in practice. They include

1. The typical investment opportunity has a finite—usually brief—life, while the life expectancy of a company is indefinite.
2. The typical investment opportunity promises stable or perhaps declining cash flows over time, while the ability of a company to reinvest earnings customarily produces a growing cash flow.
3. The cash flows from a typical investment belong to the owner, while the cash flows generated by a company go to the owner only when management chooses to distribute them. If management decides to invest in Mexican diamond mines rather than pay dividends, there is little a minority owner can do other than sell out.

As the problems in the accompanying boxes demonstrate, these practical differences introduce potentially large errors into the valuation process and make the resulting FMV estimates highly sensitive to small changes in the discount rate and the growth rate employed.

Comparables

Granting that present value approaches to business valuation are conceptually correct but difficult to apply, what are the alternatives? One popular technique involves comparing the target company to similar publicly traded firms. Imagine shopping for a used car. The moment of truth comes when the buyer finds an interesting car, looks at the asking price, and ponders what to offer the dealer. One strategy, analogous to a present value approach, is to estimate the value of labor and raw materials in the car, add a markup for overhead and profit, and subtract an amount for depreciation. A more productive approach is comparison shopping. Develop an estimate of fair market value by comparing the subject car to similar autos that have recently sold, or are presently available. If three, similar-quality 1982 T-Birds have sold recently for $3,000 to $3,500, the buyer has reason to believe the target T-Bird has a similar value. Of course, comparison shopping provides no information about whether 1982 T-Birds are really worth $3,000 to $3,500 in any fundamental sense; it only indicates the going rate. However, in many instances this is sufficient. (Another tactic recommended by some is to skip the valuation process entirely and proceed directly to bargaining by asking the dealer what he wants for the car, and responding, "B——t, I'll give you half that." This probably works better for cars than companies, but don't rule it out entirely.)

Use of comparables in business valuation requires equal parts art and science. First, it is necessary to decide which publicly traded companies are most similar to the target and then to determine what the share prices of the publicly traded companies imply for the FMV of the firm in question. The equity valuation equation discussed above offers a useful starting point. It says that comparable companies should offer similar future dividend streams and similar business and financial risks. The former assures comparable cash flows, and the latter, comparable discount rates. (It is useful to note that comparable companies need not be the same size, for as will be demonstrated below, our results can be scaled to eliminate this factor.)

In practice, these guidelines suggest we begin our search for comparables by considering firms in the same, or closely related, industries with similar growth prospects and capital structures. With luck, the outcome of this exercise will be four to six, more or less, comparable publicly traded companies. Considerable judgment will then be required to decide what the comparables imply as a group for the fair market value of the target. Table 9–2 offers an abbreviated look at the process. It presents relevant data on a target company and four publicly traded comparables from the same industry.

Review of the figures suggests the target company has experienced better growth over the past five years than all but one of the comparables, has an above-average return on equity, and a representative capital structure. On balance, it would appear the target firm is in the upper range of the companies represented.

TABLE 9–2
Comparison of Target Firm and Four Comparables

	Target Company	Publicly Traded Comparables			
		Co. 1	Co. 2	Co. 3	Co.4
Assets ($ millions)	$120	$390	$680	$70	$250
Book value of equity ($ millions)	75	222	300	41	200
Earnings ($ millions)	15	40	60	7	18
Dividends ($ millions)	3	18	18	4	8
5-yr growth in earnings	17%	12%	19%	6%	11%
Return on equity	20%	18%	20%	17%	9%
Debt/assets ratio	38%	43%	55%	41%	21%
Stock price per share ($)	? ?	150	25	17	42
Price/earnings ratio	? ?	12×	15×	9×	10×
Shares outstanding (millions)	1.5	3.2	36	3.71	4.29
Market value of equity ($ millions)	? ?	480	900	63	180

Problem: Using the Price-to-Dividends Ratio to Adjust for Size

It might appear that because the present value formula discounts dividends, not earnings, we should use the price-to-dividends ratio rather than the price-to-earnings ratio to adjust for size. Calculate the price-to-dividends ratio for the four publicly traded companies in Table 9–2. How does the variability of this ratio across the four firms compare with the variability of the price-to-earnings ratio? What does this suggest about use of the price-to-dividends ratio to scale for size?

Answer: The price-to-dividends ratios for the four companies are 27, 50, 16, and 23. The largest of these ratios is 3.1 times the smallest. This compares with only 1.7 times for the price-to-earnings ratios. Because price usually correlates more closely with earnings than dividends across similar firms, the price-to-earnings ratio is usually thought to be the better indicator of long-run dividend-paying ability.

To convert this qualitative judgment into an estimated fair market value, we need to adjust for size. Observe from the price-to-earnings ratios that investors are paying between $9 and $15 per dollar of current earnings for the comparable firms' shares. If the risks and growth prospects of these firms are roughly similar to those of the target, it should command a similar ratio. Indeed, if we believe the company is in the upper range of those portrayed, a ratio of 14× might be appropriate. At this multiple, the implied fair market value of equity is $210 million (14[price/earnings ratio] × $15 million earnings).

Lack of Marketability.   An important difference between owning stock in a publicly traded company and a private one is that the publicly traded shares are more liquid. They can be sold quickly for cash without significant loss of value. Because liquidity is a valued attribute of any asset, it is necessary to reduce the FMV of a private company estimated by reference to publicly traded comparables. Without boring you with details, a representative lack-of-marketability discount is on the order of 25 percent. Hence, a more accurate estimate of the fair market value of the target company in Table 9–2 is $158 million (.75 × $210 million).[2] Of course, if the purpose of the valuation is to price an initial public offering of common stock, the shares will soon be liquid, and no discount is required.

CORPORATE RESTRUCTURING

Having now reviewed the basics of business valuation, let's see what they tell us about corporate takeovers and restructurings.

We have noted on several occasions that buying a minority interest in a company differs fundamentally from buying control. With a minority interest, the investor is a passive observer; with control, she is able to restructure the corporation and perhaps make a fortune in the process. Indeed, the two situations are so disparate that it is appropriate to speak of stock as selling in two separate markets: The market in which you and I participate trades claims on future dividends; the second market, in which Boone Pickens and other corporate raiders participate— *the market for control*—trades a more valuable commodity. In addition to claims on future dividends, the buyer in this market also gains the privilege of structuring the company as he or she wishes. Because shares trading in the two markets are really different assets, they naturally sell at different prices.

The Premium for Control

Figure 9–3 illustrates this two-tier market. From the perspective of minority investors, the fair market value of the company is *m,* the present value of cash flows to equity, given current control. However, to an individual seeking control, the FMV is

---

[2]Shannon P. Pratt, *Valuing A Business: The Analysis and Appraisal of Closely Held Companies* (Homewood, Ill.: Dow Jones-Irwin, 1981).

FIGURE 9–3
FMV of a Corporation to Investors Seeking Control May Exceed FMV to Minority Investors

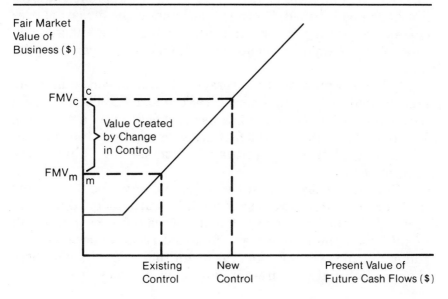

c, which may be well above m. The difference, $c - m$, is the value of control. It is the maximum premium over the minority FMV a raider will pay to gain control. It is also the expected increase in shareholder value created by the change in control. If a raider pays FMV_c for the target, all of the increased value will be realized by existing shareholders. But at any lower price, part of the increased value accrues to the raider.

What Price Control? After determining the FMV_m of a target, the raider's next task is to decide how large a control premium he can afford to pay. The following simple equation suggests one useful approach when the target is privately held.

$$\text{FMV}_c = \text{FMV}_m + \text{Enhancements},$$

where c refers to a controlling interest and m to a minority interest. It says the value of controlling interest in a business equals the FMV of the business under present stewardship, plus whatever enhancements to value the new buyer envisions. If the buyer intends no changes in the business now or in the future, the enhancements are zero, and no premium over FMV_m can be justified. On the other hand, if the buyer believes current leadership is squandering shareholders' money on ill-advised schemes and delusions, enhancements can be quite large.

Table 9–3 presents the average premiums paid in mergers and acquisitions over the period 1981–mid-1986. The premium in the most recent period is 47.1 percent, down from a whopping 70.7 percent in 1981. Evidently, acquirers believe the changes they contemplate will significantly increase the value of the acquired firm.

Putting a price tag on the value enhancements resulting from a change in control is a straightforward undertaking conceptually. Make a detailed list of all the ways free cash flow will be increased and business and financial risks reduced as a result of the takeover; estimate the magnitude and timing of these changes; calculate the present value of each; and sum.

$$\text{Enhancements} = \text{PV\{All value-increasing changes due to takeover\}}.$$

TABLE 9–3
Average Premiums Paid in Mergers and Acquisitions
(1981–First-Half 1986)

Year	Number of Transactions	Average Premium over Stock Price One Month before Announcement
1981	129	70.7%
1982	154	63.7
1983	155	47.1
1985	294	52.5
1986	116	47.1

Source: "Payments and Premiums," *Mergers & Acquisitions* (November/December 1986), p. 12.

Avoiding Dilution in Earnings Per Share

A popular alternative approach to determining how much one company can afford to bid for another looks at the impact of the acquisition on the acquirer's earnings per share (EPS). Popularity is about all this approach has to recommend it, for it grossly oversimplifies the financial effects of an acquisition, and it rests on an inappropriate decision criterion.

Suppose the following data apply to an acquiring firm, A, and its target, T, in an exchange-of-shares merger; that is, A will give T's shareholders newly printed shares of A in exchange for their shares of T.

	Co. A	Co. T	Merged Company
Earnings ($ millions)	$100	$20	$130
No. of shares (millions)	20	40	26
Earnings per share ($)	5.00	0.50	5.00 (minimum)
Stock price ($)	70	5	
Market value of equity ($ millions)	1,400	200	

The suggested decision criterion is that, at a minimum, A should avoid dilution in EPS. If earnings of the merged firm are forecasted to be $130 million, the figures above indicate that A can issue as many as 6 million shares without suffering dilution ([$130 million/ $5.00] − 20 million). At $70 per share, this implies a maximum price of $420 million for T ($70 × 6 million), or a 110 percent premium ([420 − 200]/200). It also suggests a maximum exchange ratio of .15 shares of A for each share of T (6 million/40 million).

The obvious shortcomings of this simplistic approach are first, that earnings are not the cash flows that determine value, and second, that it is grossly inappropriate to base an acquisition decision on only one year's results. Doing so is comparable to making investments because they promise to increase next year's profits. If T's growth prospects are sufficiently bright, it may be perfectly reasonable to sacrifice near-term EPS in anticipation of long-run gains. Business valuation is tough in practice, but this is no reason to use flawed techniques just because they are tractable.

Controlling Interest in a Publicly Traded Company.
If we are willing to assume that the pre-acquisition stock price
of the target firm reasonably approximates its FMV_m—or at
least that we are unable to detect when the approximation is
unreasonable—this formula can also be used to value controlling interest in a publicly traded company:

FMV_c = Market value of business + Enhancements.

A particular virtue of this formula for valuing acquisition
candidates is that it forces attention on the specific improvements anticipated from the acquisition and the maximum price
one should pay for them. This perspective reduces the possibility
that an exuberant buyer will become carried away during spir-
ited bidding and overpay.

The Battle for Free Cash Flow

We conclude (or at least I conclude) that the best way to value a
public company for acquisition purposes is to add the present
value of all benefits attributable to takeover to the target's
current market value. So, you ask perceptively, What are the
anticipated benefits motivating today's takeovers and restructurings? While neither space nor patience warrant a complete
listing, three possible enhancements appear sufficiently fundamental and frequent to merit review. I will refer to them as *tax
shields, incentive effects,* and *controlling free cash flow.*

Tax Shields. Many restructurings appear motivated by
the desire to make more extensive use of depreciation and interest tax shields. As noted in Chapter 6, the tax deductibility of
depreciation and interest expenses reduce a company's tax bill,
and hence may add value. Investment manager Warren Buffett
puts it more directly when he observes, "If you can eliminate
the government as a 46 percent partner," the business will be
far more valuable.

Consider the following restructuring. Pertinent data for
Herb Bird, Inc., a mature publicly traded company, appear
below.

Herb Bird, Inc. ($ millions)

Annual EBIT	$ 25
Market value of equity	200
Long-term debt	0
Fixed plant and equipment	100
Annual depreciation	10

Global Investing Corp. believes Bird may be ripe for a leveraged buyout and has approached management with a proposal to form a new corporation, called NEWCO, to purchase all of Bird's equity. Because Bird's cash flows are very stable, Global figures NEWCO can finance most of the purchase price by borrowing $190 million on a 10-year loan at 10 percent interest. The loan payments will be interest-only for the first five years. In addition, Global believes its auditors will allow NEWCO to write up the book value of Bird's fixed plant and equipment to a fair market value of $160 million on acquisition. This will result in a $6 million increase in annual depreciation for the next 10 years. The value of the anticipated tax shields to NEWCO, discounted at a 12 percent rate, is shown below.

Year	Increase in Interest Expense	Increase in Depreciation	Tax Shield @ 34% Tax Rate
1	19.00	6.00	8.50
2	19.00	6.00	8.50
3	19.00	6.00	8.50
4	19.00	6.00	8.50
5	19.00	6.00	8.50
6	19.00	6.00	8.50
7	15.89	6.00	7.44
8	12.46	6.00	6.28
9	8.70	6.00	5.00
10	4.56	6.00	3.59
		PV @ 12% =	$43.81

The figures suggest that NEWCO can bid up to $243.81 million—a 22 percent premium—to purchase Bird. Global's equity investment will be as high as $53.81 million ($243.81 million value of firm − $190 million value of liabilities), implying a post-acquisition debt-to-assets ratio of 78 percent. This, believe it or not, is conservative financing by recent standards. LBOs are indeed aptly named.

Note that if increased tax shields are the objective, an LBO is not the only way to attain them. Bird can generate much the same effect by simply issuing debt and distributing the proceeds to owners as a large dividend, or by a share repurchase. This was Colt Industries' strategy in 1986 when they floated a large debt issue to finance distribution of a special $85 per share dividend. To put this number in perspective, Colt's stock traded for only $67 just prior to announcement of the restructuring. After recapitalization, Colt faced a negative net worth of $1 billion and $1.6 billion in long-term debt. But what's to fear from a mountain of debt as long as you have the cash flow to service it? And if you don't, your creditors have so much at stake in your company they are more likely to behave like partners than policemen.

Nor must a leveraged buyout necessarily involve a takeover. Many LBOs are initiated by incumbent management who team up with outside investors to purchase all of the company's stock and take it private. Management risks its own money in return for a sizable equity position in the restructured company.

The pros and cons of financial leverage were examined in Chapter 6, where we concluded that capital structure policy involves a judicious balancing of the tax and growth benefits of debt financing against the increased expected cost of bankruptcy. Restructurings involving extensive increases in financial leverage are implicitly saying that many companies have overestimated the cost side of this equation. Although through mid-1987 many LBOs have been wildly profitable, the next significant recession will likely provide the first real test of this high-leverage thesis.

Incentive Effects. Tax shield enhancements are clearly just a game: to the extent that shareholders win, we, the people (in the form of the U.S. Treasury) lose. And if this were the only gain to restructuring, the phenomenon would not command serious public attention. Best that we eliminate the tax benefits of restructuring and get back to producing goods and services instead of stocks and bonds.

The other two potential payoffs from corporate restructuring are not so easily dismissed, however. Both involve free cash flow and both are premised on the contention that unless otherwise constrained, many managements will not spend free cash flow in the best interests of owners. Restructuring is thus seen as a weapon by which shareholders gain control of free cash flow, or at least force managements to use the cash flow in ways that increase shareholder value. Moreover, restructuring is seen as a boon not only to shareholders but to the entire economy, for to the extent that shareholders succeed in forcing management to increase value, the economy's resources are allocated more efficiently. Let us explore this reasoning in more detail below.

Before restructuring, the life of a senior manager at Herb Bird, Inc., may well have been an enviable one. With very stable cash flows, a mature business, and no debt, management had no pressing reason to improve performance. They could pay themselves and their employees generously, make sizable corporate contributions to charity, and if the president were so inclined, sponsor an Indy race car or an unlimited hydroplane. Alternatively, if they wanted to grow, the company could buy growth by sacrificing profitability. This might involve making some uneconomic investments, but, hey, as long as cash flows are strong, almost anything is possible.

According to Samuel Johnson, the certainty of hanging in a fortnight focuses the mind wonderfully. Restructuring has a similar consequence, for it fundamentally changes the world of Bird senior executives. Because they have probably invested much of their own resources in equity of the restructured company, management's own material well-being is tied closely to that of the business. Moreover, the huge debt-service burden that restructuring frequently creates forces management to generate healthy cash flows or face bankruptcy—no more "corpocracy" at Bird. The carrot of ownership and the stick of possible financial ruin create significant incentives for management to maximize free cash flow and to spend it for the benefit of owners.

Controlling Free Cash Flow. Many hostile takeovers occur in mature or declining industries. Because investment opportunities in these industries are low, affected businesses often have large free cash flows. At the same time, industry decline creates real concern in the minds of executives about the continued survival of their organization. And although the proper strategy from a purely economic perspective is to shrink or terminate the business, management may take another tack. Out of a deep commitment to the business and concern for employees, the community, and their own welfare, managers may continue to fight the good fight by reinvesting in the business, despite the poor returns. The purpose of restructuring in these instances is brutally basic: to wrest control of free cash flow away from management and put it in the hands of owners. This is essentially the story of Gulf Oil.

The Board of Directors

One piece of the puzzle remains: How does incumbent management gain control of the firm in the first place? In theory, managers should be incapable of acting in opposition to owners for at least two reasons. First, if a company operates in highly competitive markets, management has very little discretion; it must maximize profits or be driven from the industry. Second, all corporations have boards of directors with the power to hire and fire management and the responsibility to represent owners' interests.

Theory, however, differs from reality. Most corporations operate in less than perfectly competitive markets, and most corporate boards are not an effective, independent shareholder voice. Primarily because of the vagaries of the proxy process for shareholder voting, most directors are more closely affiliated with incumbent management than with owners. Many are inside directors, others have significant ties to the enterprise other than ownership, and in most instances, directors are more beholden to incumbent management than to shareholders for their seat on the board. Consequently, while the board may aid management in running the company, it is seldom an independent voice for shareholders. Or as one professional director put it, "The most important skill a board member can have is the ability to yawn with his mouth shut."

The Gulf Oil Takeover

Pickens' attack on Gulf should no longer seem mystifying. Gulf's pre-attack $39 stock price was the value of a share to minority investors, given James Lee's stewardship, while the $80 stock price included control. Clearly, neither price was necessarily incorrect or irrational.

Pickens attacked Gulf because its financial performance was the worst among major oil companies and because he believed incumbent management was ignoring the new realities of the business. OPEC-engineered price increases in 1973 and 1979 simultaneously reduced demand for oil and created large windfall profits for oil companies. The result was excess capacity and large free cash flows, a volatile mixture. Despite the excess capacity and sharply rising costs of domestic exploration, Gulf and others in the industry continued to spend heavily on domestic exploration and development. Indeed, between 1978 and 1982 Gulf's annual outlays for exploration more than doubled to over $2.5 billion. That these outlays were economically unwarranted is indicated in a study of rates of return on exploration and development for 30 large oil firms over the period 1982—84. The study concluded that on average the industry did not "earn even a 10 percent return on pretax outlays."[3] Inasmuch as 10 percent pretax is far below its cost of capital, the research implies that each dollar Gulf spent on exploration destroyed shareholder value. Pickens's strategy was simply to create value by turning off the exploration spigot and redirecting free cash flow to shareholders. It is interesting to note that one of Standard Oil's first acts after acquiring Gulf was to curtail sharply Gulf's exploration activities.

Gulf management's primary objective appears to have been corporate survival in a shrinking market, and a continuing supply of domestic crude oil was seen as necessary to achieve this goal. In essence, management saw Gulf first and foremost as a venerable business at risk, and only secondarily as a financial

---

[3]As reported in Michael C. Jensen, "The Corporate Takeover Controversy: Analysis and Evidence," *Midland Corporate Finance Journal* (Summer 1986), p. 17.

investment responsible for generating competitive returns for its owners. Pickens and the other bidders for Gulf reversed these priorities, saying in effect that a corporation's fundamental purpose is to create value for its owners and that continued survival is contingent on the achievement of this objective.

As debate topics go, the question of whether management should have broader social responsibilities than simply creating shareholder value is among the more intriguing. Like many important societal questions, however, the issue has tended to be resolved more on the basis of power than of logic. Throughout much of this century, incumbent management has retained the power to interpret its responsibilities broadly and to treat shareholders as only one of several constituencies possessing a claim on the corporation. As the Gulf takeover illustrates, power has now begun to swing toward shareholders, and many managements have responded by taking the goal of value-creation more seriously—hence the birth of corporate restructuring.

Several factors combined to make Pickens's bid for Gulf feasible and, more generally, to enhance shareholder control of corporations. One was the Reagan administration's accommodating views on antitrust enforcement. Another was the newfound proclivity of banks to finance highly levered, contested takeovers. Indeed, banks oversubscribed the $14 billion loan package used by Standard Oil to acquire Gulf by 30 percent.

A third force facilitating Pickens's bid was the emergence of the high-yield, or junk, bond market. As noted in Chapter 5, a *junk bond* is any bond rated below investment grade. For Pickens's raid on Gulf, investment banks put together $2 billion in commitments, meaning that if the takeover met certain conditions, the banks were prepared to sell $2 billion of junk bonds on Pickens's behalf. This and a $200 million equity investment by Penn Central lent considerable weight to Pickens's crusade.

Could It Happen To My Company? You bet. With the possible exception of IBM and Exxon, no public company today is so large it can ignore the threat of takeover.

The long-run economic consequences of corporate restructuring are yet to be determined. In the meantime, this chapter suggests two strategies to those managements intent on avoiding hostile takeover. First, look at your company as an investment as well as a business; work to increase free cash flow; and avoid uses of free cash flow that reduce firm value. In other words, take value-creation seriously. Second, work to assure that your board of directors truly represents the interests of owners, and that owners have confidence in the board's commitment on their behalf. While not eliminating the threat of takeover, these strategies will reduce the disparity of interest between managers and owners, and in the process will remove a principal rationale for hostile takeover.

CHAPTER SUMMARY

1. The topic of this chapter has been corporate restructuring, defined loosely as any major episodic change in capital structure or ownership including mergers, takeovers, leveraged buyouts, divestitures, and stock repurchases. A sizable increase in hostile takeovers and preemptive restructurings prompted by these takeovers appears to be fundamentally altering corporate America.

2. The motivations fueling corporate restructuring are to be found in the study of business valuation—the art of valuing all or part of a business.

3. For publicy traded firms, the *market value of equity* is the price per share of common stock times the number of shares outstanding. The *market value of the firm* equals the market value of equity plus the market value of liabilities similarly calculated.

4. An asset's *fair market value* (FMV) is an abstract ideal defined as the price at which the asset would trade among two rational individuals, each in command of all information necessary to value the asset and neither under any pressure to trade.

5. The FMV of a business is usually the higher of its liquidation value or its going-concern value, where liquidation value is the cash generated by selling the business' assets individually and going-concern value is the pres-

ent worth of expected future cash flows generated by the business.

6. Three techniques for estimating the going-concern value of equity are: (1) estimate the present value of expected cash flows to equity, (2) estimate the present value of cash flows to the firm and subtract the value of liabilities, and (3) infer the value of equity from the prices at which the shares of comparable, publicly traded firms trade.

7. The price of common stock in public markets is that paid for a minority interest. A raider is justified in paying a premium above this minority value to gain control of a firm if he believes that in so doing he can enhance its value. The maximum premium equals the present value of all value-increasing changes contemplated by the raider.

8. Free cash flow equals the operating cash flow available to the firm after financing all worthwhile investment opportunities. The principal benefits motivating today's restructurings appear to be: (1) increased interest tax shields from debt financing, (2) increased incentive effects from increasing management's ownership of the company, and (3) owner control of free cash flow.

9. Hostile takeovers are presently the subject of an intense public policy debate. At issue is whether takeovers should be encouraged as a way to oust ineffective managements, or discouraged as inequitable and detrimental to long-run economic performance.

ADDITIONAL READING

Jensen, Michael C. "The Corporate Takeover Controversy: Analysis and Evidence." *Midland Corporate Finance Journal* (Summer 1986): 6–32.

Harry Truman's proverbial 'one-armed economist'; none of this "on the one hand but then on the other hand" from Mike Jensen. This article is a cogent, tightly reasoned, provocative review of the empirical literature on corporate takeovers and a strong statement in support of the virtues of an unfettered market for corporate control. If you only read one article on the topic, make it this one.

Lowenstein, Louis. "No More Cozy Management Buyouts." *Harvard Business Review* (January/February 1986): 147–56.

The author reviews several recent, management-led leveraged buyouts and expresses justifiable concern about the opportunities they create for serious abuse of shareholder rights.

Pratt, Shannon P. *Valuing A Business: The Analysis and Appraisal of Closely Held Companies.* Homewood, Ill.: Dow Jones-Irwin, 1981. 424 pages.

A detailed road map of how to value a closely held company. A wealth of practical detail on sources of data and applied valuation approaches. Relevant primarily for valuing small firms.

Rock, Milton R. *The Merger and Acquisition Handbook.* New York: McGraw-Hill, 1987. 544 pages.

Forty-eight articles on virtually every aspect of mergers and acquisitions, edited by the editor in chief of the periodical *Mergers & Acquisitions.* See especially "Discounted Cash Flow Valuation" by Alfred Rappaport.

CHAPTER PROBLEMS

1. Below is a recent income statement for ABC Company.

Net sales	$1,000
Cost of sales	
(including depreciation of $100)	600
Gross profit	400
Selling and admin. expenses	
(including interest expense of $60)	200
Income before tax	200
Tax	68
Income after tax	$ 132

Calculate ABC's free cash flow in this year assuming it spent $80 on new capital equipment and increased working capital $40. Assume these were positive NPV investments.

2. The following information is available about Russell Brewing Company.

Stock price	$8 per share
Common shares outstanding	10 million
Current liabilities	$15 million
Market value of long-term liabilities	$60 million
Weighted average cost of capital	14%

An investment company is confident that by terminating Russell's money-losing "fruit-flavored beer coolers," and by selling the women's hosiery division, free cash flow can be increased $4 million annually for the next decade. In addition, they estimate that an immediate, special dividend of $10 million can be financed by the sale of the hosiery division.

a. Assuming these actions do not affect Russell's cost of capital, what is the maximum price per share the investment company would be justified in bidding for control of Russell? What percentage premium does this represent?

b. Conduct a sensitivity analysis of your answer to a by assuming the cost of capital is 15 percent and the increased cash flow is only $3.5 million per year.

3. A capital goods manufacturer has decided to expand into a related business. Management estimates that to build and staff a facility of the desired size and to attain capacity operations would cost $250 million in present value terms. Alternatively, the company could acquire an existing firm or division with the desired capacity. One such opportunity is the division of another company. The book value of the division's assets is $140 million and its earnings before interest and tax are presently $30 million. Publicly traded comparable companies are selling in a narrow range around 13 times current earnings. These companies have debt-to-asset ratios averaging 40 percent with an average interest rate of 10 percent.

a. Using a tax rate of 34 percent, estimate the minimum price the owner of the division should consider for its sale.

b. What is the maximum price the acquirer should be willing to pay?

c. Does it appear that an acquisition is feasible? Why or why not?

    d. Would a 30 percent decline in stock prices to an industry average price-to-earnings ratio of 9.1 change your answer to *c*? Why or why not?

    e. Referring to the $250 million price tag as the replacement value of the division, what would you predict would happen to acquisition activity when market values of companies and divisions fall below their replacement values?

4. A grocery chain with a 10 percent debt-to-assets ratio and a times interest earned of seven is concerned about the possibility of losing its independence in a raid. As part of its defense, management elects to sell $100 million of new debt and to repurchase some of its common stock. This will increase the debt-to-assets ratio to 60 percent and will cut times interest earned to two.

    a. Do you think this restructuring will reduce the company's vulnerability to a takeover? Why or why not?

    b. Do you think the restructuring will create value? If so, how?

    c. If the tax rate is 34 percent, the interest rate is 12 percent, and the debt will be rolled over as it matures (i.e., assume the debt is outstanding in perpetuity), estimate the present value of the tax shield created by the restructuring at a discount rate of 14 percent.

    d. What percentage decline in earnings before interest and taxes could the company sustain and still cover its interest expenses prior to the restructuring? What is the comparable figure after the restructuring? If you were a well-capitalized competitor, anxious to increase market share, what do these numbers suggest might be an interesting strategy to use against this firm?

5. Breakup value is an increasingly popular notion among financial analysts. A multiproduct company's breakup value equals the cash one could realize by splitting the company into two or more independent firms and disposing of each separately. A company becomes a candidate for takeover when its market value falls below its breakup value. It appears that leverage buyout specialists Kohlberg, Kravis, and Roberts will profit handsomely from the acquisition and dismemberment of Beatrice Foods.

a. In what ways do you think that simply breaking up a company and selling the parts creates value?
b. If the sum of the free cash flows of the enterprises created by the breakup equals the cash flow of the company prior to breakup, might breakup still create value?

Appendixes

APPENDIX A
Present Value of $1 Discounted at Discount Rate k, for n Years

Period (n)	\	\	\	\	Discount rate (k)	\	\	\	\	\	\	\
	1%	2%	3%	4%	5%	6%	7%	8%	9%	10%	11%	12%
1	0.990	0.980	0.971	0.962	0.952	0.943	0.935	0.926	0.917	0.909	0.901	0.893
2	0.980	0.961	0.943	0.925	0.907	0.890	0.873	0.857	0.842	0.826	0.812	0.797
3	0.971	0.942	0.915	0.889	0.864	0.840	0.816	0.794	0.772	0.751	0.731	0.712
4	0.961	0.924	0.885	0.855	0.823	0.792	0.763	0.735	0.708	0.683	0.659	0.636
5	0.951	0.906	0.863	0.822	0.784	0.747	0.713	0.681	0.650	0.621	0.593	0.567
6	0.942	0.888	0.837	0.790	0.746	0.705	0.666	0.630	0.596	0.564	0.535	0.507
7	0.933	0.871	0.813	0.760	0.711	0.665	0.623	0.583	0.547	0.513	0.482	0.452
8	0.923	0.853	0.789	0.731	0.677	0.627	0.582	0.540	0.502	0.467	0.434	0.404
9	0.914	0.837	0.766	0.703	0.645	0.592	0.544	0.500	0.460	0.424	0.391	0.361
10	0.905	0.820	0.744	0.676	0.614	0.558	0.508	0.463	0.422	0.386	0.352	0.322
11	0.896	0.804	0.722	0.650	0.585	0.527	0.475	0.429	0.388	0.350	0.317	0.287
12	0.887	0.788	0.701	0.625	0.557	0.497	0.444	0.397	0.356	0.319	0.286	0.257
13	0.879	0.773	0.681	0.601	0.530	0.469	0.415	0.368	0.326	0.290	0.258	0.229
14	0.870	0.758	0.661	0.577	0.505	0.442	0.388	0.340	0.299	0.263	0.232	0.205
15	0.861	0.743	0.642	0.555	0.481	0.417	0.362	0.315	0.275	0.239	0.209	0.183
16	0.853	0.728	0.623	0.534	0.458	0.394	0.339	0.292	0.252	0.218	0.188	0.163
17	0.844	0.714	0.605	0.513	0.436	0.371	0.317	0.270	0.231	0.198	0.170	0.146
18	0.836	0.700	0.587	0.494	0.416	0.350	0.296	0.250	0.212	0.180	0.153	0.130
19	0.828	0.686	0.570	0.475	0.396	0.331	0.277	0.232	0.194	0.164	0.138	0.116
20	0.820	0.673	0.554	0.456	0.377	0.312	0.258	0.215	0.178	0.149	0.124	0.104
25	0.780	0.610	0.478	0.375	0.295	0.233	0.184	0.146	0.116	0.092	0.074	0.059
30	0.742	0.552	0.412	0.308	0.231	0.174	0.131	0.099	0.075	0.057	0.044	0.033
40	0.672	0.453	0.307	0.208	0.142	0.097	0.067	0.046	0.032	0.022	0.015	0.011
50	0.608	0.372	0.228	0.141	0.087	0.054	0.034	0.021	0.013	0.009	0.005	0.003

APPENDIX A *(concluded)*

Period (n)							Discount rate (k)						
	13%	14%	15%	16%	17%	18%	19%	20%	25%	30%	35%	40%	50%
1	0.885	0.877	0.870	0.862	0.855	0.847	0.840	0.833	0.800	0.769	0.741	0.714	0.667
2	0.783	0.769	0.756	0.743	0.731	0.718	0.706	0.694	0.640	0.592	0.549	0.510	0.444
3	0.693	0.675	0.658	0.641	0.624	0.609	0.593	0.579	0.512	0.455	0.406	0.364	0.296
4	0.613	0.592	0.572	0.552	0.534	0.515	0.499	0.482	0.410	0.350	0.301	0.260	0.198
5	0.543	0.519	0.497	0.476	0.456	0.437	0.419	0.402	0.320	0.269	0.223	0.186	0.132
6	0.480	0.456	0.432	0.410	0.390	0.370	0.352	0.335	0.262	0.207	0.165	0.133	0.088
7	0.425	0.400	0.376	0.354	0.333	0.314	0.296	0.279	0.210	0.159	0.122	0.095	0.059
8	0.376	0.351	0.327	0.305	0.285	0.266	0.249	0.233	0.168	0.123	0.091	0.068	0.039
9	0.333	0.308	0.284	0.263	0.243	0.225	0.209	0.194	0.134	0.094	0.067	0.048	0.026
10	0.295	0.270	0.247	0.227	0.208	0.191	0.176	0.162	0.107	0.073	0.050	0.035	0.017
11	0.261	0.237	0.215	0.195	0.178	0.162	0.148	0.135	0.086	0.056	0.037	0.025	0.012
12	0.231	0.208	0.187	0.168	0.152	0.137	0.124	0.112	0.069	0.043	0.027	0.018	0.008
13	0.204	0.182	0.163	0.145	0.130	0.116	0.104	0.093	0.055	0.033	0.020	0.013	0.005
14	0.181	0.160	0.141	0.125	0.111	0.099	0.088	0.078	0.044	0.025	0.015	0.009	0.003
15	0.160	0.140	0.123	0.108	0.095	0.084	0.074	0.065	0.035	0.020	0.011	0.006	0.002
16	0.141	0.123	0.107	0.093	0.081	0.071	0.062	0.054	0.028	0.015	0.008	0.005	0.002
17	0.125	0.108	0.093	0.080	0.069	0.060	0.052	0.045	0.023	0.012	0.006	0.003	0.001
18	0.111	0.095	0.081	0.069	0.059	0.051	0.044	0.038	0.018	0.009	0.005	0.002	0.001
19	0.098	0.083	0.070	0.060	0.051	0.043	0.037	0.031	0.014	0.007	0.003	0.002	0
20	0.087	0.073	0.061	0.051	0.043	0.037	0.031	0.026	0.012	0.005	0.002	0.001	0
25	0.047	0.038	0.030	0.024	0.020	0.016	0.013	0.010	0.004	0.001	0.001	0	0
30	0.026	0.020	0.015	0.012	0.009	0.007	0.005	0.004	0.001	0	0	0	0
40	0.008	0.005	0.004	0.003	0.002	0.001	0.001	0.001	0	0	0	0	0
50	0.002	0.001	0.001	0.001	0	0	0	0	0	0	0	0	0

APPENDIX B   **Present Value of an Annuity of $1 for _n_ Years, Discounted at Rate _k_**

Period (n)	1%	2%	3%	4%	5%	6%	7%	8%	9%	10%	11%	12%
1	0.990	0.980	0.971	0.962	0.952	0.943	0.935	0.926	0.917	0.909	0.901	0.893
2	1.970	1.942	1.913	1.886	1.859	1.833	1.808	1.783	1.759	1.736	1.713	1.690
3	2.941	2.884	2.829	2.775	2.723	2.673	2.624	2.577	2.531	2.487	2.444	2.402
4	3.902	3.808	3.717	3.630	3.546	3.465	3.387	3.312	3.240	3.170	3.102	3.037
5	4.853	4.710	4.580	4.452	4.329	4.212	4.100	3.993	3.890	3.791	3.696	3.605
6	5.795	5.601	5.417	5.242	5.076	4.917	4.767	4.623	4.486	4.355	4.231	4.111
7	6.728	6.472	6.230	6.002	5.786	5.582	5.389	5.206	5.033	4.868	4.712	4.564
8	7.652	7.325	7.020	6.733	6.463	6.210	5.971	5.747	5.535	5.335	5.146	4.968
9	8.566	8.162	7.786	7.435	7.108	6.802	6.515	6.247	5.995	5.759	5.537	5.328
10	9.471	8.983	8.530	8.111	7.722	7.360	7.024	6.710	6.418	6.145	5.889	5.650
11	10.368	9.787	9.253	8.760	8.306	7.887	7.499	7.139	6.805	6.495	6.207	5.938
12	11.255	10.575	9.954	9.385	8.863	8.384	7.943	7.536	7.161	6.814	6.492	6.194
13	12.134	11.348	10.635	9.986	9.394	8.853	8.358	7.904	7.487	7.103	6.750	6.424
14	13.004	12.106	11.296	10.563	9.899	9.295	8.745	8.244	7.786	7.367	6.982	6.628
15	13.865	12.849	11.939	11.118	10.380	9.712	9.108	8.559	8.061	7.606	7.191	6.811
16	14.718	13.578	12.561	11.652	10.838	10.106	9.447	8.851	8.313	7.824	7.379	6.974
17	15.562	14.292	13.166	12.166	11.274	10.477	9.763	9.122	8.544	8.022	7.549	7.102
18	16.398	14.992	13.754	12.659	11.690	10.828	10.059	9.372	8.756	8.201	7.702	7.250
19	17.226	15.678	14.324	13.134	12.085	11.158	10.336	9.604	8.950	8.365	7.839	7.366
20	18.046	16.351	14.877	13.590	12.462	11.470	10.594	9.818	9.129	8.514	7.963	7.469
25	22.023	19.523	17.413	15.622	14.094	12.783	11.654	10.675	9.823	9.077	8.422	7.843
30	25.808	22.396	19.600	17.292	15.372	13.765	12.409	11.258	10.274	9.427	8.694	8.055
40	32.835	27.355	23.115	19.793	17.159	15.046	13.332	11.925	10.757	9.779	8.951	8.244
50	39.196	31.424	25.730	21.482	18.256	15.762	13.801	12.233	10.962	9.915	9.042	8.304

Discount rate (k)

APPENDIX B *(concluded)*

Discount rate (k)

Period (n)	13%	14%	15%	16%	17%	18%	19%	20%	25%	30%	35%	40%	50%
1	0.885	0.877	0.870	0.862	0.855	0.847	0.840	0.833	0.800	0.769	0.741	0.714	0.667
2	1.668	1.647	1.626	1.605	1.585	1.566	1.547	1.528	1.440	1.361	1.289	1.224	1.111
3	2.361	2.322	2.283	2.246	2.210	2.174	2.140	2.106	1.952	1.816	1.696	1.589	1.407
4	2.974	2.914	2.855	2.798	2.743	2.690	2.639	2.589	2.362	2.166	1.997	1.849	1.605
5	3.517	3.433	3.352	3.274	3.199	3.127	3.058	2.991	2.689	2.436	2.220	2.035	1.737
6	3.998	3.889	3.784	3.685	3.589	3.498	3.410	3.326	2.951	2.643	2.385	2.168	1.824
7	4.423	4.288	4.160	4.039	3.922	3.812	3.706	3.605	3.161	2.802	2.508	2.263	1.883
8	4.799	4.639	4.487	4.344	4.207	4.078	3.954	3.837	3.329	2.925	2.598	2.331	1.922
9	5.132	4.946	4.772	4.607	4.451	4.303	4.163	4.031	3.463	3.019	2.665	2.370	1.948
10	5.426	5.216	5.019	4.833	4.659	4.494	4.339	4.192	3.571	3.092	2.715	2.414	1.965
11	5.687	5.453	5.234	5.029	4.836	4.656	4.486	4.327	3.656	3.147	2.752	2.438	1.977
12	5.918	5.660	5.421	5.197	4.988	4.793	4.611	4.439	3.725	3.190	2.779	2.456	1.985
13	6.122	5.842	5.583	5.342	5.118	4.910	4.715	4.533	3.780	3.223	2.799	2.469	1.990
14	6.302	6.002	5.724	5.468	5.229	5.008	4.802	4.611	3.824	3.249	2.814	2.478	1.993
15	6.462	6.142	5.847	5.575	5.324	5.092	4.876	4.675	3.859	3.268	2.825	2.484	1.995
16	6.604	6.265	5.954	5.668	5.405	5.162	4.938	4.730	3.887	3.283	2.834	2.489	1.997
17	6.729	6.373	6.047	5.749	5.475	5.222	4.988	4.775	3.910	3.295	2.840	2.492	1.998
18	6.840	6.467	6.128	5.818	5.534	5.273	5.033	4.812	3.928	3.304	2.844	2.494	1.999
19	6.938	6.550	6.198	5.877	5.584	5.316	5.070	4.843	3.942	3.311	2.848	2.496	1.999
20	7.025	6.623	6.259	5.929	5.628	5.353	5.101	4.870	3.954	3.316	2.850	2.497	1.999
25	7.330	6.873	6.464	6.097	5.766	5.467	5.195	4.948	3.985	3.329	2.856	2.499	2.000
30	7.496	7.003	6.566	6.177	5.829	5.517	5.235	4.979	3.995	3.332	2.857	2.500	2.000
40	7.634	7.105	6.642	6.233	5.871	5.548	5.258	4.997	3.999	3.333	2.857	2.500	2.000
50	7.675	7.133	6.661	6.246	5.880	5.554	5.262	4.999	4.000	3.333	2.857	2.500	2.000

Glossary

accelerated depreciation Any *depreciation*[1] that produces larger deductions for depreciation in the early years of a project's life.

acceptance criterion Any minimum standard of performance in investment analysis (cf. *hurdle rate*).

accounting income An economic agent's *realized income* as shown on financial statements (cf. *economic income*).

accounting rate of return A figure of investment merit, defined as average annual cash inflow divided by total cash outflow (cf. *internal rate of return*).

accounts payable (payables, trade payables) Money owed to suppliers.

accounts receivable (receivables, trade credit) Money owed by customers.

accrual accounting A method of accounting in which *revenue* is recognized when earned and expenses are recognized when incurred without regard to the timing of cash receipts and expenditures (cf. *cash accounting*).

acid test (quick ratio) A measure of *liquidity,* defined as *current assets* less inventories divided by *current liabilities.*

---

[1]Words in italics are defined elsewhere in the glossary.

aftertax cash flow Total cash generated by an investment annually, defined as profit after tax plus depreciation, or equivalently, operating income after tax plus the tax rate times depreciation.

allocated costs Costs systematically assigned or distributed among products, departments, or other elements.

annuity A level stream of cash flows for a limited number of years (cf. *perpetuity*).

asset turnover ratio A broad measure of asset efficiency, defined as net sales divided by total assets.

bankruptcy A legal condition in which an individual's or company's assets are assumed by a federal court official and used to pay off creditors.

benefit-cost ratio *Profitability index.*

β-risk (systematic risk, nondiversifiable risk) Risk that cannot be diversified away.

bond Long-term publicly issued debt.

bond rating An appraisal by a recognized financial organization of the soundness of a *bond* as an investment.

book value The value at which an item is reported in financial statements (cf. *market value.*)

book value of equity The value of *owners' equity* as shown on the company's balance sheet (cf. *market value of equity*).

break-even analysis Analysis of the level of sales at which a firm or product will just break even.

breakup value The value one could realize by dividing a multibusiness company into a number of separate enterprises and disposing of each individually.

business risk Risk due to uncertainty about investment outlays, operating cash flows, and salvage values without regard to how investments are financed (cf. *financial risk*).

call option Option to buy an asset at a specified exercise price on or before a specified maturity date (cf. *put option*).

call provision Provision describing terms under which a bond issuer may redeem bond in whole or in part prior to maturity.

capital The amount invested in a venture (cf. *capitalization*).

capital budget List of planned investment projects.

capital consumption adjustment Adjustment to historical-cost depreciation to correct for understatement during inflation.

capital rationing   Fixed limit on capital that forces company to choose among worthwhile projects.

capital structure   The composition of the liabilities side of a company's balance sheet. The mix of funding sources a company uses to finance its operations.

capitalization   The sum of all long-term sources of financing to the firm, or equivalently, total assets less current liabilities.

cash accounting   A method of accounting in which changes in the condition of an organization are recognized only in response to the payment or receipt of cash (cf. *accrual accounting*).

cash budget   A plan or projection of cash receipts and disbursements for a given period of time (cf. *cash flow forecast, cash flow statement, pro forma forecast.*)

cash cow   Company or product that generates more cash than can be productively reinvested.

cash flow   The amount of cash generated or consumed by an activity over a certain period of time.

cash flow cycle   The periodic transformation of cash through *working capital* and fixed assets back to cash.

cash flow forecast   A financial forecast in the form of a *sources and uses statement.*

cash flow from operations   Cash generated or consumed by the productive activities of a firm over a period of time; defined as profit after tax plus *noncash charges* minus noncash receipts.

cash flow principle   Principle of investment evaluation stating that only actual movements of cash are relevant and that they should be listed on the date they move.

certainty-equivalent   A guaranteed amount of money that a decision maker would trade for an uncertain cash flow.

close off the top   Financial jargon meaning to foreclose the possibility of additional debt financing.

collection period   A ratio measure of control of *accounts receivable,* defined as accounts receivable divided by credit sales per day.

common shares   *Common stock.*

common-size financial statements   Device used to compare financial statements, frequently of companies of disparate size, whereby all balance sheet entries are divided by total assets and all income statement entries are divided by net sales.

common stock (common shares) Securities representing an ownership interest in a firm.

comparables A method for estimating the *fair market value* of a closely held business by comparing it to one or more comparable, publicly traded firms.

compounding The growth of a sum of money over time through the reinvestment of interest earned to earn more interest (cf. *discounting*).

conglomerate diversification Ownership of operations in a number of functionally unrelated business activities.

constant-dollar accounting System of inflation accounting in which historical-cost items are restated to adjust for changes in the general purchasing power of the currency (cf. *current-dollar accounting*).

constant purchasing power The amount of a currency required over time to purchase a stable basket of physical assets.

consumer price index (CPI) An index measure of inflation equal to the sum of prices of a number of assets purchased by consumers weighted by the proportion each represents in a typical consumer's budget.

contribution to fixed cost and profits The excess of *revenue* over *variable costs*.

control ratio Ratio indicating management's control of a particular current asset or liability.

conversion ratio Number of shares for which a *convertible security* may be exchanged.

conversion value Market value of shares investor would own if he or she converted one convertible security.

convertible security Financial security that can be exchanged at the holder's option for another security or asset.

corporate restructuring Any major episodic change in a company's capital or ownership structure.

correlation coefficient Measure of the degree of comovement of two variables.

cost of capital (opportunity cost of capital, hurdle rate, weighted-average cost of capital) Return on new, average-risk investment that a company must expect in order to maintain share price. A weighted average of the cost to the firm of individual sources of capital.

cost of debt   *Yield to maturity* on debt; frequently after tax, in which event it is one minus the tax rate times the yield to maturity.

cost of equity   Return equity investors expect to earn by holding shares in a company. The expected return forgone by equity investors in the next best, equal-risk opportunity.

cost of goods sold (cost of sales)   The sum of all costs required to acquire and prepare goods for sale.

coupon rate   The interest rate specified on interest coupons attached to bonds. Annual interest received equals coupon rate times the *par value* of the bond.

covenant (protective covenant)   Provision in a debt agreement requiring the borrower to do, or not do, something.

coverage ratio   Measure of financial leverage relating annual operating income to annual burden of debt (cf. *times interest earned ratio, times burden covered ratio*).

cumulative preferred stock   *Preferred stock* containing the requirement that any unpaid preferred dividends accumulate and must be paid in full before common dividends may be distributed.

current asset   Any asset that will turn into cash within one year.

current-dollar accounting   System of inflation accounting in which historical-cost items are restated to adjust for changes in the price of specific item (cf. *constant-dollar accounting*).

current liability   Any liability that is payable within one year.

current portion of long-term debt   That portion of long-term debt that is payable within one year.

current ratio   A measure of *liquidity,* defined as current assets divided by current liabilities.

days sales in cash   A measure of management's control of cash balances, defined as cash divided by sales per day.

debt (liability)   An obligation to pay cash or other goods or to provide services to another.

debt capacity   The total amount of debt a company can prudently support, given its earnings expectations and equity base.

debt-to-assets ratio   A measure of *financial leverage,* defined as debt divided by total assets (cf. *debt-to-equity ratio*).

debt-to-equity ratio   A measure of *financial leverage,* defined as debt divided by shareholders' equity.

default   To fail to make a payment when due.

default premium The increased return on a security required to compensate investors for the risk the company will default on its obligation.

deferred tax liability An estimated amount of future income taxes that may become payable from income already earned but not yet recognized for tax-reporting purposes.

delayed call Provision in a security that gives the issuer the right to call the issue but only after a period of time has elapsed (cf. *call provision*).

depreciation The reduction in the value of a long-lived asset from use or obsolescence. The decline is recognized in accounting by a periodic allocation of the original cost of the asset to current operations (cf. *accelerated depreciation*).

dilution The reduction in any per share item (such as earnings per share or book value per share) due to an increase in the number of shares outstanding either through new issue or conversion of outstanding securities.

discount rate Interest rate used to calculate the *present value* of future cash flows.

discounted cash flow The method of evaluating long-term projects that explicitly takes into account the time value of money.

discounted cash flow rate of return *Internal rate of return.*

discounting Process of finding the present value of future cash flows (cf. *compounding*).

diversifiable risk That risk that is eliminated when an asset is added to a diversified portfolio (cf. β-*risk*).

diversification The process of investing in a number of differing assets.

dividend payout ratio A measure of the level of dividends distributed, defined as dividends divided by earnings.

earnings (income, net income, net profit, profit) The excess of revenues over all related expenses for a given period.

earnings per share (EPS) A measure of each common share's claim on earnings, defined as earnings available for common divided by the number of common shares outstanding.

earnings yield *Earnings per share* divided by stock price.

EBIT Abbreviation for earnings before interest and taxes.

economic income   The amount an economic agent could spend during a period of time without affecting his or her wealth (cf. *accounting income*).

efficient market   A market in which asset prices instantaneously reflect new information.

equity (owners' equity, net worth, shareholders' equity)   The ownership interests of common and preferred stockholders in a company; on a balance sheet, equity equals total assets less all liabilities.

equivalence   Equality of value of two cash flows occurring at different times if the cash flow occurring sooner can be converted into the later cash flow by investing it at the prevailing interest rate.

expected return   Average of possible returns weighted by their probability.

fair market value (FMV) (intrinsic value)   An idealized *market value* defined as the price at which an asset would trade between two rational individuals, each in command of all of the information necessary to value the asset and neither under any pressure to trade.

figure of merit   A number summarizing the investment worth of a project.

Financial Accounting Standards Board (FASB)   Official rule-making body in accounting profession.

financial flexibility   The ability to raise sufficient capital to meet company needs under a wide variety of future contingencies.

financial leverage   Use of debt to increase the expected return and the risk to equity (cf. *operating leverage*).

first-in, first-out (FIFO)   A method of inventory accounting in which the oldest item in inventory is assumed to be sold first (cf. *last-in, first-out*).

Fisher effect   Proposition that the nominal rate of interest should approximately equal the real rate of interest plus a premium for expected inflation (cf. *real amount, nominal amount*).

fixed cost   Any cost that does not vary over the observation period with changes in volume.

fixed-income security   Any security that promises an unvarying payment stream to holders over its life.

forcing conversion   Strategy in which a company forces owners of a convertible security to convert by calling the security at a time when its call price is below its conversion value (cf. *call provision, convertible security*).

free cash flow   The *cash flow* available to a company after financing all worthwhile investments. It is defined as operating income after tax plus depreciation less investment. The presence of large free cash flows is said to be attractive to a corporate raider.

frozen convertible (hung convertible)   *Convertible security* that has been outstanding for several years and whose holders cannot be forced to convert because its *conversion value* is below its call price (cf. *forcing conversion*).

funds   Any means of payment. Along with cash flow, funds is one of the most frequently misused words in finance.

gains to net debtors   Increase in debtor's wealth due to decline in purchasing power of liabilities.

general creditor   Unsecured creditor.

going-concern value   The *present value* of a business' expected future *aftertax cash flows*. The going-concern value of *equity* is the present value of cash flows to equity, while the going-concern value of the firm is the present value of cash flows to all providers of capital.

gross margin percentage   Revenue minus cost of goods sold divided by revenue.

hurdle rate   Minimum acceptable rate of return on investment (cf. *acceptance criterion, cost of capital*).

historical-cost depreciation   *Depreciation* based on amount originally paid for asset.

income   *Earnings.*

income statement (profit and loss statement)   A report of a company's revenues, associated expenses, and resulting *income* for a period of time.

inflation premium   The increased return on a security required to compensate investors for expected inflation.

insolvency   The condition of having debts greater than the realizable value of one's assets.

internal rate of return (IRR)   *Discount rate* at which project's *net present value* equals zero. Rate at which funds left in a project are *compounding* (cf. *rate of return*).

internal sources Cash available to a company from *cash flow from operations*.

inventory turnover ratio A measure of management's control of its investment in inventory, defined as *cost of goods sold* divided by ending inventory, or something similar.

inventory valuation adjustment Adjustment to historical-cost financial statements to correct for the possible understatement of inventory and *cost of goods sold* during inflation.

investment bank A financial institution specializing in the original sale and subsequent trading of company securities.

investment value Value of a *convertible security* based solely on its characteristics as a fixed-income security and ignoring the value of the conversion feature.

junk bond Any *bond* rated below investment grade.

last-in, first-out (LIFO) A method of inventory accounting in which the newest item in inventory is assumed to be sold first (cf. *first-in, first-out*).

leveraged buyout (LBO) Purchase of a company financed in large part by company borrowings.

liability An obligation to pay an amount or perform a service.

liquid asset Any asset that can be quickly converted to cash without significant loss of value.

liquidation The process of closing down a company, selling its assets, paying off its creditors, and distributing any remaining cash to owners.

liquidation value The cash generated by terminating a business and selling its assets individually. The liquidation value of equity is the proceeds of the asset sale less all company liabilities.

liquidity The extent to which a company has assets that are readily available to meet obligations (cf. *acid test, current ratio*).

liquidity ratio Any ratio used to estimate a company's *liquidity* (cf. *acid test, current ratio*).

market for control The active, competitive trading of controlling interests in corporations, effected by the purchase or sale of sizable blocks of common stock.

market line (securities market line) Line representing relationship between *expected return* and β-*risk*.

market value The price at which an item can be sold (cf. *book value*).

market value of equity   The price per share of a company's *common stock* times the number of shares of common stock outstanding (cf. *book value of equity*).

market value of firm   The market value of *equity* plus the market value of the firm's liabilities.

monetary asset   Any asset having a value defined in units of currency. Cash and accounts receivable are monetary assets; inventories and plant and equipment are physical assets.

multiple hurdle rates   Use of different *hurdle rates* for new investments to reflect differing levels of risk.

mutually exclusive alternatives   Two projects that accomplish the same objective, so that only one will be undertaken.

net income   *Earnings.*

net monetary creditor   Economic agent having *monetary assets* in excess of *liabilities.*

net monetary debtor   Economic agent having *monetary assets* less than *liabilities.*

net present value (NPV)   *Present value* of cash inflows less present value of cash outflows. The increase in wealth accruing to an investor when he or she undertakes an investment.

net profit   *Earnings.*

net sales   Total sales revenue less certain offsetting items such as returns and allowances and sales discounts.

net worth   *Equity,* shareholders' equity.

nominal amount   Any quantity not adjusted for changes in purchasing power of the currency due to inflation (cf. *real amount*).

noncash charge   An expense recorded by an accountant not matched by a cash outflow during the accounting period.

nondiversifiable risk   β-*risk, systematic risk.*

operating leverage   Fixed operating costs that tend to increase the variation in profits (cf. *financial leverage*).

opportunity cost   Income forgone by an investor when he or she chooses one action opposed to another. Expected income on next best alternative.

opportunity cost of capital   *Cost of capital.*

option   See *call option, put option.*

over-the-counter (OTC) market   Informal market in which securities not listed on organized exchanges trade.

owners' equity   *Equity.*

paid-in capital   That portion of *shareholders' equity* that has been paid-in directly, as opposed to earned profits retained in the business.

par value   An arbitrary value set as the face amount of a security. Bondholders receive par value for their bonds on maturity.

payables period   A measure of a company's use of trade credit financing, defined as accounts payable divided by purchases per day.

payback period   A crude figure of investment merit and better measure of investment risk, defined as the time an investor must wait to recoup his or her initial investment.

perpetual growth equation   An equation representing the *present value* of a *perpetuity* growing at the rate of *g* percent per annum as next year's receipts divided by the difference between the *discount rate* and *g*.

perpetuity   An *annuity* that lasts forever.

plug   Jargon for the unknown quantity in a pro forma forecast.

portfolio   Holdings of a diverse group of assets by an individual or a company.

preferred stock   A class of stock, usually fixed-income, that carries some form of preference to income or assets over *common stock* (cf. *cumulative preferred stock*).

premium for control   The premium over and above the existing *market value* of a company's *equity* an acquirer is willing to pay to gain control of the company.

present value   The present worth of a future sum of money.

price-to-earnings ratio (P/E ratio)   Amount investors are willing to pay for $1 of a firm's current earnings. Price per share divided by earnings per share over the most recent 12 months.

principal   The original, or face, amount of a loan. Interest is earned on the principal.

private placement   The raising of capital for a business through the sale of securities to a limited number of well-informed investors rather than through a public offering.

pro forma statement   A financial statement prepared on the basis of some assumed future events.

profit center An organizational unit within a company that produces revenue and for which a profit can be calculated.

profit margin The proportion of each sales dollar that filters down to *income,* defined as income divided by *net sales.*

profits *Earnings.*

profitability index (benefit-cost ratio) A figure of investment merit, defined as the *present value* of cash inflows divided by present value of cash outflows.

protective covenant *Covenant.*

public issue (public offering) Newly issued securities sold directly to the public (cf. *private placement*).

put option Option to sell an asset at a specified exercise price on or before a specified maturity date (cf. *call option*).

quick ratio *Acid test.*

range-of-earnings chart Graph relating *earnings per share* (EPS) to earnings before interest and taxes (EBIT) under alternative financing options.

rate of return Yield obtainable on an asset.

ratio analysis Analysis of financial statements by means of ratios.

real amount Any quantity that has been adjusted for changes in the purchasing power of the currency due to inflation (cf. *nominal amount*).

realized income The earning of income related to a transaction as distinguished from a paper gain.

retained earnings (earned surplus) The amount of earnings retained and reinvested in a business and not distributed to stockholders as dividends.

return on assets (ROA) A measure of the productivity of assets, defined as *income* divided by total assets. A superior but less common definition includes interest expense and preferred dividends in the numerator.

return on equity (ROE) A measure of the productivity or efficiency with which shareholders' equity is employed, defined as *income* divided by *equity.*

return on invested capital (ROIC) A fundamental measure of the earning power of a company that is unaffected by the way the company is financed. It is equal to earnings before interest and tax times one minus the tax rate, all divided by *debt* plus *equity.*

return on investment (ROI)   The productivity of an investment or a profit center, defined as *income* divided by *book value* of investment or *profit center* (cf. *return on assets*).

residual income security   A security that has last claim on company income. Usually the beneficiary of company growth.

residual profits   An alternative to *return on investment* as a measure of *profit center* performance, defined as *income* less the annual cost of the capital employed by the profit center.

revenues   *Sales.*

rights of absolute priority   Specification in bankruptcy law stating that each class of claimants with a prior claim on assets in liquidation will be paid off in full before any junior claimants receive anything.

risk-adjusted discount rate (cost of capital, hurdle rate)   A *discount rate* that includes a premium for risk.

risk aversion   An unwillingness to bear risk without compensation of some form.

risk-free interest rate   The interest rate prevailing on a default-free bond in the absence of inflation.

risk premium   The increased return on a security required to compensate investors for the risk borne.

sales (revenue)   The inflow of resources to a business for a period from sale of goods or provision of services (cf. *net sales*).

secured creditor   A creditor whose obligation is backed by the pledge of some asset. In liquidation, the secured creditor receives the cash from the sale of the pledged asset to the extent of his or her loan.

Securities and Exchange Commission (SEC)   Federal government agency that regulates securities markets.

semistrong-form efficient market   A market in which prices instantaneously reflect all publicly available information.

senior creditor   Any creditor with a claim on income or assets prior to that of *general creditors*.

sensitivity analysis   Analysis of effect on a plan or forecast of a change in one of the input variables.

shareholders' equity   *Equity, net worth.*

shelf registration   SEC program under which a company can file a general-purpose prospectus describing its possible financing plans for up to two years. This eliminates time lags for new public security issues.

simulation (Monte Carlo simulation) Computer-based extension of *sensitivity analysis* that calculates the probability distribution of a forecast outcome.

sinking fund A fund of cash set aside for the payment of a future obligation. A bond sinking fund is a payment of cash to creditors.

solvency The state of being able to pay debts as they come due.

sources and uses statement A document showing where a company got its cash and where it spent the cash over a specific period of time. It is constructed by segregating all changes in balance sheet accounts into those that provided cash and those that consumed cash.

spontaneous sources of cash Those liabilities such as accounts payable and accrued wages that arise automatically, without negotiation, in the course of doing business.

spread Investment banker jargon for difference between the issue price of a new security and the net to the company.

statement of changes in financial position A financial statement showing the sources and uses of working capital for the period.

stock *Common stock.*

stock option A contractual privilege sometimes provided to company officers giving the holder the right to purchase a specified number of shares at a specified price within a stated period of time.

standard deviation of return A measure of variability. The square root of the mean squared deviation from the *expected return.*

striking price (exercise price) The fixed price for which a stock can be purchased in a call contract or sold in a put contract (cf. *call option, put option*).

strong-form efficient market A market in which prices instantaneously reflect all information public or private.

subordinated creditor A creditor holding a debenture having a lower chance of payment than other liabilities of the firm.

sunk cost A previous outlay that cannot be changed by any current or future action.

sustainable growth rate   The rate of increase in sales a company can attain without changing its profit margin, assets-to-sales ratio, debt-to-equity ratio, or dividend payout ratio. The rate of growth a company can finance without excessive borrowing or issuing new stock.

tax shield   The reduction in a company's tax bill caused by an increase in a tax-deductible expense, usually depreciation or interest. The magnitude of the tax shield equals the tax rate times the increase in the expense.

times burden covered   A *coverage ratio* measure of *financial leverage,* defined as earnings before interest and taxes divided by interest expense plus principal payments grossed up to their before-tax equivalents.

times interest earned   A *coverage ratio* measure of *financial leverage,* defined as earnings before interest and taxes divided by interest expense.

trade payables   *Accounts payable.*

underwriting syndicate   A group of *investment banks* that band together for a brief time to guarantee a specified price to a company for newly issued securities.

unrealized income   Earned income for which there is no confirming transaction. A paper gain.

variable cost   Any expense that varies with sales over the observation period.

volatility   β-*risk.*

warrant   A security issued by a company granting the right to purchase shares of another security of the company at a specified price and for a stated time.

weak-form efficient market   A market in which prices instantaneously reflect information about past prices.

weak-form efficient market   Cost of capital.

weighted-average cost of capital   *Cost of capital.*

with-without principle   Principle defining those cash flows that are relevant to an investment decision. It states that if there are two worlds, one with the investment and one without it, all cash flows that differ in these two worlds are relevant and all cash flows that are the same are irrelevant.

working capital (net working capital) The excess of current assets over current liabilities.

working capital cycle The periodic transformation of cash through current assets and current liabilities and back to cash (cf. *cash flow cycle*).

yield to maturity The *internal rate of return* on a bond when held to maturity.

Index